Speaking of Flying

Personal Tales of Heroism, Humor, Talent and Terror from 44 Unique Aviators

Produced by Diane Titterington

Cover layout by Diane Titterington.
Jacket cover artwork by Frank Loudin, Mark Postlewaite, Rick Herter, Mark Short & Matthew Waki

Book design by Diane Titterington.

Please visit and bookmark our web site at
www.aviationspeakers.com
for any additional speaker updates.

This book may be ordered on the web site or at 800-437-7080.

Contents

Dedication

To the pilots who flew these tales
and shared them.

To the designers, builders and mechanics
who give us the gift of flight.

Preface

Hangar flying soars to new heights in this book.

The writers are professional speakers whose aviation tales have dazzled and delighted audiences around the world for decades.

After hearing hundreds of fascinating anecdotes and stories, I've gathered some of the funniest, most thrilling, scariest, daring, and revealing of these tales. Here you will find the history and mystery, the excitement and the challenges of aviation's greatest moments, as told by the pilots.

Diane Titterington

You will also discover real heroes in these stories. Some have tiptoed around death's door and danced with lady luck more than once. And these high-spirited pilots are full of shenanigans too. Amazingly, these tall tales are true!

Each chapter is presented in the unique style of its author. You will see the very human side of aviation, and the men and women who have devoted their lives to flying. If you wish to read the stories with the writer's voice in mind, audio for each author can be heard at www.aviationspeakers.com.

Though you may read it all the way through, this is not a book you will finish any time soon. You will most likely find yourself reading it again. With each reading you will find new meaning, new emotion, and new insights.

It is my great pleasure to bring you *Speaking of Flying*.

BRIGADIER GENERAL ROBIN OLDS USAF (RET.)

FIRST TRAIN - MID MAY, 1944

Hell! We wanted to kill something!

At least that's what we lieutenants wanted. But no, for the past two weeks we had just sailed along at 10 to 15 thousand feet as though all the Germans were on leave in Russia. It got so we welcomed the occasional bursts of flak. At least the Jerries knew we were there and the black puffs off to the sides made us feel a little bit important.

I'd get so damned mad and frustrated I'd take off my oxygen mask to get the cuss words out. We'd been told to observe radio discipline. What the bosses meant was, "Shut up. Don't say anything." No matter what we saw sitting or moving around down below. We passed trucks barreling down tree-lined roads, trains stopped in patches of woods, wisps of steam giving them away. We saw deserted-looking airfields given away by small buildings backed up against the surrounding forests. Large and small marshaling yards with goods wagons sitting still, just waiting to be pounced on. All sorts of lucrative and tempting targets. But *Highway* kept sailing along as though we were still over England.

Our squadron CO, Major Miller Herren, was a good guy, though I wasn't quite sure we brand-new first lieutenants were in any position to judge. But our naïve impressions were all positive. Major Herren worked long hours getting us organized to ship out. He trained us hard, and we liked that. His manner with all of us was direct and to the point. He didn't tolerate slackness and he inspired us to do our best. We weren't afraid of him, meaning we judged him to be fair, not like some of the men we had already experienced in our short careers. Best of all, he flew the P-38 with us and more than once had proved his skill and guts in the wild blue yonder.

But now we had a problem. It wasn't the major losing face by not leading us into battle the way we thought he should and wanted him to do. It wasn't thinking he was showing a timid streak by not getting at the enemy. It was something different. We thought the boss was under some kind of pressure not to expose us to the wily Hun. Maybe he was getting the word from Group or higher.

The situation was downright embarrassing. What were the old time Groups over here thinking about this brand-new 479th? Our daily ops reports must have them snickering. I'd already started reading all of theirs and those guys were shooting up everything in sight, even getting into an occasional aerial fight with the Germans. It was a creeping awful feeling, like we'd be judged to be pantywaists afraid to join the big boys.

Our frustration and sense of outrage kept growing. We had to shoot at something! We had to get into the scrap before we were permanently branded. I could just see it coming.

"Daddy, what did you do in the war?"

Or...

"You say you were in the 479th back in '44? Wasn't that the chicken outfit that never fired its guns? Oh, yeah, now I remember. 'Scuse me pal, I see a friendly face down at the end of the bar." And he walks away not even bothering to hide his laughter.

Not for me, and not for the last time in my life the old devil got behind me and gave me a shove.

"Newcross Lead, this is Newcross Blue 3. I've got a train at eight o'clock. I'm going down. Will you cover me?"

"Roger Blue 3," came the response.

I was already on my way, fangs out and trigger finger curled. A quick check of the armament switches, a fast look around for other aircraft, and a full powered shallow drive toward that blessed train... the train that was going to get me in this damned war or get me court martialed, probably both.

A hard bank to the right, pull the pipper through the length of the goods wagons, put it a bit above the aim point to allow for range, roll wings level as the sight stops dead on the engine's boiler. Squeeze off a burst and see the HEI (high explosive incendiary) sparkling all over that old engine. Watch a fountain of smoke and steam burst out of the stack and jink away to set up for another pass, this time on the goods wagons.

Coming around to line up I thought about the train crew and was glad I hadn't aimed at the engineer's cab. In all likelihood the trainmen were Frenchmen. It sure wouldn't be nice to shoot up some guy forced to drive old Hitler's freight around France in broad daylight as these guys were doing.

On the next pass I raked my .50 caliber bullets along a part of the stalled train. It was great seeing the sparkles light up the wagons, but disappointing to see nothing blow up. For more than a year, Pathé news had featured film clips of trains blowing up during strafing passes. Spectacular stuff and heady impressions for a 21 year-old novice.

As I pulled around for a third pass and checked over my shoulders for flak, what did I see but the entire train light up from end to end. Then I saw the whole dammed squadron had come down on the target. My initiative had been too much for the rest of the

troops. I hadn't heard anything on the radio so this was pure reflex on their part. Talk about mass relief! No frustrations left in that bunch. They all banged away at what must have been the most shot-up train in the entire war.

"Newcross Blue, this is Newcross Lead. Pull up! Pull up and regroup." Major Herren's voice felt like slivers of ice.

The guilt set in as the squadron formed up. We returned to base in silence, cold silence. We were left to stew and wonder... and I guess I did most of the stewing and wondering. Hell, he couldn't fire all of us—or could he? Certainly I would be fair game. No doubt about that. But there was still the satisfaction of having finally fired my guns. I thought of the happy look I would soon see on my armorer's face when he saw the powder marks on my P-38's nose.

I was right. The armament corporal was one happy troop. But that joy was short-lived. By the time I shut down my engines I was in the depths thinking my career as a great fighter pilot was about to end within the week. The ride back around the perimeter track to the debriefing was not exactly marked with exuberance. Someone tried to talk about our great contribution to Hitler's demise, but his remarks were less than half-hearted and no one else was in a talking mood.

It crossed my mind I might jump off the jeep and head for the woods, but that was out of the question. Music was music and the sooner faced the better.

Debriefing was grim. S-2, old Mother Horton, kept at us and stretched the whole procedure beyond belief. Finally it ended and in the hush my name was spoken softly... quietly... with menace.

"Olds, come over here."

I got up and stood at attention in front of the Boss.

"You broke formation. You disobeyed regulations. You defied my authority. You exposed the squadron to unwarranted risk, and for all I know, you attacked an unauthorized target."

The Major was really mad, angrier than any of us had ever seen him. His voice was low and steely and his eyes blazed as they stared into mine. I had visions of steel bars and rock piles.

Major Herren went on. Things grew darker. The room shrank, the ceiling came down over my head. All I could see were those steely blues boring into mine. Thank God for plebe year. I stood at attention and tried to bore right back. I heard the Major's words, but I concentrated on keeping my eyes locked on his.

Finally, "Well, what do you have to say for yourself? Give me one good reason not to draw up court martial charges right this minute!"

A small ray of light broke into the dark, a chink of hope in the wall of despair. He actually wanted me to say something. From plebe days I knew that was no small mistake on the Boss's part. He had given me an opening, right in front of the whole squadron.

On the football field I had learned aggressiveness often made up for size and sometimes a blind side block carried the play.

"Sir," I said, "I called you. I said, 'Newcross Lead, this is Newcross Blue 3. There is a train at eight o'clock. I'm going down. Will you cover me?' and you said 'Roger, Blue 3.' So I went down and attacked the train."

Major Herren glared at me. He clenched his fists and his face turned red. He looked as though he was about to explode. Now it was his turn to feel frustration. He opened his mouth to speak and nothing came out. He tried again and only sputtered. Finally he managed, "God damn you, Olds, I wasn't the one who said 'Roger!'"

It was chilly around the Mess for a while, but the Major was a fair man and though he didn't say so, he knew he had been out-maneuvered. Of course, I never told anyone it was impossible not to recognize my wingman's voice when he said, "Roger." An Okie twang is an Okie twang, even over France.

Sadly, Major Herren was killed later that summer. We respected him and we knew we had lost something and somebody important in our lives.

MIXING IT UP IN WORLD WAR II

My father served as a pilot in France in World War I, so I grew up with combat aviation in my blood. He was responsible as much as anything else for my burning desire to be a pilot. He was always a strong advocate of air power and, among many other achievements, had been the commander of the 2nd Bomb Group, the first unit to operate the B-17. I graduated from West Point in June 1943, receiving my wings and started operational training almost right away on the Lockheed P-38 Lightning fighter. This experience seemed to take forever. In May 1944, however, I was assigned to England as a member of the 479th Fighter Group (434th Fighter Squadron). We were stationed at RAF Wattisham. We quickly worked up to combat status, carrying out a lot of interdiction type flying over France and Germany prior to D-Day. June 5th was a day never to forget. We were sent out to cover the armada headed for Normandy and were back the following day to provide escort for the invasion itself.

I had still to experience my first actual aerial combat, an event that took place early on the morning of August 13, somewhere close to Montmirail in France. This involved a surprise attack I pulled off, jumping two FW-190s down at ground level. After a brief but hectic fight I was able to down both of them. Things moved faster after that. Just a couple of weeks later my wingman and I attacked a group of Messerschmitt 109s. There were between 55 and 60 of them and we had a heck of a fight. The MEs were headed for the bomber stream. The engagement began at 28,000 feet over Muritz Zee, and, in the usual fashion for such affairs, finished on the deck. By then, we were close to Rostock on the Baltic. During the battle, I was able to bag three MEs while my wingman was responsible for two destroyed. But what I remember most was the trip home. It was long, slow and cold, my canopy having departed during a high G, high speed pullout. Things worked out, however, this being only my second combat, it resulted in the award of the Silver Star.

That fall we converted to P-51s and I continued on to fly a total of two combat tours, many of them characterized by engagements every bit as colorful. Many of the operations were long range escort missions for bombers on deep penetration missions. We also had engagements with the ME 262 jet, frequently the missions involved strafing runs on German facilities and airfields.

MIXING IT UP IN VIETNAM

On May 3, 1967, we were penetrating from the Gulf of Tonkin to a target that lay alongside the railroad northeast of Hanoi. Our eight F-4Cs were providing escort coverage for a force of F-105s that were in action striking a marshalling yard. Just short of the target we were hit by a group of some 16 MiG 17s. A swirling battle ensued, with a member of my flight immediately taking hits and being forced to bail out. I managed to bag one of the MiG 17s early on in the fight, which turned out to be the

longest aerial battle I have experienced. The enemy was most aggressive and well disciplined. However, low fuel ("bingo") finally forced us to disengage, but halfway to the coast I turned back by myself to engage the MiG pilot who had seemed to be directing traffic from a vantage point on the deck below the general melee. I caught him and downed him with one Sidewinder heat-seeking missile, then turned for the Gulf and that desperately-needed aerial tanker.

Biography

BRIGADIER GENERAL ROBIN OLDS USAF (RET.)

Brigadier General Robin Olds is rated a triple ace, having a World War II tally of 13 aerials, 11.5 during airfield strafing runs and, in North Vietnam, four confirmed aerials destroying two MiG 17s and two MiG 21s. In his 30 years of U.S. Air Force service, he flew some 65 different aircraft, including the Spitfire and Typhoon, the P-51, P-80, F-86, Gloster Meteor, F-101C, P-38, F-4 and many other aircraft. Combat missions included 107 in two tours during World War II and 152 in Vietnam, of which 115 were over North Vietnam. He earned his second oak leaf cluster to the Silver Star on January 2, 1967 during his famous "MiG Sweep." His third oak leaf cluster to the Silver Star was for "exemplary airmanship, extraordinary heroism and indomitable aggressiveness" in a low-level bombing run against the Thai Ngyen steel mill blast furnaces. He was awarded the Air Force Cross for his part in the famous Paul Doumier Bridge Raid. "General Olds is one of the top Air Force leaders in American history," states General Steve Ritchie. He is one of our best-loved military leaders. Robin is a powerful, charismatic and witty speaker.

GENERAL OLDS' MANY DECORATIONS INCLUDE:
Air Force Cross
Distinguished Service Medal with one oak leaf cluster
Silver Star with three oak leaf clusters
Distinguished Flying Cross with five oak leaf clusters
Air Medal with 40 oak leaf clusters
Distinguished Flying Cross (RAF)
Croix de Guerre (France)
Distinguished Service Order (South Vietnam Air Force)
Air Gallantry Medal with Gold Wings (South Vietnam)

BRIGADIER GENERAL ROBIN OLDS USAF (RET.)

DICK RUTAN

PERMISSION TO FLY BY?

In 1967-68, I flew aerial combat missions in an F-100, the North American Super Saber, in the Republic of North Vietnam and the Republic of South Vietnam. The F-100 became the Air Force's first operational supersonic airplane back in the 1950s and it was used extensively in Vietnam.

Our missions over North Vietnam lasted from four to six hours and required multiple aerial refuelings. We refueled from a tanker circling off the coast of North Vietnam over the Gulf of Tonkin. The drill was simple: run strike reconnaissance, refuel, run back in. We saw a lot of ground fire, MiGs, surface to air missiles, and a lot of excitement.

During one mission, I flew into North Vietnam and one of my drop tanks would not feed. I couldn't use the fuel in the tank and I didn't want to carry the extra weight, so I flew over a suspected truck park and jettisoned the tanks. The empty tank probably didn't do any damage, but the full one might have found a target of opportunity. I completed my mission with double the refuelings.

Most of the pilots flying combat missions in Vietnam were barely 20 years of age. We saw death on every mission and most of us didn't know if we were going to make it back ourselves. We were pretty blasé, devil-may-care, go get 'em types, and we didn't pay a lot of attention to regulations. So if we saw an opportunity to do something rowdy, we'd do it.

On the way back to our base in South Vietnam, I got an idea. The F-100 is a supersonic fighter, but it's only supersonic without the drop tanks. What an opportunity! Wouldn't it be interesting to fly over the base supersonic? Wouldn't it be interesting to just lay a good supersonic boom across the base? After all, reasoned my 20-year-old brain, what could it hurt? The Viet Cong shelled the base every day. Charges and mortars exploded inside the base every night. What harm could another couple of boom-booms do?

Preparations are being made on an F-100 before Dick's flight from Phu Cat air base in South Vietnam

I flew across the base at about 20,000 feet, kicked in the afterburner and got the F-100 supersonic. I turned and made my pass, rolling my wings back and forth to make sure I went directly over the complex. Then I looked back and noticed that the airplane had slipped subsonic. I didn't know if this happened over the base or after passing it. I didn't know if I boomed the base or not. So I came around again and repeated the entire pass, this time a little bit lower. I made sure that I had a good solid supersonic shock wave established and drilled right across the base.

I thought to myself, "Boy, this will really boom them. Really get their attention. Ha, ha, ha, ha. Some good prank."

I came around and landed, then taxied the plane to the ramp. I, the crusty combat veteran, sat in the cockpit basking in the euphoria of the fly-by. Yeah, me, the 20-year-old captain, wearing my "Go To Hell" fighter pilot hat, twisting my big long handlebar mustache.

Up walked a full colonel. I don't remember whether he was the wing commander or somebody more important, but he was one of the big colonels on the base. He stood there with a frown on his

face and looked at me as I got out of the airplane. "Rutan," he says, "I'm going to assume that since you are the only person who's been flying without drop tanks that you are the one responsible for booming our base. I want you to report to your squadron commander immediately upon your debriefing."

That's all he said, so as I walked up to my commander's station, the military professional thought, "Oh, boy, am I going to get chewed out now." But then the 20-year-old pilot retorted, "Who cares? What are they going to do with me? Send me to North Vietnam and let me get shot?"

My squadron commander's name was Col. Stanley Manlock. He was such a crazy guy. We all called him Col. Stopcock. When I walked into his office, he looked at me and said, "Rutan, you boomed the base. They aren't mad that you did that. But when you boomed the base, all the Vietnamese personnel got scared so bad, they all dove into the bunkers. It took us all afternoon to talk them into getting out of the bunkers. But by the time we got them back out, it was too late to put them back to work. So we put them back on the bus and drove them off the base. So from now on, we would appreciate it if you didn't come back and drill the base."

WHAT LOST PROP OVER TEXAS?

Denial: when you find yourself in an impossible situation, you look around and see no other alternative, your mind shuts down and tells you this horrible thing is *not* happening.

Early one Sunday morning in mid-Texas, I took off in my little Long EZ (a single engine airplane with a wood propeller in the back) on my way to Venezuela to film a commercial at Angel Falls. We started out very early, climbed through the thick summer fog at ground level, and then leveled off at 10,000 feet and headed towards Brownsville to clear Customs. It was calm and nice that morning, until I started feeling a vibration, very slight at first. When I reduced the power, the vibration went away. Then I'd restore power, and after maybe half a minute or so, the vibration returned. Then I reduced the power again and the vibration went away.

Something was definitely wrong. I called Air Traffic Control to request the weather at the different fields around me. At Austin, the closest recovery base, the fog was so thick the birds were walking. About this time the vibration started to get really noticeable. As the airplane started shaking more, I'd pull back the power more. Finally the power was almost back to idle. I trimmed up the airplane for best glide speed. ATC told me the nearest airport where I could possibly make an instrument approach was San Antonio, Texas, 60 miles away.

I turned towards San Antonio. The airplane shook and vibrated horribly. It got worse with every passing second. The power was all the way back at idle. We were on top of a thick, solid fog layer that went all the way to the ground. I realized we were in deep trouble.

POP! I turned over my right shoulder and watched the propeller and spinner tumble end over end and drop into the solid layer below.

I knew what this meant: a total engine failure, on top of a solid fog layer, no hope of making a safe landing in any kind of field. There were absolutely no choices. We had major problems.

Since the horrible problem, the severe vibration, was gone, my mind went into denial. The vibration is gone, therefore every-

Long EZ

thing should be okay. So I turned around and looked south toward Brownsville. Even though I had just seen the prop tumble away from the back of the airplane, I relaxed, took a deep breath and said, "Boy, sure glad that's over with."

I reached down and pushed the throttle in to continue our way to Brownsville. Without a prop, the engine screamed to life. The terrible noise obliterated the denial. I shut off the mags, the fuel, the engine, and began to deal with the emergency.

I pressed on and was just able to see the barest outline of a tiny airfield below us. With a little piece of airmanship, a little bit of luck and a smile from above, I was able to land on that little airport in terrible weather without any further damage to the airplane.

A GODDESS OVER THE INDIAN OCEAN

Everyone knows the Voyager around-the-world flight was a nine day nonstop record, but not everyone knows just how grueling it was to be locked up in that small cabin for those nine days. Even with all the training and preparation, years and thousands of hours flown, the best of us can be taken by surprise—or fatigue.

Voyager had just crossed the Malay Peninsula, just south of Thailand. When the sun went down, I could see the southern tip of India way off in the distance. It was a long, dark, moonless night. We were flying out across the Indian Ocean in the early morning hours just off the coast of Somalia, around day four,

Voyager

about an hour before sunrise. It was Jeana, my copilot's turn to sleep. While I flew the plane in that dark void, I began to think how ominous the African continent appeared. What would it hold for us? I've visited most parts of the world, seen Asia and Europe many times, but I had never been to Africa.

As we sat off the coast of Somalia it was very black. The air was crystal clear. We were cruising between 10,000 and 12,000 feet—just about the same conditions when I was shot down in my fighter plane in Vietnam. I began to imagine being attacked by a renegade African fighter pilot, someone who might want to make a name for himself at the expense of the very fragile and very vulnerable Voyager. I looked up and down the coast of Somalia and wondered why there were no lights. Why was it so very dark and forbidding that morning? At that moment I saw something flash across the canard. It sounded and looked just like a missile that had been fired at us and missed. Maybe it was my imagination. As I saw the missile go by, I turned around. Right behind us was the brightest aircraft landing light I had ever seen.

I thought we were being tracked by an enemy fighter. My first reaction was to grab the stick, turn off the autopilot, go into afterburner, pull up sharply, roll to the left, and get into the vertical rolling scissors. Reverse. Reverse. Get them in gun range and blow my adversary out of the sky.

Then I remembered where I was. The Voyager couldn't turn at all. Well, it could just barely turn, much less manage a vertical aerial engagement. So I sat there, tensing up, waiting for the next missile to fire and hit us. Then I called mission control. I told them we were being shot at and tracked by an unknown aircraft at our six o'clock position. It didn't dawn on me to ask why would somebody shoot at us and display a large landing light. Nor did I realize any airplane that had the capability of firing missiles certainly couldn't fly with us at such a slow speed. This logic never occurred to me. Of course, I had slept only one or two hours in the last four days. Maybe it was fatigue.

Maybe it was my imagination. I kept turning around and making shallow "S" turns to try to maneuver to see what the tracking airplane would do. Each time I moved it pretty much stayed in the same spot. It didn't fire again. It didn't do anything. It just sat there with its brilliant landing light shining on the back of Voyager.

Enough of this, I thought. I put Voyager into a full left 90-degree left turn away from Somalia. As I rolled out of the steep turn, the bright light was now off my left wing tip. That seemed strange. It couldn't sit there off the wing tip. I started to look at it more carefully. Finally, I recognized the *fighter plane* that had just shot a missile at us.

My adversary was the morning star, the planet Venus.

How embarrassing. Guess it can happen to anyone—even Voyager.

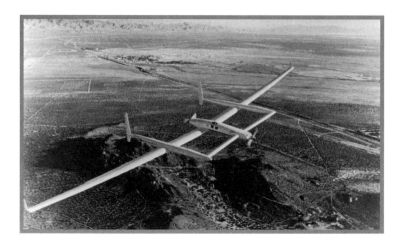

CAN ANYONE GIVE US A LIFT BACK TO MOJAVE?

The Voyager project was a very intense volunteer effort. We were only a month away from the close of our weather window and everyone on the project had been working around the clock to get the mission in the air. Everyone was so immersed in the operation of the airplane, getting it ready and fueled, getting the food and provisions on board, making sure all the equipment worked, no one had any time to think about the outside world. No one knew if the press would cover our flight. We didn't have the time to contact them.

Fortunately, some folks outside our mission group informed the press and we received overwhelming media coverage. But during the flight I was not aware of the tremendous media interest in the Voyager flight. Neither Jeana nor I knew that CNN was broadcasting hourly reports all over the world. We were entirely focused on flying Voyager.

On the ninth day, we crossed from night into the early dawn light just over Los Angeles. As we watched the lights of Los Angeles slip underneath our nose, we finally realized we had made it around the world.

We came across Long Beach, El Monte and Mt. Wilson. When we reached Edwards Air Force Base, Palmdale and Lancaster, the high desert was covered with a moderately high overcast and another cloud bank with tops of about 8,000 feet. That cloud bank extended all the way over to the edge of Edwards Air Force Base, blocking our view of the usual traffic. Upon seeing Edwards I knew we were home. I started to think of all the aviation activities located at Edwards, the test pilot training school, supersonic development and training, contractor operations, NASA operations, the space shuttle recovery—it's a very, very busy place.

Edwards is also located right in the middle of a restricted area... I panicked. We hadn't made prior arrangements. We didn't have prior permission to land at Edwards Air Force Base!

Then I thought, well, we have to land there. Where else are we going to land? Maybe if I'm very polite and very amenable, maybe... just maybe, they will let me land.

I called the tower, and said, "Edwards Tower, this is Voyager One, we are 25 miles south, inbound, and we would like permission to enter your restricted area." And then I thought, if I don't bother them too much, maybe I could talk them into letting us come in there and land without permission.

I added, "No problem, I know you're busy. Now I just kinda would like to work my way around your traffic... without bothering anybody. I'll just land on the northern dry lake and I won't get in anybody's way." I crossed my fingers hoping they would allow us to come in.

The tower sounded confused when he answered. "Voyager One, this is Edwards Tower. Sir, we have canceled flying for today. They are all here waiting for your return."

When we were still on top of the cloud bank, just before I called Edwards, I reminded my copilot we had left our cars back at Mojave. We were both hoping someone would be around to give us a ride back to Mojave and our cars. When we flew to the edge of the cloud bank at about 10,000 feet, we looked down for the first time at Edwards' Muroc dry lake and its 15,000-foot runway, the same runway we had just taken off from nine days earlier. There below us, lining the edge of the dry lake runway stood tens of thousands of people! It reminded us of a space shuttle landing.

Then I knew that, yes, there was going to be somebody around to give us a ride back to Mojave. We also began to realize that our lives were going to be very different. When we landed we learned of the huge interest in Voyager, not only in the aviation community, but also within the general and international press. Thanks to this great interest and outpouring of affection, we were able to go on a lecture tour and pay off the debts that we incurred. And, yes, we did get a ride back to our cars.

WHAT ARE BEST FRIENDS FOR?

After my Vietnam conflict days, I pulled a tour of duty in England at Lakenheath Air Base, the same airport that sent B-17's into Germany during World War II. One day I pulled an assignment to fly a functional flight test in an F-100 that had received extensive maintenance and a new engine. I took off alone and climbed to above 40,000 feet where I finally broke out on top of the horrible, typical English winter weather. Somewhere over the North Sea, I began performing some routine engine checks.

During the negative G checks, an oil sample bottle that a crew chief had inadvertently dropped into the oil tank became lodged in the oil pickup line. All oil flow to the engine instantly stopped. I reduced the throttle, called "Pan-Pan-Pan," and began the long descent back to Lakenheath. The Ground Control Approach (GCA)

By Rainer Hanxleden

controller told me the weather was very bad, ceilings 900 feet, about two or three miles visibility and light rain.

Halfway down the GCA glide path, 12 1/2 minutes after the sample bottle became lodged in the oil line, the engine seized. As I broke out of the clouds, barely above the minimum altitude to bail out, I heard a big explosion and a sickening grinding noise. Then fire shot out both ends of the airplane and the huge compressor stalled, blowing my feet off the rudder pedals and dirt up into my face. Then came more fire at the front of the doomed F-100.

I was able to just level off as the airspeed bled down to almost a stall. I reached and grabbed the ejection seat handles and ejected from the dying F-100. My parachute opened. I swung two times and into the trees before I hit. I glanced over my shoulder and saw the F-100 go into the trees ahead of me and blow up.

Meanwhile, the mobile controller on the runway had seen the airplane come out of the clouds with its landing light on and crash in the trees about two or three miles short of the runway. No one saw a parachute. The controller hollered, "No chute, no chute, get out there quick!" Everybody knew if you didn't bail out and the airplane crashed in a fireball, there was no chance of survival.

I came crashing down through the trees and my parachute and I landed right next to a typical English bloke trimming trees in the Queen's forest, literally at his feet. He had heard the explosion, saw the rocket seat go out, and here before him stood this man in a white helmet with a gold visor and oxygen mask on—a spaceman. As I ripped off my helmet, I hollered, "My name is Major Rutan and I am alive!" I grabbed my emergency bailout kit to get to my emergency radio. I pulled the handle and there was a loud hissing noise as the life raft started to inflate. It scared the man so bad he started running. I took off my parachute harness and went running after him. I said, "Come back, come back! I need your help!" He reluctantly came back and helped me get the parachute down out of the trees and the radio out. Then I made a radio call. "This is flight test *Ring Dove Two-one*, I'm down. I'm okay."

At the time, I didn't know that my parachute had not been spotted. My good buddy, who works in helicopter rescue, knew I was coming home with a bad engine. He was airborne in his helicopter at the time and heading for the crash site. Underneath his helicopter is a round pressurized container that holds a lot of fire fighting suppressant. His job was to land that unit right next to the crash site, where the helicopter rotor would blow suppressant into the flames. The firefighter corpsman would don his gear and fight his way through the fire into the cockpit, pull the pilot out, and drag him back out of the flames.

When the mobile controller had said to get out there quick, he inadvertently jettisoned the fire suppression bottle before he went tearing out there. He knew his good friend Dick Rutan, whose wife was two weeks overdue with their second child, was caught in the fireball. As he orbited the burning wreckage, the thought that he had just lost a very good friend was overwhelming. And then he heard my call on the radio, "Hey, come out and get me!" He thought I was inside the fireball calling for him, then he realized that he dropped the fire suppressant container.

All he could do was sit there and watch the crash burn. Then he heard me call again. He called, not believing that I survived the accident. I answered him.

And then in disbelief he called, "Where are you?"

I said, "I bailed out about two miles short."

"You bailed out? You're okay, you're out of the fireball?"

And then with a great sigh of relief, we finally rendezvoused. I was picked up and returned to the based unhurt.

Dick's attempt for a third around-the-world record in the Global Hilton balloon.

Biography

DICK RUTAN

Dick Rutan made history in December of 1986 after completing a nine day, three minute and forty-four second round-the-world, non-stop and non-refueled flight, setting an absolute world's record that still holds today. Setting the storm-battered Voyager down on the dry lakebed at Edwards Air Force Base, he successfully completed a six-year quest, doubling the previous world distance record. President Ronald Reagan awarded Dick the Presidential Citizen's Medal of Honor at a special ceremony for the Voyager Team four days after the landing. The Medal of Honor has been presented only sixteen times in the history of the United States. Dick received his student pilot's license, soloed and received his driver's license on his 16th birthday. He flew 325 missions in Vietnam, 105 of them as a member of the Super Sabre FAC, a high-risk operation commonly known as the "MISTYS." Dick was hit by enemy ground fire on his last mission and was forced to eject from his burning F-100, to be later rescued. Before retiring from the Air Force in 1978, Lt. Col. Rutan was awarded the Silver Star, five Distinguished Flying Crosses, 16 Air Medals and a Purple Heart. Dick continued his experimental adventures in aviation. In 1997, his "Around the World in 80 Nights" tour was successfully completed in two small experimental Long EZ aircraft. In 1998, his third attempt at an around-the-world record ended dramatically with an emergency parachute jump from a pressurized capsule suspended under a 110-foot hot air/helium balloon after experiencing a dangerous fabric tear. This was Dick's third life-saving parachute jump.

DR. JERRY COCKRELL

"THE GRADUATE" AS FLIGHT INSTRUCTOR

Author's note: This story is true in every detail.

Thinking back on the many aspiring pilots I instructed while working my way through undergraduate school, it now seems a bit odd that I didn't have even *one* female student. Our FBO had many college students and locals who were interested in learning to fly, and had a contract to teach Army, Navy and Air Force Flight Instruction Program students as well, but no females.

After graduation, I decided to instruct and fly charter at a large FBO in my hometown while waiting for fall and graduate school. The wife of one of our students expressed great interest in also learning to fly, but she wanted a different instructor in order to minimize comparisons and competition. The duty was assigned to me, and on a bright Saturday morning in June I met my new student, *Mrs. Robinson.* (No kidding!)

When Mrs. R came gliding up to the picnic table/outdoor pilot lounge in front of the office, I totally lost what little composure could be ascribed to a hotshot, 21-year-old instructor. I knew she would be a good pilot—she already knew how to glide. I knocked over three chairs just trying to stand up when she asked where she could find *her* flight instructor, Jerry. The woman was SPECTACULAR! She was the most striking lady I had ever seen in real life! She had looks, figure and style. Although I had never really cared for perfumes, she was followed by just a hint of an essence that complemented her beauty and instantly made me dizzier than jet fuel.

In addition to my own wide eyes and slack jaw, all the other guys had a similar reaction. I fumbled through an introduction, knowing I was the immediate envy of my fellow instructors. I couldn't believe this stroke of luck, and I certainly wasn't about to complain.

I had often wondered what differences I might encounter when instructing a female student, but loss of composure hadn't been on the list. I totally forgot the classroom briefing for lesson one, failed to sign the airplane out, and left the student packet and keys in the office. That was just for openers.

As we walked over to the Cessna 150, all eyes were on us. One thing that never occurred to me, as a professional instructor, was suggesting that Mrs. R dress differently for future lessons. The need for this should have been obvious when two lineboys ran their tugs into each other while watching us cross the ramp. Mrs. R's short, short-shorts and silky "almost" top would have been great for just about any other casual setting. They were a major distraction and potential hazard in the flight training environment.

Other instructors and even students began checking the training schedule to see when Mrs. R was signed up for a lesson so they could observe what she *wasn't* wearing that day. Neither before, nor since, had I seen so much student interest in the preflight inspection of an aircraft. I must admit, this process took on a totally new meaning for all of us. I'm certain no one who witnessed this daily ritual will ever visually check the fuel quantity in a Cessna 150 without thinking of Mrs. R. It was a sight to behold.

Until meeting Mrs. R, I thought of myself as a pretty darn good instructor, and as professional as three years of experience would allow. However, I have to admit my failings and weaknesses. When Mrs. Robinson showed up, I just lost it. Consider, for a moment, the combination of human factors at work here. Her movie star attractiveness and my 21-year-old naivete; her intoxicating perfume and my testosterone.

In spite of the unbelievable distraction, Mrs. R was actually making some progress as a student pilot. One pilot task that I recognized as a problem area (for me, not her) was in making coordinated turns. It came to my attention when I asked Mrs. R. to make *left* turns. We would dutifully clear the area before the turn

In 1968, I took my dad, Jim Cockrell, flying in my PT-17 Stearman. It had been 25 years since dad's last Stearman flight, during his primary flight training in WWII.

and *every* time she turned the control yoke to the left her "almost" top would pop wide open. I'm somewhat ashamed to admit it, but I looked. The devil made me do it!

I soon learned a lesson about situational awareness. It happened during our postflight discussion following lesson number six. When I asked Mrs. R if she had any questions about anything we had covered thus far in her training, she said she had only one concern. "My husband and I didn't really want to compare our flight training experiences," she said, "but he did tell me that his instructor covered left *and* right turns pretty early in the program. I was just wondering when *we* might be doing right turns."

The humiliating reality was almost as overwhelming as my first meeting with Mrs. R. Aspiring, as I did, to being a top-notch, really professional instructor and having to face this major mistake was devastating.

After thinking the situation through for several days, I decided that the ethical thing to do was to switch Mrs. R to another instructor. I also decided to confide in and seek counsel from our chief instructor, a highly experienced and respected instructor, 55 years of age. He listened thoughtfully to my quandary and concerns and finally agreed with my decision. Since Mrs. R was about due for a phase check, he would fly with her and break the news about a new instructor. I just couldn't face her.

I peered dejectedly out of the flight office window as they crossed the ramp to begin the phase check. I was a failure!

That was the last time I saw either of them. They ran off to Mexico together. They were last seen in a climbing left turn

Biography

DR. JERRY COCKRELL

Dr. Jerry Cockrell is a psychologist, 12,000 hour pilot and one of the funniest speakers in aviation. His qualifications include B-737 Captain, CRM & Check Airman Instructor, B-737 Simulator Instructor, CFI and Advanced Ground Instructor ratings and DC-3 type rating. Dr. Cockrell's Ph.D. is in psychology and education. He gives a hilarious banquet-keynote presentation and uses funny and amazing true stories to teach safety, human factors and awareness. Folks laugh and enjoy themselves, then later realize they have learned a great deal and they remember the lessons. As one of the earliest developers of CRM (crew resource management) in 1977 and one of the foremost educators on the subject, Jerry serves as an expert witness in the area of human factors in numerous aviation accident areas. Dr. Cockrell has traveled to all 50 states, England, Germany, Saudi Arabia, Nigeria, Zimbabwe, Mexico and Canada delivering his insightful and humorous presentations. He toured for the Air Safety Foundation (a division of AOPA) for many years teaching various pilot programs and flight instructor revalidation clinics.

WILLIAM G. (BILL) RHEAMS

THE CHAMP

I had flown the B-17 in World War II and, because of that experience in the old Flying Fortress, in 1953 I was transferred to Lajes Field on the Island of Terceira, in the Azores. I did a three-year tour there with the 57th Air Rescue Squadron, flying the B-17 with a 35 foot boat slung underneath it.

When I first got to the Azores, I began as a copilot for an older pilot and I learned a great deal from this man. The most important thing I learned was never to swap stories with him.

He had the most remarkable ability to wind up a flight with a bottle of Scotch whisky and a water glass. Didn't matter where we were, he'd show up with his bottle and his glass. He'd just sit there, sip his Scotch, and tell stories. I knew the routine, so I wasn't surprised when, after a long, tedious flight to French Morocco, he came into my room with a bottle of Scotch in one hand and a water glass in the other. He turned a straight-backed chair around, sat in it with his arms over the back, with the bottle in one hand and the glass in the other, grunted and took a sip.

I knew that a story was coming, so I relaxed and waited. He didn't disappoint me.

He said, "You know, Bill, you remind me of a copilot I had in World War II. We only flew together on one mission. That was a raid on Schweinfurt that was really bad. Just before we reached the coast, on the way back, number three engine got hit and started to burn. I pulled the fire bottle, but it didn't do any good. It just kept on burning. I tried everything I knew to put the fire out, but nothing worked. I knew that I only had a couple of minutes left before the fire burned through the firewall, reached the fuel tank, and we blew up. I had to do something, and do it quick.

"We had reached the Channel by this time, so I elected to ditch. I tried to remember what they taught us about ditching a B-17, but I was excited—and a little scared, too—so, when I tried to put the airplane down on a wave, I did it wrong. We bounced back up in the air, but the water pouring over the wing put the fire out, so I just opened the throttles and went on home."

Well, he SAID that was the way it happened.

RESCUE

There are times that it is possible to look back and see that a particular event was a turning point in the course of your life. It is extremely rare that an event is identified as such while it is taking place. There was a flight on June 4, 1953, that was clearly such a major turning point for me, and I knew that it was, even before I made the decision to take the mission. Perhaps the fact that I fully expected to die had something to do with it.

I arrived in the Azores June 1, and was given a day or two to clear onto the base. On June 4, a major Atlantic storm began blowing. About eight times a year, the Azores are lashed with hurricane force winds, as major weather disturbances sweep across the North Atlantic. This one was particularly vicious.

While the native Portuguese were boarding up windows and doors, and base personnel were heading to the gym for safety, Parker Mudge came to me and said that we had a mission. He said that he would take the flight as aircraft commander, but that he needed a copilot. Because of the hazardous weather conditions, he would take only a volunteer.

Parker was our operations officer, the pilot in charge of aircraft operations. He was then, and was until the day he died, an impressive man. About 10 years older than the rest of us, he had been an active pilot since the 1930s. He wore two sets of wings, one for the RCAF, and those of the USAF. He had a most extraordinary flying history and was at first not well liked, because he demanded the absolute maximum proficiency of his pilots. Later, we recognized that, because of his demands, we had become better pilots than we had any reason to expect to be. He became one of the most respected officers in all of Air Rescue—and deservedly so.

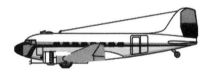

I didn't know all of that yet. I had been there only three days. At the time, the winds were up over 60 knots, projected to go well over 90 knots, and this guy wanted to go fly? I thought he had lost his mind. Fortunately, before I decided not to volunteer, I asked him what the mission was. We stood there with the wind about to blow us away, and he told me about this incredible situation.

There was a ship making its way across the North Atlantic. It was an MSTS ship, that is, a civilian ship leased to the U.S. Navy. It carried mostly freight, but on board as the only passengers were the young wife of a U.S. sailor stationed at Port Layote, in French Morocco, and their 18-month-old son. They were enroute to Port Layote to join the sailor and live there on the base.

As they approached the Azores, the child became quite ill and turned a surprising shade of yellow. The ship's crew became concerned. Rumor mounted upon rumor, and they told the captain that the child had spinal meningitis, that they would all become infected and die. The captain panicked. They were approaching the Island of San Miguel, so the captain put the woman, her child and her baggage in a lifeboat and rowed to the shore. He put the woman out of the lifeboat and on the beach, put her baby in her arms, her baggage at her feet, and rowed back to the ship. He steamed away, leaving this poor girl and her sick baby alone on a strange beach in the middle of the ocean, with a powerful storm making up.

Needless to say, she was in shock. A Portuguese fisherman came walking up the beach and recognized that she was in terrible trouble. He spoke no English and she spoke no Portuguese, but he recognized that she was speaking English. He motioned to her to follow him, and, carrying her baggage, he led her to a nearby village where there was someone who did speak English.

She told her story, but it was hard to believe. Lord love them, the Portuguese are the guttiest sailors in the whole world. It was inconceivable to them that any ship's captain would abandon a passenger on a beach for any reason, least of all because her child was sick and needed help. But there was that obviously sick youngster. They took her across the island to Punta Delgada, the capital of San Miguel, and brought her to the U.S. Consul there. By radio, he called Air Rescue at Lajes Field, some 130 nautical miles to the northwest, and requested evacuation of the mother and child for treatment at the military hospital there—there were no modern hospital facilities on San Miguel.

Parker was very careful to explain to me all the hazards to be faced in accomplishing the evacuation: night was coming on. There were no real radio aids for navigation, so we would have to fly below the clouds and above the waves—the base of the clouds was at about 100 feet, and the waves were 30 feet high. The winds were of hurricane force and were projected to become considerably worse. Very heavy turbulence could be expected, and he had no idea what the strip at San Miguel would be like after we got there.

After all that, he looked me right in the eyes and asked, "Well?"

There comes a time in your life when you either have to put up, or forever live with the knowledge you are less than the man that you want to be. I figured that I was going to die, but I could not abandon that poor girl, either. I told Mudge, "Major, there's no way that we can survive this flight—not in weather like this—but, yes, I'll go. We can't leave her on the beach. We've got to try."

There was no "stout fellow" or back slapping, or anything of that sort. Parker just nodded, said, "Let's go" and headed down the hill to the aircraft parking ramp. Enroute, he said that he'd rather take a Gooney Bird than a Seventeen. It takes less runway, and is made for rough field landings.

We climbed in Air Force C-47 Number 5937, and were in the midst of our startup procedure when a car came up to the aircraft carrying a flight nurse. She was a transient, just passing through Lajes enroute to another station, when she heard about our mission and volunteered to go with us. I must say a word here about military flight nurses. They are absolutely the bravest, finest, most professional, most caring, wonderful gift that God has ever bestowed on mankind. If I knew better and stronger adjectives, I would use them. I am far from alone in my admiration of these extraordinary women.

Parker tried to explain to her the hazards involved, but all she said was, "She'll need a nurse."

We strapped her down laying across the bucket seats, one belt across her knees, one across her waist, and one across the chest. Without it, the turbulence we expected to encounter would have beaten her to death in the back of the airplane. She had stopped at the hospital and had a bag of emergency medical supplies, which we stored securely in a space in the radio compartment.

By this time, the winds were up over 70 knots, and were directly across the runway. There was no way possible for the C-47 to overcome such a crosswind component, so Parker opened the throttles, and we took off right there on the parking ramp. Actually, he opened the throttles, pulled back on the control column, and we jumped up in the air, virtually zero launch. We leveled off at the base of the clouds, at about 200 feet, and turned southeast towards San Miguel. Away from the island, the ceiling dropped down to about 100 feet, with occasional clouds right down to the water. Every now and then, we would have spray from a particularly large wave splash over the windshield.

Major Parker B. Mudge and Bill Rheams

The turbulence was so violent that it took both Parker and me on the controls at the same time to keep the airplane reasonably on course and off of its back. There was a strange calm in the cockpit. Even though Parker and I were using all of our flying skills and every bit of our physical strength in flying the aircraft, we performed our duties of pilot and copilot in a business-as-usual manner. I told Parker later that I could actually feel Someone say to me, "Don't worry about it, Bill. You're doing good work. I'll take care of you." Parker didn't comment on this strange confession of mine. He merely nodded. He had had the same experience. That's the only reasonable answer to why we survived the mission.

It took about an hour of the most furious flying I had ever imagined possible for us to reach San Miguel. Our arms were like lead, from fighting the aircraft, and we were both bathed in pools of sweat. The poor nurse in the back of the aircraft had been hanging on for dear life, even though she was strapped down like a piece of cargo. We were all bruised black and blue from being thrown against the safety belts. I have no idea how the aircraft stood up to the punishment it took.

Before we left, Parker had established with the consul a radio frequency for air-to-ground communications. As we approached

Bill Rheams (far left) and crew members at Lajes Field in the Azores.

San Miguel, Parker called him. The consul stated that the wind was blowing so hard that he could hardly stand up, and that it was blowing directly across the landing strip. There was no possibility of our landing there. Parker asked him if there was a valley somewhere on the island that was protected from the wind, one that had an open field, such as a cow pasture. The consul had us wait a minute while he conferred, then said that, yes, there was one on the other side of the island. Parker told him to move the mother and her baby there, and to line up cars and trucks with their headlights on to act as a runway for us. The consul agreed.

By the time we had fought our way around the island to the other side, the consul had a collection of cars and trucks in a grassy valley, saw my flashing the landing lights, and guided us in. It was pitch dark. We were in and out of clouds and blinding rain all the way down to the ground, and we knew that we were landing between two mountains that we could not see, but we could taste.

Somehow—I don't know how—we made it safely to where the consul and our passengers were waiting. Parker had me load the passengers, while he kept the engines running, and flew the aircraft, there on the ground, to keep the howling wind from making the airplane fly. The speed of the wind going over our wings was in excess of our normal takeoff speed.

I spoke briefly to the consul, then helped the mother and her child into the aircraft, preparatory to tying them down. That's when I found out that that poor girl had never been in an airplane in her life. She had never flown before, and she was going to take a ride like this one!

The flight nurse sailed in, took over, and opened her medical bag. She smiled at the mother, said, "Good night!", and gave her a shot that would knock out a horse. We tied the mother down as we had the nurse for the trip down, then I tied the nurse down again and handed her the child. She held that kid in her arms all the way back to Lajes.

All this time, Parker had been fighting to keep the airplane on the ground. It was bouncing, wiggling, and jumping all over the place, as it was battered by hurricane force winds. He waved goodbye to the consul, taxied up just a little to get out of the way of the vehicles, then opened the throttles. We jumped into the air, then sweated making a steep turn in the violent turbulence, trying to get out to sea without running into the invisible mountains.

The trip back was considerably worse. The winds were now at 90 knots, the sea was higher, the ceiling was lower, and the rain was blowing in sheets, mixing with the spray from the sea, just below our belly. All I can say is, we had *Help* on the way back. That, coupled with Parker's superb flying skills, and the incredible strength Donald Douglas built into his airplane.

We made it back to Lajes. Landed right there on the parking ramp in an almost perfect zero length ground roll, and were immediately tied down by waiting airmen. The ambulance took the mother and child up to the hospital, and the nurse, Parker and I retired to the bar at the Officers Club for some medication of our own.

Shortly, the call went out for whole blood. The problem with the child wasn't spinal meningitis, at all. He had an Rh factor mismatch. They changed the blood in that kid like you change the oil in your car. They pumped new blood in one side, while they pumped the old blood out of the other.

The next morning, the nurse, Parker and I went to the hospital to see how our passengers were doing, and the doctors told us that the child would have died in another hour-and-a-half had we not gone out and brought him in. We went to the mother's room and found the child playing happily in a playpen, and the mother a wreck.

When she saw us, she began to cry. She tried her best to say thank you, but she couldn't. She just held our hands and kissed each of us. Regardless of how long I live, I will never forget the look in that young mother's eyes.

BOATING IN THE SAHARA

Because of other duties, besides flying, I was required to travel from Lajes to the 7th Air Rescue Group in Tripoli, Libya (this was in the early 50s, and Libya was still friendly). I did this regularly, and while it was convenient to be able to fly my own aircraft and travel at my own schedule, it was a long, exhausting trip in a 150-mile-an-hour B-17. Flight planning called for a 1,200 mile leg from Lajes to Sidi Slimane, French Morocco, and refuel. The first checkpoint out of Sidi Slimane, on the leg to Tripoli, was the ancient city of Fez, followed by Taza, just before the Atlas Mountains.

If the weather was good, we could avoid climbing over the mountains by going through the Taza Pass. While the mountains were more or less 13,000 feet high, the mile wide Taza Pass was at only 6,000. There was a radio beacon at Taza that was positioned to guide aircraft through the pass. Even if the visibility was poor, we never used it. If we couldn't see the pass with our unaided eyes, we climbed up over the mountains. The radio beacon was manned by Communist sympathizers and, if you identified yourself as a United States Air Force aircraft, they would distort the signal so as to fly you right into the mountains.

To provide rescue for survivors down at sea, our B-17 carried a 35 foot boat under the aircraft, slung from bomb shackles in the

bomb bay. It was quite a boat. It had an engine with fuel. A mast and sails were folded up inside the boat. It contained a wealth of survival supplies, and, when it was dropped, it came down gently on three large parachutes. While the boat was heavy, it didn't add too much to aerodynamic drag. Being a boat it was built to cut through the water. It did, however, reduce the rate of climb, and we were well past Fez and just about over Taza and the mountains by the time we reached 18,000 feet.

Our problems began when we got over the mountains. We were still in the clouds, and high enough to pick up ice. Normally, this would be no problem. Our de-icing and anti-icing equipment was quite capable of shedding the ice from the wings and the props. But there was no way to get the ice off of the boat. As time went by and the ice built up, it not only added a great amount of weight, it deformed the aerodynamic shape of the boat, and it became a giant wedge that we had to push through the air.

By the time the ice had grown to the point it was threatening our ability to stay in the air, we had passed the mountains, out of the clouds, and into the clear, dry air of the Sahara Desert. I thought that, since deserts are hot, I'd drop down to just over the sand, and let the heat of the Sahara melt the ice.

That's what I did, but it didn't work out quite the way we thought it would. That's when I found out what a wonderful ablative material ice really is. The surface of the ice melted, taking all of the heat with it, leaving the ice beneath just as cold as it had been. There was no way that the ice would melt in time, and, given our overweight condition, the thermals rising from the hot sand were threatening to bounce us into a stall. The farther we flew into the desert, the stronger the thermals became, until there was only one answer: I had to drop the boat. That's what I did. Staggering up to 1,500 feet, I pulled the salvo handle that dropped the boat, and it left the aircraft, taking all of our problems with it. I circled, watched the parachutes open and the boat land gently on the sand, then flew on to Tripoli with no further problem.

This does bring a thought to mind, though. There, several hundred miles deep in the Sahara Desert, is a sailboat in full bloom. I like to think of the effect this will have on some poor Arab, coming up over a dune on his camel and seeing a sailboat sitting there. What will happen to him when he goes back to his tribe and tells his chief what he saw?

BAD DINNER SELECTION

In March of 1954, the 59th Air Rescue Squadron, stationed at Dhahran, Saudi Arabia, found all of its SA-16 aircraft grounded due to propeller problems. The 57th Air Rescue Squadron was ordered to send one of its B-17s to Dhahran immediately to provide coverage of the Arabian area. Parker Mudge took the mission, and I went with him as copilot.

It is approximately 5,000 nautical miles from the Azores to Dhahran, and we flew some 28 flying hours straight on through. We stopped briefly in French Morocco for fuel and some food, then flew over the Atlas Mountains to the Mediterranean by way of Oujda in Algeria, followed the coastline for all of the long leg to Alexandria, Egypt, then turned south for Cairo.

We arrived at the international airport in Cairo much after dark, and I took the crew off to find the dining room, while Parker arranged for refueling. Working out the procedures for payment for the gas took some neat negotiations, and Parker was very good at that. He joined us in the main dining room, and we drank some welcome glasses of iced tea.

The airport in Cairo was one of the most exotic places I had ever seen. Music played over the loudspeakers 24 hours a day, with western music being played for the first 15 minutes of an hour, Arabic music the second 15 minutes, Central African the third 15 minutes, and Far Eastern music the last 15. Then the sequence started all over again. Needless to say, I was fascinated.

When the menu was presented, it was in Arabic, and none of us had any idea what it said. The people at the table next to us all had the same dish, a sort of curried rice with a meat in the middle. It looked good, so we waved our hands to the waiter, indicating that we all wanted the same thing.

That's when Parker spoke up. He said that he had an ironclad rule that the pilot and the copilot never ate the same thing. That made sense to me, so I looked around at some other tables, saw something that looked edible, pointed to it, then back to me. The waiter nodded his understanding, and left to place our order. Sign language is wonderful, if everyone is patient.

Just as our food was served, my attention was diverted and, hungry as I was, I totally lost all thoughts of eating. Two men entered the restaurant and were seated at a table right next to me. The first was a huge black man, obviously from Central Africa. He had on a western style dress shirt and slacks, no tie, and open-toed Arab type sandals. He had a lion's skin over his shirt and slacks, tied at his waist with a wide leather belt in which he carried a huge dagger. He had gold earrings in his ears, a small bone through his nose, and his teeth were filed to sharp points.

The second man was a tiny Italian diplomat dressed to the nines in a formal dress coat, vest with gold chain, striped pants, spats, gloves and a monocle. He wore a neat, thin mustache.

As they took their seats, they were arguing heatedly in what I can only guess was Swahili. The giant African drew his dagger and was gesticulating with it right under the nose of the Italian. With this vicious knife being waved less than an inch from the tip of his nose, the tiny Italian never blinked, nor did he lower his voice. To this day, I remain in awe of the sheer nerve of that little man.

The entire time that Parker and the other three crew members were eating, I stared in fascination at the two men arguing at the table next to me. How could I possibly think of food, when this was going on? I couldn't, so it was something of a surprise when Parker said, "Let's go." I hadn't eaten anything. It had been 15 hours since I had eaten at French Morocco, and I wouldn't have a chance for anything for at least another seven more, so I was sure to be starving before we reached Dhahran. Well, what the hell, it was worth it for the show I had just witnessed.

We took off in the middle of a very black night and headed east. About an hour out of Cairo, Parker became ill. He had a terrible case of food poisoning—so bad that he could only lie on the floor of the airplane and writhe in agony. He was the sickest man I had ever seen. There was not the remotest possibility of his functioning as a pilot. It demonstrated in the most dramatic fashion the wisdom of his prohibition against the pilot and copilot eating the same thing. Had I done so, or maybe had I eaten what I had ordered, there would have been nobody left to fly the aircraft. We would have all died. Had my fascination with the ultimate odd couple actually saved all of our lives? I think so.

I flew the entire leg to Dhahran alone, with Parker lying on the floor in just terrible shape. We arrived at Dhahran at daybreak, and Parker struggled into the other pilot's seat for the landing. I told the tower operator of Parker's problem, and asked for medical attention. We landed. I taxied up to the ramp, and Parker was hauled off to the hospital, where they pumped him out good and proper.

The rest of us went by stake body truck to the mess hall for breakfast, but even though I hadn't eaten for 20-odd hours, I was still hesitant about breakfast, thinking about what had happened to Parker.

I will say this: in all the years since this flight, I never, *never*, have allowed my copilot to eat the same thing that I did. Actually, I try to have him eat at a different place and at a different time.

It's not "Live and learn." It's "Learn and live."

A MATTER OF PERSPECTIVE

For a month we remained tightly on the base at Dhahran, Saudi Arabia. Any emergency that would require B-17 air rescue service would also demand a very short reaction time. When we finally got a day off, what did we do? Why, we went flying. We checked out a helicopter and took an aerial tour of the area. There really is nothing better for touring around than a helicopter. We checked out an H-19 complete with a pilot. Parker flew as copilot, and the navigator and I flew as rear seat passengers. We had a grand old time. Parker brought himself up to currency in a helicopter. The navigator and I sat with our feet hung out of the door which gave us a bird's eye view of the desert. We flew over an oasis near the ancient town of Qatif. It looked like it came straight out of a Hollywood movie, with its minarets and walled homes, and date palms rising right out of the sand. It was fascinating.

The town of Hufhuf is several thousand years old, and it presented an even more romantic vista. We flew low over the town, taking photographs of everything in sight. There was a magnificent old mosque at the edge of an enormous courtyard, with a large number of people coming in and going out of it. We hovered in front of the mosque at an altitude of 500 feet, taking pictures from every angle. The people below gathered together into a tight crowd, talking excitedly and pointing at the helicopter.

The navigator said, "Hey, that's nice. They're all waving at us."

Parker jerked the airplane away from the courtyard so violently that he almost threw the navigator and me out of the door. "Waving, hell. They're SHOOTING at us."

A VERY BUSY MAN

I thoroughly enjoyed my tour at Patrick Air Force Base, in Florida. This was at the very beginning of the missile test program, and everything was new and interesting. The missile range was put on the coast of Florida because there was a chain of islands in the Caribbean upon which to build a string of tracking stations. The second tracking station out of Cape Canaveral was on the island of Eleuthera, a lovely, long, thin island. At that time the only landing strip was in the middle of the island.

I flew a C-54, the equivalent of the civilian DC-4, into Eleuthera with some regularity. The schedule of our flights to supply the tracking station there coincided exactly with that of a small British airline, so both aircraft arrived at the island at the same time. Since I was military, and the small DeHavilland Dove was civilian, I always signaled to the Dove pilot that I would circle and permit him to land first. He was very appreciative of this courtesy.

It was a courtesy, and I intended it to be so, but I did it, too, so that I could watch what followed. The Dove was the only airplane the airline had, and the pilot was the only employee. He performed all of the normal airline functions, but he did them in a typically British manner, with great formality.

His routine never varied. He landed the aircraft, taxied up to the tiny terminal building, parked and shut down the engines. He climbed out of the aircraft, assisted the passengers down the steps, then opened the baggage compartment. He removed his pilot's cap, put it in the baggage compartment, took the baggage handler's cap out of the compartment, put it on and carried the baggage into the terminal.

He gave the baggage to the arriving passengers, then put the baggage handler's cap onto a shelf in the ticket seller's booth, removed the ticket seller's cap from the shelf, put it on and sold tickets to the departing passengers. Once that was done, he returned the ticket seller's cap to the shelf, removed the baggage handler's cap, put it on and carried the baggage out to the airplane.

At the aircraft, he loaded the baggage, put the baggage handler's cap back in the compartment, took out his pilot's cap, put it on, entered the aircraft, taxied out and took off.

All of this was done with great seriousness. He performed each function properly, and required of himself the proper uniform for each individual job.

I arrived one day, and as usual, circled to let him land first. When I landed and walked over, I saw that his right arm had been injured and was hanging helpless in a sling. He performed all of his usual functions with his normal efficiency, but I had to comment on the difficulty of doing them with only one arm.

"Yes," he said, "it does get a bit trying, at times."

NAME, RANK, AND SERIAL NUMBER

How do you describe a giant? Many have said that General Doolittle was small. He wasn't small, only quite short. He was exceptionally well muscled, for having such a short frame, but then he had been an acrobat and a boxer. He was very soft spoken. At times, he was somewhat hard to hear, but then, everybody paid attention when he spoke, so he didn't really have to speak loudly. His actions not only spoke for him, they thundered down through the history of aviation.

I met General Doolittle only once, in 1959. That meeting formed the unquestioned highlight of my life as an aviator—he flew with me as copilot for a couple of hours. At the time, he was Chairman of the President's Scientific Advisory Committee, and the entire Committee was visiting the Atlantic Missile Range for a tour of Cape Canaveral and a few of our downrange stations. After their tour of the Cape, our squadron flew them downrange. There were about 50 of them in all, and we divided the committee into two parties and flew them in very loose formation in two C-54s. I was chosen to fly one of the aircraft.

Our first leg was to Eleuthera, some 300 nautical miles downrange. As we were passing Grand Bahama, one of the scientists on board asked if he could say something over the radio to his friend in the other aircraft. Since we were far enough out at sea that our UHF radio signals would not reach land and could not disturb any other traffic, I told the crew chief to rig up a headset and microphone in the passenger compartment, and asked the other aircraft to do the same thing. The world's top scientists then chatted up a storm, behaving like little kids with their first Christmas walkie-talkies.

The crew chief came back to the flight deck and said that General Doolittle would like to know if he could come up front.

"What do you mean, can he come up front? He can have the whole damned airplane, if he wants it! You tell him that I'd be honored."

General Doolittle came onto the flight deck and, before I could ask him to do so, the copilot jumped out of the right seat and indicated that it was Doolittle's if he wanted it. Doolittle grinned, climbed in, and stuffed all the cushions he could find behind and under himself. He called them shims. I turned off the autopilot, shook the wheel, and waved for him to fly the aircraft. He unbuttoned his vest, put his feet up on the instrument panel, and took the controls. It warms my heart to this day to think about the sheer joy that shone on his face. There were no budgets, no meetings, no engineering, no politics. Just a true aviator doing what he was born to do—fly.

The sky was a beautiful cloudless blue, the air was smooth, and we flew on for a bit, enjoying the chatter of our world famous passengers cutting up on the radio like a bunch of kids. It turned out that there was an instructor from the Air Force seaplane training base at West Palm Beach who was flying far enough out to sea that he could hear our chatter. He thought it was some of his students talking.

He came over the radio, "The pilots breaking radio discipline will give me their names, rank and serial numbers."

General Doolittle and I looked at each other and grinned. I did nothing to interfere with the radio chatter.

The instructor got a little hot when the chatter continued, and he transmitted, "Look, I told you I want the names, rank and serial numbers of the pilots disregarding radio discipline. I want you to know I'm a major!"

That was too good to pass up, and I reached for the microphone. Doolittle waved his finger at me in a negative, pointed to himself, and took up the mike.

"I'll be happy to: Doolittle, James H., Lieutenant General, United States Air Force retired." (He had three stars at the time. The President gave him his fourth star later.) He recited his serial number then said, "And now, major, I'd like to have your name and serial number."

There was a long silence, and I fully expected that that would be the end of it. But, the major must have been more of an OK guy than it first appeared. He came back, "There ain't no way you're Jimmy Doolittle, but there ain't no way I'm gonna give you my name and serial number, either."

We were both laughing so hard it was difficult to fly the airplane. Actually, that ended it. We were approaching Eleuthera. Doolittle went into the back, and the copilot climbed in his seat.

How do you describe a giant? You can try, but it's not enough.

HIGH STAKES

During World War II, the C-47, the military version of the venerable DC-3, served well in flying the Hump, the route over the Himalayas that carried people and supplies from India to China. All of the flights were hazardous. Some were downright peculiar as well.

On one particular flight, the pilot, a friend of mine named Leroy Lovegrove, was struggling to get his old Gooney Bird high enough to fly over the mountains, rather than through the passes. He was, as usual, over gross weight, with the rear of the aircraft full of Chinese laborers. About an hour into the flight, there was a commotion in the passenger cabin. The balance of the aircraft shifted from normal to tail heavy, the flight instruments fluctuated momentarily, then the balance returned to normal.

Things were quiet for a half hour, then the same thing happened again: Leroy could hear a great deal of jabbering and squabbling in the back. The balance of the aircraft shifted to the rear, the instruments fluctuated, then the balance returned to normal. Then silence for a half hour. When this whole situation was repeated for a third time, Leroy had to go in the back and see what was happening.

The Chinese laborers had become bored with the long flight, and they began gambling. However, they had no money, or anything else of value, with which to gamble, so they agreed that the loser of the game would be thrown out of the airplane. Everyone else was considered to be a winner, because they would not be the one thrown out. The change in the balance of the aircraft was caused by the passengers escorting the loser to the back door, and the fluctuation in the instruments was caused by the opening of the back door when the loser was thrown out—the alternate static source for the instruments is just behind the cargo door.

The squabbling and commotion was the result of the loser discovering that he was the one to be thrown out. He didn't want to go.

SKIING THE AMAZON

Bruce Webster has a long background in aviation, and is a quiet, dignified man of enormous talent and ability. Fortunately, he is also possessed of great aplomb. In 1980, Bruce was engaged in a commission that tested that aplomb mightily.

Two pilots were flying a Falcon Jet along the Amazon River in South America and, having made some serious navigational errors, they became lost. As time wore on, and they flew farther and farther without discovering where they were, their fuel supply became dangerously low, and they realized that they would have to put the airplane down. They were in a really remote area. There were huge trees everywhere, but one emergency landing site did present itself, an area of extensive swamp with mud flats that ran right down to the river. They figured that it would be better to go in while they still had some fuel, and thus power to control the landing. They looked over the area carefully, decided on a place with more water than trees, and went in gear up. The airplane settled onto the swamp quite gently, and skidded to a stop. The pilots slogged their way to the Amazon, hitched a ride on a passing boat, and returned to civilization.

The insurance company paid off the claim as a total loss and assumed title to the wreckage. From the pilot's description of the aircraft's condition, it seemed that it was worth salvaging, so the insurance company commissioned Bruce to travel to South America and retrieve the aircraft. Bruce went to Brazil, hired a barge and tug, and had a crane put on board the barge.

The tug pulled the barge up the Amazon to the crash site, tied up alongside the mud flats, and Bruce waded through the mud flats and the swamp to inspect the aircraft. He found it sitting on its belly in excellent condition. However, it was three miles from the river, so it would have to be moved to be within reach of the crane.

His original intent was to use water buffaloes to drag the airplane across the swamp and mud to the barge, but they proved to be too wild. Next he hired 50 natives to try to pull or push it across, but they couldn't budge it. In looking at the situation, Bruce thought that in dragging the airplane on its belly, much further damage could be done. So he cut some 30 foot trees, split them lengthwise in half, and deposited them alongside the aircraft. He jacked up the airplane, then cleaned out the engines, ran a thorough check, and everything seemed to be in working order.

He fired up the engines, put the landing gear down and got a three green, all down and locked signal. He climbed down out of the cockpit, put a split log under each landing gear, and tied them tightly to the wheels with cable. When all was secure, he lowered the aircraft off of the jacks so that it rested on its wheels on the split logs.

The weight of the jet had sunk the logs slightly, so that the natives could not break the airplane loose. Bruce thought that it would be a good idea to use the power of the engines to help, so he cracked the throttles a little, but the airplane just stayed there. He opened the throttles a bit more—still nothing. He opened the throttles all the way, and the aircraft broke free and began to move over the swamp. The logs acted as skis and slid along over the muck, then planed over the patches of water, gaining speed all the way. Bruce just kept it going, aiming the aircraft towards the barge. Hey, why quit, it was working!

When he hit the slick mud flats along the river bank, the drag of the swamp muck was replaced by the almost frictionless wet mud clay. The aircraft accelerated like it was shot from a sling. Before he could do anything about it, Bruce found himself out in the Amazon River, water skiing a Falcon Jet, supported only by speed and three split logs.

He didn't dare reduce the throttles, fearing he'd slow down and sink. Working furiously, he manipulated the plane with the flight controls and asymmetric power. The Falcon Jet came roaring up the river much to the astonishment of the wide-eyed people on the barge. With incredible skill, he pointed the aircraft at the mud flats beside the barge. Just when a crash seemed inevitable, he popped out of the river onto the flats, slid right alongside the barge and chopped the throttles. The aircraft came to rest immediately next to the barge, in a perfect position for the crane to reach out and lift it on board.

Bruce shut the engines down. Completely hiding his pounding pulse, he stepped out of the aircraft. With great nonchalance he said to the crane operator, "Here y'are."

FRIENDLY FORTRESS

Off and on, from 1944 to 1960, the B-17 had taken me safely across oceans, deserts, jungles, through hurricanes and sand-storms, and always got me home—always. It's not hard to under-stand why I love that airplane.

Last winter, an old B-17 from the Confederate Air Force flew into town. It was a cold, blustery winter's night, filled with fog and a fine mist. I went to the airport alone. It was eight o'clock, pitch dark, and the airport was totally deserted. There, in a place all by itself on the ramp, was the old Fort, lighted only by the glare of a security light. I stood there in the mixture of rain, fog and mist for more than an hour, all alone with the airplane.

Surely a machine can have a soul?

BIG FELLA

For three and a half years, I owned the XC-99. It was the cargo version of the ten engine B-36 and the only one made. The XC-99 had six engines on the back of the wings pushing, but didn't have the B-36's four jets on the wing tips. With multiple decks, it would carry 100,000 pounds of cargo 8,000 miles non-stop. The aircraft was big and efficient but standard loading and unloading procedures reduced its efficiency considerably. To speed turnaround time, the XC-99 was the first aircraft to use containerized freight. It carried an enormous amount of freight to Frankfurt and Greenland for the Air Force for about seven years. At the time, the XC-99 was the largest aircraft ever to fly operationally. The only larger aircraft was the Spruce Goose. The XC-99 was retired at Kelly Field in San Antonio. I wanted to scrap it, but the head of the American Aviation Research Association wanted it as a museum. We were discussing this option when I received a letter from the tax assessor. Since I owned an airplane with a stated

The XC-99. To appreciate the size, look directly down
from the tail at three people standing beneath it.

The XC-99

worth of $8,000,000 U.S., I was to pay personal property taxes on that amount. My donation to the AARA was expedited. Unfortunately I didn't have the taxable income to use against my new $8,000,000 U.S. tax credit.

Bill Rheams, yesterday.

Biography

WILLIAM G. (BILL) RHEAMS

William G. (Bill) Rheams' first ride aloft was in a Ford Tri-motor in 1929. He flew the B-17 in World War II, again in Air Rescue—with a 35 foot boat slung under it—and on the Atlantic Missile Range in support of the missile launches from Cape Canaveral. He flew several thousands of hours all over the world in dozens of aircraft types, primarily heavy, four- to ten-engine bombers and transport aircraft.

Bill has spent a lifetime in aviation: as a pilot and as a specialist in the recovery of people, missile capsules, nose cones, and various things dropped in the ocean—not always where they were supposed to be. He has acted as a consultant to several airlines in the United States and in Latin America, and has owned, at one time or another, a couple of his own airlines.

Rheams is well qualified to tell and write Outrageous Airplane Stories. He brings his peculiar sense of humor to these stories. He is as fascinated by aviation as he was on the day he soloed, 55 years ago. Bill says, "Nothing ordinary has ever happened to me."

KENT S. JACKSON

SACKS, DUIs & VIDEOTAPE

When considering what stories I could contribute for this book, my first impulse was to write about flying sacks of checks at night. None of my experiences as an aviation attorney have burned into my memory as clearly as the lightning flashes of embedded thunderstorms rolling across the Midwest past midnight. "Center, has anyone reported the conditions ahead of me?" "Negative, they have radar. They've already deviated away from there." During one such night of "thundersnow," I seriously wondered if a lightning strike would take care of the ice buildup on the wings that the boots couldn't handle.

But mushing sacks of checks in a Piper Seneca through snow can't compare with the unique flying adventures that others have contributed to this book, so instead of writing about contests with Mother Nature, I choose to write about fights with Big Brother.

Defending pilots and companies from the FAA and the IRS is serious business, but even when careers and millions of dollars are at stake, humor can appear as magically as St. Elmo's Fire.

Sometimes, the jokes are lost on the unknowing.

Several years ago, I represented a pilot facing emergency revocation of his commercial certificate for accumulating three DUIs (driving while under the influence citations). The legalities of his defense were complex and speculative. I escorted him into the courtroom like a "dead man walking." Then the judge entered, serious and authoritative in his black robe. A black robe with a tiny difference. A "QB" pin. (A QB, or Quiet Birdman, is a member of a unique social organization of male pilots.) My client grabbed my shoulder with a paralyzing grip and whispered intensely: "He's a QB. They drink like fish!"

After winning the case, I dismissed the QB pin explanation, and assured my client that we won the case on the basis of my sharp instincts and legal research. At least, that's how I prefer to remember it.

Sometimes, the whole case sounds like a joke. The following comes directly from an actual case involving an FAA Emergency Order of Revocation. Only the names have been changed. Not to protect the innocent, but changed anyway.

The basic facts are not in dispute. Bob was pilot-in-command of a DC-3, carrying cargo and operating under Part 135 of the FARs. The flight had landed at Kanawha County Airport and was taxiing toward the ramp when it approached a group of cadets who were assembled on a closed runway in connection with a mock aircraft accident drill. Bob himself described what happened next: "I turned to my copilot and I said something to the effect, 'Drive for a minute', or 'You've got it' or, 'It's your airplane', and then I stood, threw the window open and dropped my trousers with my back to the window." From the record, it appears that the episode lasted five to seven seconds, that the aircraft was taxiing at a speed of 5 to 10 mph, and that the plane passed within approximately 75 feet of the cadets.

The incident was filmed by a person on the closed runway and the videocassette was introduced into the record.

Bob, following the incident, told the investigating FAA inspector that the copilot was laughing so hard that he was slumped down in the seat and therefore was hard to see on the videotape.

The key allegation against Bob:

Your actions, under the facts and circumstances set forth above, demonstrate that you are not a person of good moral character.

"Good moral character" is a specific requirement for holding an Airline Transport Pilot's certificate, and because Bob's butt had appeared prominently on the evening news, the FAA felt compelled to ground Bob for good.

I would have paid Bob for the privilege of taking this case to court, but the privilege went to Harry Riggs, Jr., a friend and mentor who has been protecting the rights of pilots for decades. It is hard to sum up Harry Riggs in one sentence, but the bottom line is this: If you ever stick your bare butt out a cockpit window, Harry Riggs is best suited to save it.

If the FAA and the NTSB had the authority to dispense punishment to fit the crime, a wooden paddle would have provided poetic justice in this case. Unfortunately, the law limited the judge to either revoking the pilot's certificate, or merely suspending it. Revocation kills a pilot's career in the air, and that's what the FAA was trying to do to Bob.

Harry Riggs argued to Judge Jane Doe that Bob's juvenile stunt amounted to mere stupidity, not a lack of good moral character. The FAA didn't have much to say on the subject, so they kept replaying the videotape of Bob's butt, hoping that the facts would speak for themselves. Judge Jane was apparently impressed by both. Two direct quotes:

"I do not find that the act of mooning comes up to the level requiring the revocation of an ATP. We have not yet reached the point where stupidity alone is grounds for revocation of an ATP."

"That beautiful sight was captured by a video camera...."

After winning the case, Harry dismissed the "beautiful sight" comment and assured his client that they had won solely on the basis of Harry's sharp instincts and legal research. At least, that's how Harry prefers to remember it.

Biography

KENT S. JACKSON

Kent Jackson is an aviation attorney, author and ATP with flight experience in Part 91 and 135 operations. A partner in the law firm Jackson & Murphy, L.L.C., he practices solely in aviation law. He has represented numerous pilots, flight departments and corporations in FAA enforcement proceedings, IRS excise tax audits and aviation accident litigation. Admitted to practice in Kansas and Missouri, Mr. Jackson advises clients from coast to coast on all aspects of

aviation law, including FAA and IRS considerations of aircraft acquisition, operation and leasing. He has co-authored all three volumes of *Federal Aviation Regulations Explained* with Joseph T. Brennan, a retired FAA attorney. Illustrating and explaining the policies behind the regulations with specific situations, the books reference a variety of sources, including the Federal Register, AIM, FAA Advisory Circulars, NTSB Decisions and FAA Chief Counsel Opinions. Mr. Jackson has written for *Inside Air Charter, Lawyer-Pilot's Bar Association Journal, Flight Training Magazine,* and *Business Aviation Management Journal.* He is Chairman of the NBAA Tax Committee and an Adjunct Professor at CMSU. In his speaking, Mr. Jackson simplifies and presents complex subjects in a fresh and enjoyable manner.

GORDON BOWMAN-JONES

DON'T KEEP IT SHORT

During my first trip to Launceston, Tasmania to narrate the Unlimited Air Races, I was offered a visit to the airport control tower. As we were ascending the steps, it was explained to me that contrary to the U.S., Australian control towers were typically operated by private contractors under the auspices of the C.A.A. (Civil Aviation Authority).

"As a matter of fact," noted my guide, "the C.A.A. inspectors are up there now for their annual inspection." As we entered the tower, I overheard a transmission from an arriving pilot, "Lawney Tower, this is Vee Haitch Oscar Bravo Hotel inbound for landing."

One of the C.A.A. inspectors immediately grabbed the microphone from the startled controller, puffed up his chest and announced, "This is the C.A.A. speaking, please refrain from the use of abbreviated names for aviation facilities. It is in direct contravention of C.A.A. regulations and is likely to confuse other pilots in the area. Thank you very much!"

I should note that during my arrival in Launceston, our pilot had used the diminutive term "Lawney Tower" during his radio calls and it had seemed to me slightly out of place at the time.

There was a moment of silence as the occupants of the tower nervously glanced at each other, then suddenly a new voice blared from the radio, "The C.A.A. are all numbskulls." The inspector turned a deep crimson color and again snatching up the microphone boomed, "Whoever that was, I want your name, address, aircraft registration and pilot certificate numbers immediately!"

There was no pause this time, the same voice came back immediately, loud and clear, "See? I told you!"

WHAT ARE THE POSSIBILITIES FOR PROMOTION?

A number of Australian airlines run shuttle flights between major cities with modern fleets of aircraft. Much like the New York to Washington or San Francisco to Los Angeles corridors, the Melbourne to Sydney route is quite busy with numerous daily flights.

Following typical procedure, a shuttle flight crew chose to alternate landings and takeoffs for the four backward and forward flights that day, with the first officer taking honors for the first landing in Sydney. There was a brisk crosswind at Mascot Airport that morning and the first officer had his hands full with the aircraft bouncing and skipping its way down the runway. As it came to rest, the captain picked up the cabin microphone and announced, "Ladies and gentlemen, that somewhat tentative return to earth was performed entirely by your first officer!" The first officer, somewhat humbled, chose to stay in the cockpit until the last of the passengers had deplaned.

The return flight to Melbourne was without incident. This time the captain took the controls for the landing. Well, you've guessed it. The captain made an almost identical landing in Melbourne. He ballooned out of his flare, eventually falling to the ground with a bone-crunching thud.

The first officer could barely contain himself. As the aircraft lurched off the runway, he gleefully grabbed the cabin microphone and said, "Ladies and gentlemen, the superlative piece of airmanship that you just experienced was courtesy of your aircraft captain!"

The captain was aghast, "What did you do that for?" he demanded.

"Well, you did it to me!" replied the first officer, righteously raising the cabin microphone.

"I know I did!" bellowed the captain. "But I didn't press the #@$&% mic button!"

NOW YOU SEE IT - NOW YOU DON'T

When the F-117 Stealth fighter was still a rarity at air shows, I developed a very convincing routine around an imaginary fly-by of that elusive bird. As I narrated, I would detail the aircraft's progress inbound, and deliver a bogus technical rundown on the stealth technologies and features employed on the F-117. I started out using the routine to fill time, but I quickly developed a reputation for being able to put one over on some of the most informed aviation enthusiasts.

I hadn't done it before at the Redding, California airshow, so when I saw "Stealth Fly-By - Gordon Bowman-Jones" on the program, with a 12 minute time slot allocated for it, I asked the show organizers about it.

The organizers told me they had heard all about my Stealth fly-by routine and wanted to include it in the program. The routine was something that I normally did on the spur of the moment, when and if it seemed appropriate. I couldn't think of a tactful way to get out of it, so I reluctantly agreed to perform it on cue. As the show progressed, it came time for the Stealth fly-by. The Air Boss winked at me with a broad grin and reported, "Stealth fighter inbound from the south, 35 miles." I began my routine.

"Ladies and gentlemen, our Stealth has reported 35 miles to the south. We've checked with San Francisco radar and they tell us that there is absolutely nothing on their screens, so he's definitely on the way. The Stealth fighter employs the latest DSR audio technology to effectively mask the sound of its huge F-404

engines. This technique, developed by NASA, strategically places high-powered direct sonic radiators on the skin of the aircraft. These are connected to huge 10 megawatt solid state amplifiers in the bomb bay. Over a period of 48 hours, NASA engineers recorded a perfect silence inside a soundproof anechoic chamber. This recorded perfect silence is then continuously played back at very high volume through the DSRs, effectively masking the sound of those massive F-404 engines."

I continued my dialog, being careful to explain that the Stealth would also be practically invisible because of the polarized rear projection visual masking. I told the audience, confidentially, of a trick I had learned from the aircraft's designers. Holding one's head 90 degrees to the horizon would partially defeat the polarizing masks. The Air Boss gestured southward. "I think I see it," he said, "just above the tree line." Scanning the audience, I noted the majority of the viewer's heads were tilted 90 degrees to the horizon, also pointing excitedly to the south. I grinned to myself. This looked liked the best one I had pulled off yet!

"Here it comes, just low over the horizon," I shouted, theatrically building to a crescendo as the ecstatic audience, now pressed up to the ropes, were pointing hundreds of video and still cameras to the south. I extended my arm to track the imaginary pass down the flight line for the audience. And there it was for real. I was dumbfounded. The bat-shaped, midnight black profile passed in front of me and all I could do was stare up at it slack-jawed. From the corner of my eye I saw the show organizers rolling about in laughter, and then it dawned on me. It was a real F-117 and the whole carefully orchestrated practical joke... WAS ON ME!

DON'T TRY THIS AT HOME

One of the funnier acts I had the pleasure of describing as an air show narrator was the infamous "inebriated flying farmer act" at the Livermore, California air show in the mid 1970's. The act began with a battered looking Piper Cub sitting in the middle of the spectator area, door ajar and toilet rolls spilling from the aircraft. Official looking line personnel pushed the derelict looking Cub aside to the apron.

Various officials came to the announcer's stand, purportedly looking for the owner of the plane and explaining to the audience that the "farmer pilot" was potentially dangerous. He had been spotted in a local drinking establishment, they reported, where he was observed consuming huge amounts of whiskey and loudly proclaiming that he could fly the pants off any pilot at the air show.

The whole ruse was obviously a setup, but we had a lot of fun with it.

On cue, a figure clad in a denim bib overall, bright red checkered shirt and a straw hat broke from the crowd line and started weaving toward the Cub. It was a sorry sight as he fell repeatedly trying to get into the airplane, gesticulating wildly for people to get out of his way. I was, of course, playing my part to the hilt, building up the audience for the madcap flying routine to follow. I pleaded for a volunteer from the crowd to go out and stop him. We had two shills planted in the front row ready to go.

As the shills started running toward the aircraft to "try to stop him," they were quickly overtaken on the ramp by one of Livermore's finest, speeding out on his police motorcycle. It was magnificent. Wasting no time, the policeman grounded his bike, dismounting on the run as the big cruiser slid across the asphalt on its side. The unsuspecting "farmer" had no time for explanations. Proudly displaying his civic responsibility the officer rushed the "drunken farmer" from behind, spun him around, and cold-cocked him on the spot with a single mighty blow! With the pilot out cold, the crowd wildly applauded approval for their new hero. Some never knew the unconscious pilot was part of the show.

THERE WAS MAGIC IN THE AIR

In the early 1900s aviators in Europe and the United States rode magic carpets made real by Orville and Wilbur Wright. Aircraft manufacturers sprang up as fast as Internet sites do today, and there was no shortage of bold souls and daredevils to pilot their flimsy and unstable products.

Although powered flight was then an almost daily occurrence in France, England and the United States, controlled, powered flight had eluded all Australian attempts for more than a year after the Wright brothers made their leap into history. The Australian authorities' official definition of "controlled, powered flight" called for an aeroplane to rise from the ground under its own power, fly a figure-eight pattern around two pylons erected half a mile apart, then alight safely back at its original point of departure.

The breakthrough came in 1910 when an amateur aviator from the United States arrived in Australia, bringing with him a French designed and built Voisin biplane. He was actually in Australia on unrelated business, but had scheduled enough time to demonstrate his "other passion" during his visit.

On March 16, 1910 the aviator took his aircraft to Ballarat, the site of the Great 1860 Australian Gold Rush, about 65 miles northwest of Melbourne in Victoria. Assistants erected the pylons to specifications on the outskirts of Ballarat as the aviator prepared his machine for flight. After officials had inspected the pylons, they stood with a small audience of onlookers and watched as the pilot steered his fragile craft around the prescribed course, becoming the first man ever to perform controlled flight in Australia.

The pilot landed to the cheers of his small audience and, as he stepped down from his flying machine, bowed almost theatrically. Truth is many times stranger than fiction and, although it was duly recorded in the history books, I have often wondered how many of the witnesses to that momentous flight believed what they saw. They had good reason not to, for the pilot was not world renowned as an aviator, but as a master of magic and illusion— the great Harry Houdini!

AS THE WORLD TURNS

There is no sweeter sound to my ears than the harmony between a radial engine and a whirling propeller, but as Homer warned us in the *Odyssey*, the Siren's song can mask some sharp and nasty teeth.

In the Army for a day, Gordon flies on a Dust-Off mission.

The summer marine layer had temporarily lifted to 2,000 feet at Half Moon Bay, California. My friend Jay offered me a ride across the hill to San Carlos airport to pick up my airplane and leave his there. The afternoon marine stratus had forced me to divert there the day before, and he wanted to avoid the morning scud for an early flight the following day. Our brief window of opportunity opened so we hurried to prepare his Ryan PT-22 for the short flight.

Jay performed the preflight inspection while I secured the hangar. As I walked toward the aircraft, he was already seated in the rear cockpit waiting to be propped. As an antique airplane pilot and enthusiast, I had propped many different aircraft, including the Ryan. I was fully aware of the dangers and knew many instances of lost limbs, and even lost lives, attributed to using the "Armstrong" starter method.

The Ryan is a little different from other aircraft of the era. Powered by a five cylinder Kinner radial engine, the ignition system features impulse couplings on the magnetos for easy starts.

The engine is primed by throttle and there is no idle cutoff on the mixture control. The engine is stopped by simply turning off the magnetos.

Although there are various techniques for starting the Ryan, I prefer to use my standard method for all aircraft. Check switches OFF, check for hydraulic lock while pulling the prop through all cylinders, prime as necessary, position the propeller at 10 o'clock then call for MIXTURE RICH, THROTTLE CRACKED, HOT AND BRAKES.

The Ryan doesn't need much to get it started, but a healthy pull from the 10 o'clock position assures a good clean start for any engine. If it doesn't start, reposition the prop by holding the opposite tip at arm's length while walking away from it. Repeat as necessary. The basic safety message was solidly ingrained in me. Always treat a propeller as though it was hot!

I had checked switches OFF and pulled the propeller through as Jay pumped the throttle to prime the engine. I spotted fuel from the overflow and advised Jay that it was primed. "OK, pick your blade," he replied. The propeller was in an almost vertical position. I was mentally positioning it for the starting swing. Instead of grasping the tip and walking away, I gingerly inched the propeller a short distance forward, preparing to call HOT AND BRAKES.

My mind was about a millisecond behind the opposite blade as it struck and smashed my hand. It probably took me another full second to realize the engine had started. The next few seconds expanded rapidly in ultra slow motion. The Kinner was running at about 600 RPM, but I was able to carefully consider each blade as it passed inches from my face. What happened? The engine couldn't be running. But it was.

Reality in the shape of those big Fahlin blades slapped the front of my jeans. Standing on tiptoes I was just tall enough to be pulled up hard against the spinner. I could feel the heat as the friction burned a hole in my shirt then ground on into my shoulder. My mind had reached maximum processing speed and was now fully interred in that incredible zone where a lifetime of images flashes by in juxtaposition with immediate reality. I had to get away from it. I tried bouncing away from it but the pull was too strong and I was overbalanced forward. Each time I was pulled back I hit the spinner harder. I knew that I couldn't stand on my tiptoes much longer, but if I relaxed I would go through the prop.

I did the only thing I could. I moved my left leg forward to push myself away. It was like being hit by an 18-wheeler. The blade struck my thigh and threw me into the air. I vividly recall looking down on the airplane and noting Jay struggling to stop the engine. The spinning propeller was now directly below me. I was twisting in the air like a high diver who has suddenly realized there is no water in the pool. I don't know if it was pure luck or if I somehow managed to change my trajectory, but I fell through the prop in the direction it was turning. It slapped me hard in the back, batting me to the ground as I came down.

I realized I was completely paralyzed. I was sure I had lost my leg and probably my hand as well. My face was pressed against the asphalt and I couldn't move my head. I remember a giant ant, next to my eye in the moonscape that was the ramp from an altitude of less than an inch, then focused away.

It was very quiet. Jay had managed to stop the engine by turning off the fuel. I saw his feet, then momentary darkness as he took off his leather jacket, threw it over me and rushed to call an ambulance. Still peacefully quiet, I could hear birds. Am I bleeding to death? How do I stop it, I can't move?

I heard faint sirens in the distance. Then a fire truck arrived. I'm not on fire. An ambulance pulled up directly behind me. Now there are people around me. I can hear them. No one wants to move me. Do they know I'm conscious? What limbs have I lost, how will my life change without a leg and a hand? I want to ask someone but I'm afraid to because I don't want my fears confirmed. Am I dying?

I see the ambulance attendant. I still can't move but I realize I might be able to talk. He thinks I'm unconscious. I'm thinking about how to phrase the question, but more about how to brace for the answer. "Can you save my leg?" I mush out from my immobile mouth.

He appears startled. "It looks awfully bad," he replies.

Now I'm ready. "Can you put it back on?"

"Oh! It's still attached, but you're going to have some really good scars," he said.

"How about my hand?"

He pursed his lips and glanced down at it. "It's busted up, but we've got some pretty good surgeons who'll fix you right up."

Relief washed over me like a warm wave. I felt incredibly lucky. I knew I would heal eventually. I was actually feeling in a good mood! The paralysis was fading and I tried unsuccessfully to sit up. "Hold on, we'll have you loaded up in a minute," the medic grinned. His partner was remarking about the lack of heavy bleeding given the severity of the leg wound. They began a technical discourse about the location of major blood vessels on the outer side of the leg and the effects of shock. I attracted their attention by waving my good hand.

"It's not that at all," I remarked sternly. "Get me to the damn hospital, I can't hold it much longer!"

The engine had started because a broken P-lead on the magneto caused it to be hot with the switches turned off. Jay could not stop the engine because the switches were already off, and there is no idle/cutoff position on the mixture control. His only alternative was to turn off the fuel and wait for the engine to stop, about three minutes.

I am now fully recovered, albeit with some nasty scars on my leg. I became proficient at writing left handed during my months of recovery.

Yes, I still prop airplanes, but just a little more carefully.

Biography

GORDON BOWMAN-JONES

Announcer and narrator Gordon Bowman-Jones is one of aviation's most experienced and professional voices in the air show business. Gordon was born in England and raised in Australia. Regular air show visitors recognize his familiar Aussie accent from the hundreds of air shows he has narrated all over the world. From New England to New Zealand and Tennessee to Tokyo, air show fans have enjoyed his vivid narratives and engaging style for 20 years.

An avid aviation historian, he is known for his wealth of knowledge related to almost anything that flies. His attention to detail provides an experienced mix of informative detail on exotic and unusual aircraft on display, along with exciting narrative on the aerobatic performers in the air. To his fellow aviators and announcers, he is known for his playful wit.

An active aviator since 1968, Gordon Bowman-Jones has owned and flown numerous aircraft from Austers and Ercoupes to Messerschmitts and MiGs, even the GULF blimp. Exploring all facets of aviation, he has pursued many flying interests, including gliding, skydiving and aerobatics.

He currently flies an award-winning 1943 Boeing Stearman PT-13D, which he fully restored in 1984 at his home base in California.

A. SCOTT CROSSFIELD

JUST ANOTHER LONG DAY

Now every pilot has a yarn or two that are favorites and can be told without tongue in cheek and with the minimum of enhancement for the purpose of "hangar story."

At the North American Aviation installation at Edwards Air Force Base on the Mojave Desert we began the rocket-powered X-15 flight test program in 1959. The X-15 was a tiger and to this day has never had its equal in speed, power or performance. Early on, before it grew up, we had some small rocket engines on it. Kind of like training wheels before the "big" engine arrived for the good stuff.

The X-15 program created a quantum jump toward learning how to provide the human factors support for pilots going to space. On every flight I wore a full pressure suit which in reality was a form-fitting flexible life support capsule essential to keep me functioning under any anticipated normal or emergency circumstance that might arise. Some of those with queasy stomachs felt it necessary that there be a medical examination prior to every flight. Dr. Toby Freedman, a dear friend, was the corporate flight surgeon in charge and when he got his emotions and pulse rate under control we would go ahead with a flight. He also was the command surgeon on the emergency helicopter in case I flunked my flight test.

The X-15 was launched from the wing of a B-52 at about 40,000 feet. Early in 1960, on the third flight, one of the rocket barrels exploded when I started it up right after launch. The possibility for that particular explosion had been lurking in those engine models for 20 years and chose this day to spoil. The explosion blew the back end out of the X-15 and the spewing fuel and liquid oxygen torched into an impressive fire trailing the airplane. Chase pilot Major White implored me to shut down. I needed little prompting because I had to get rid of the propellant load to be able to make an emergency landing on Rosamond Dry Lake without adding a much more spectacular explosion.

Most of the propellants jettisoned properly and I made a pretty good landing on Rosamond. Unbeknownst to all of us another lurking problem was a design flaw in the nose gear shock absorber. On landing, the airplane broke right behind the cockpit and instrument bay. I didn't know that. I thought the rear landing gear had collapsed. When the airplane broke the other chase pilot, Joe Walker, commented on the radio, "He broke his back."

Now it didn't occur to Dr. Freedman that Walker was referring to the airplane and not to me. Toby, bringing a corpsman with a back board, flogged the helicopter pilot mercilessly to hasten to come to my lonely scene on Rosamond. He wanted to get his friend with a broken back out of the "crash."

Meanwhile I stayed in the airplane, a heavy nickel/steel structure. It was the best place in case of more fire and explosion for a pilot partially immobilized in a pressure suit. I could see no shadow of heat or smoke on the dry lake floor with my limited rearward visibility. However, I could see what appeared to be the fastest helicopter in the world zooming across the desert. That would be Toby. They landed and he and the corpsman leaped out and began running toward my airplane. As he did, he was pointing to the X-15's midsection. I opened the canopy that was hinged in back of my head. Toby grabbed it and tried to throw it wide open so he could get a back board on his friend with a broken back.

Now what Toby didn't know, but I did, was that if the canopy was opened full, past a detent, it would arm the ejection seat. I didn't think that was too healthy for Mrs. Crossfield's son. I hung onto that canopy for dear life while this ex-football player was virtually lifting the nose of the airplane off the ground with me still strapped to the seat as the connecting link between airplane and canopy. I couldn't communicate through an oxygen mask and helmet.

It finally dawned on the good doctor that: (1) for a broken back I was showing remarkable strength and determination and (2) there must be a reason for my struggle with him. He relaxed his grip and I got my helmet open to shout, "No!" at him and it was over.

Then I had to start laughing when it began to occur to me how we had cheated our friends in the media. I could visualize their headlines:

"TROUBLE-PLAGUED X-15 BLOWS UP IN FLIGHT, BREAKS IN TWO ON LANDING, CREMATES FLIGHT SURGEON WITH EJECTION SEAT ROCKET BLAST, AND THE PILOT ENDS UP 400 FEET IN THE AIR WITH AN ARMFUL OF PARACHUTE AND NO WIND TO FILL IT."

Some days you win the right one!

Biography

A. SCOTT CROSSFIELD

Scott Crossfield is best known for being the first to fly Mach 2 and also the first to successfully fly Mach 3. He flew most of the research airplanes, including first flights in the T-39 and the X-15. Scott has received an incredible number of honors and awards for his many contributions to aviation. His list of accomplishments and credentials is mind boggling. He has a Masters degree in Aeronautical Engineering and a varied professional career. He was a Navy fighter pilot, a Chief Wind Tunnel Operator, a Chief Engineering Test Pilot, an Apollo Program System Director, a Technical Director and held several Vice President positions—all in government and industry. He was a Technical Advisor on aerospace for the U.S. Congress. His presentation *Onward and Upward* is a fascinating program on the men and machines of the most productive government research program of record, one that brought us to the threshold of space.

JULIE CLARK

WE'VE COME A LONG WAY... DOWN?

There are more women airline pilots than ever, yet even now, as a captain, I can't walk through the cabin without some passenger asking me an unusual question. Recently, a woman passenger touched my arm after a flight and asked why I wasn't "allowed" to make the PA announcement. I explained to her, it was my leg to fly. The pilot not flying normally makes the announcements. She assumed it was because I was a woman....

If people still ask such questions now, imagine how it was in 1976 when I was hired by Hughes Airwest (now Northwest Airlines). Back then, my uniform put management in a quandary until they decided to dress me like the men, right down to the men's black tie. This would, of course, make us blend right in. Fortunately, as a first officer, I could normally perform my inspection duties and be buttoned in the cockpit before the passengers were boarded. By staying out of the cabin I could keep to the job of flying, and avoid the passengers' questioning looks and curious comments.

But I couldn't avoid the passengers in the cabin forever. Once during my first year flying a DC-9, the captain ordered a visual gear inspection. We had lowered the gear in preparation for landing, but we were not getting the three-in-the-green light display needed to verify the landing gear was down and locked. In the two-crew cockpit, the duty of checking the gear went to the first officer, me. The worst part of this visual inspection was the location of the indicator, right in the middle of the passenger cabin aisleway. Our flight was full. To get to the indicator, I would have to walk by dozens of passengers and perform the inspection in front of all of them.

As representatives of the airline, pilots are required to adhere to a strict dress code, especially when interfacing with the passengers. The cockpit has a mirror for pilots to check their appearance before leaving the cockpit. Due to the nature of the inspection, I decided to bend the rules a bit and proceed without my hat and jacket, but I carefully straightened my tie. On the other side of the door, as expected, every eye was on me. I walked purposefully, but with a friendly smile, so not to alarm anyone.

All the passengers must have put away all their books and magazines in preparation for landing, because every one of them turned and watched my antics with great interest. Midway through the cabin I found the location of the inspection hole above the landing gear. Unless you fly DC-9s, you would probably never notice the snap at the carpet's edge. I undid the snap and pulled up the carpet, exposing the cap. Beneath the cap is a periscope to view the landing gear indicators. In order to ensure the landing gear is down and locked, I had to look into the periscope and make a visual check to see that the two indicators are perfectly aligned. So I knelt on my knees, leaned down, and removed the cap.

Suddenly, a quick "swish" sucked my tie down the hole and smacked my chin against the carpet. Mentally I cursed the captain for not completing the cabin decompression. When the cap was removed the higher pressure air in the cabin rushed out the hole to the lower pressure air outside, attempting to take me with it. Fortunately, I was a lot bigger than the hole.

So there I was with face smashed against the floor trying to look cool. I looked up at the passengers staring at me with interest. I smiled. "Hi." "Hello." "How are you?" "Be done in just a sec." Nobody laughed. It took about three minutes to complete decompression. It seemed like three hours. Finally with a light "sigh" the hole gave up its death grip on my tie. I visually checked the gear. It was down and locked. Then I replaced the cap and carpet and quickly returned to the cockpit. Boy, did I give that captain a piece of my mind.

Fortunately, my rug-burned chin and bruised ego quickly healed. To this day, whenever I walk down the aisle of a DC-9 and see that carpet snap, I smile.

Biography

JULIE CLARK

Julie Clark is a veteran pilot with more than 30 years of flight experience and 25,000 accident-free hours. One of the first women pilots to fly for a major airline, she captains Northwest Airline's DC-9s and MD-80s. Captain Clark is checked out in more than 65 types of aircraft, including WWII B-17s and PBY-5 flying boats. Julie was a civilian instructor at NAS Lemoore, CA, flying the military T-34 trainer for the U.S. Navy. In 1977, she purchased a T-34, sight unseen, for $18,000 at a government surplus sale in Anchorage. After flying 2,900 shaky miles home from Alaska, she began the extensive restoration. She added a 285-horsepower custom-built engine and painted the plane in her version of the Air Force One paint scheme. She also owns and operates an ex-Navy T-28 that she flies for fun when not flying air-shows. In addition to flying a reg-

ular captain's schedule for the airlines, Julie has flown 1,000 performances, averaging 23 airshows a year in her Beechcraft Mopar T-34 Mentor. Her routine is an elaborate ballet of grace and skill in the sky, with red, white and blue smoke to the sounds of Lee Greenwood singing *God Bless the USA*. This beautiful, energetic, all-American was the 1998 winner of the coveted Art Scholl Showmanship Award. Julie is an inspiration to young and old.

BRIGADIER GENERAL R. STEPHEN RITCHIE (RET.)

THUNDER OVER FLORIDA

Right after pilot training, Jack Hudson, now a pilot for Delta, and I were flying together at Eglin Air Force Base. We thought we were pretty hot stuff... two young second lieutenants flying the F-104 Starfighter. We each had some 200 hours in the T-33 (T-Bird) and about 50 hours in the F-104.

Late one night, we were returning to Eglin in the T-Bird from a cross-country flight through a line of thunderstorms. I was in the back seat, flying the airplane. Frequent lightning, piercing the darkness of the black, moonless sky, kept me hunkered down in the rear cockpit. All of a sudden, the engine overheat warning light came on!

My heart started beating faster. Shortly thereafter, the fire warning light illuminated. Fire is the pilot's worst enemy. Military pilots are trained for emergencies like this, and dread the day when they have to deal with a burning aircraft.

"Jack, we're on fire," I cried. "I've got a fire light!"

I was really frightened. Finally, he started laughing. Jack couldn't hold it any more. He had been tinkering with the warning test switch. By slowly pulling it down, he had activated the overheat light and then the fire warning light in my cockpit.

Scared the devil out of me!

LEADERSHIP THAT INSPIRES EXCELLENCE

It was one of the most carefully planned missions of the Linebacker campaign. For days, with the help of the latest special intelligence-gathering techniques, we studied the routes, orbit points, formations, and tactics of the enemy. We selected 10 May 1972 to put to the test what we had learned. At 0500 hours, the 432nd Tactical Fighter/Reconnaissance Wing briefing took place as it did every day, seven days a week. We then broke for individual briefings to review each detail of what was likely to occur during the next few hours as we prepared to launch for various destinations over North Vietnam.

I was number three, or deputy flight leader, of Oyster Flight. Oyster was the ingress flight led by Major Bob Lodge, a friend, a fellow 1964 graduate of the Air Force Academy in Colorado Springs, and one of my former students in the Air Force Top Gun school at Nellis Air Force Base, Nevada.

Our McDonnell Douglas F-4 Phantoms were the first four aircraft to penetrate North Vietnamese airspace, paving the way for the strike force to follow. Our job was to intercept and defeat enemy fighters that would attempt to prevent our strike Phantoms from dropping their highly accurate laser-guided bombs.

After a brief delay for foul weather in the target area, the mission was a go. Following tanker rendezvous shortly after takeoff to top off our fuel tanks, Oyster Flight dropped to treetop level and proceeded inbound low enough to be under enemy surveillance radar. We employed radio silence procedures to reduce the chances of being detected. Reaching our planned orbit some 25 to 30 miles west of Hanoi, we stayed below 300 feet as planned and continued radio silence. Using the latest, highly classified, high-technology equipment—available in only a few of our best airplanes—we electronically spotted a flight of four Soviet-built MiG-21s in orbit northwest of Hanoi. Intelligence had predicted the situation and our plan was to wait until the MiGs departed their holding pattern to attack our strike force as it approached from the southwest. Then we would "pop up" to meet the Soviet-built fighters head-on.

Our orbit was then below the effective altitude for surface-to-air missiles (SAMs) and heavier anti-aircraft artillery (AAA), so small arms fire and light AAA were the only nuisance as we waited.

Right on schedule, the MiG-21s departed orbit and we rolled out on a northerly heading, pointing our radar sensors skyward to achieve full system radar lock-ons at 15 miles. Our adrenaline surged as the battle developed at a closing rate of more than 1,200 miles per hour. Visual engagement was only moments away. The computer for our Sparrow radar missiles flashed that we were in range and, as briefed, our first two jets (Oyster One with Bob Lodge and Roger Locher and Oyster Two piloted by John Markle and Steve Eaves) fired head-on at seven miles.

Within seconds, fireballs and smoke trails filled the air, and debris was falling all around us. Two MiG-21s had been destroyed. Lodge and I, in Oyster One and Three, immediately turned our fighters as hard as possible to achieve rear-quarter positions on the remaining two MiGs. I locked on to the third MiG using the auto-acquisition switch on the left throttle and fired two Sparrows at a range of 6,000 feet. The second missile exploded under the fuselage of the North Vietnamese fighter, and the pilot bailed out as his aircraft burst into flames at 15,000 feet.

Meanwhile Lodge and Locher were positioning for a shot at MiG number four. What a great day it was going to be—a perfectly planned, perfectly executed mission, resulting in four American victories. But it was too good to be true. As Oyster One, piloted by a crew with over 400 combat missions (a crew largely regarded as the best in Southeast Asia), was about to claim its second MiG of the day, a flight of four MiG-19s stormed in from above and behind.

"Oyster One! Break! Break!" we screamed. "MiG-19s at six o'clock! Oyster One, Oyster One, Break! MiG-19s firing!"

But Lodge and Locher, concentrating on the MiG-21, missed our frantic calls, and 20 millimeter rounds from the MiG-19s peppered the wings and fuselage of the American fighter. Within seconds the Phantom II burst into flames and rolled.

"Bail out! Bail out!" I yelled. "Bail out!"

At 7,000 feet, upside down and on fire, the Phantom was out of control. What began as a triumph ended in tragedy. Two of America's finest young officers, and two very close friends, were going down in flames, and Oyster Two, Three and Four were being chased out by the remaining MiG-21 and the MiG-19s. It was not supposed to end that way.

Throughout the following week, we returned to the area and called on the radio, hoping that Lodge and Locher who carried survival radios with extra batteries, had somehow managed to bail out—hoping that our calls would be returned by one, or even both. But our calls went unanswered. We finally resigned ourselves to the probability that they had been killed or captured (though their names never appeared on the list released by the North Vietnamese of those taken prisoner on or after 10 May) and we were ready to give up.

Then, 22 days later, on the first of June, the strike force was in the vicinity of Yen Bai Airfield, some 60 miles northwest of Hanoi. Momentary silence filled the air, then came a piercing call. "Any U.S. aircraft, this is Oyster-Zero-Bravo—over."

We don't have an Oyster callsign today, I thought, but my backseater, Chuck DeBellevue, shouted, "My God, that's Roger Locher!" We answered, and Roger said, "Hey guys, I've been down here a long time. Any chance of picking me up?"

"You bet—you bet there is!"

Back at Udorn Royal Thai Air Base we quickly planned and launched a rescue mission. It was one of the deepest, most difficult and dangerous rescues ever attempted. There were numerous SAM sites and more than adequate AAA around Yen Bai, one of North Vietnam's most important airfields. And, of all places, Roger Locker was only five miles off the south end of the runway. The ground fire was so intense the rescue attempt had to be aborted, and Udorn was quiet that night. We knew Roger was alive. We knew he had valiantly evaded the enemy for over three weeks. And now we could not get him out. We had failed to get him out, and what was worse, the North Vietnamese had been alerted. They knew Roger was in their jungle, and now they knew where to find him.

Back at Udorn we were frustrated and discouraged. The next morning, General John Vogt, the four-star commander of Air Forces in Vietnam and Thailand, in an uncommon act of courageous leadership, canceled the strike mission to Hanoi and dedicated over 100 aircraft to the rescue of Roger Locher. Captain Ron Smith flew Sandy One, the low-altitude, on-scene commander, and a 27-year-old captain named Dale Stovall commanded Jolly 30, the lead chopper that snatched Locher from the jungle as the enemy closed in.

In a brilliant display of total commitment and unparalleled excellence, a bitter defeat became a sweet, sweet victory. On that morning, training, teamwork, discipline, and the dedication of hundreds of Americans and allies resulted in the successful return of Captain Roger Locher to friendly territory. During Locher's debriefing it was learned that, unfortunately, Bob Lodge did not make it out of the airplane. His remains were returned to the United States by the North Vietnamese government some years later.

On learning the good news, General Vogt flew from Saigon to Udorn in time to be the first among hundreds to welcome Roger back as he stepped off the rescue helicopter after 23 days in the jungles of North Vietnam. It was an experience as moving as it was magnificent. Enormous resources had been expended and many lives had been risked.

The flight surgeons rushed Locher off to the hospital, but later agreed that he could come to the Officers Club that night. The word spread and the club was packed. At 1900 hours, washed, shaven, fed, and in his "party suit," Roger walked through the front door to applause that continued for 20 minutes. Hands were shaken. Tears were shed. The camaraderie and love that bound us together in time of war had come together that morning. Enormous resources and many lives had been risked, but Roger Locher had been saved.

YOUNG AND COCKY

In the summer of 1965, I had logged almost 200 hours of T-37 and T-33 jet time during more than nine months of Air Force pilot training. As a newly licensed civilian pilot, I had flown another 50 hours in my Cessna 120, a $1,500 investment in 1965 dollars. Much of my taildragger flying was across Texas, hopping from one small strip to another. I experienced a lot of crosswind landing practice on those short runways.

Late one afternoon, while I was changing the Cessna's oil, a few construction workers sauntered over. They had finished work for the day, and one of them, who had consumed a few beers, wanted to know if he could go for a ride. I had just flown at the base and had not planned to fly my plane that day, but offered, "If you pay for the gas, I'll take you for a ride."

"So, how much?" he asked, considering it.

After some quick math I replied, "75 cents for 15 minutes." It was a deal.

We buttoned up the airplane, got in and taxied out. After take-off, I spotted a small thunderstorm over downtown Laredo, about eight miles southeast of the field. As we headed south for an overhead view of the city, I watched it move northwest and head toward the field. We flew over Laredo and then headed back to land, but by that time, the thunderstorm was right over the airport. The windsock was sticking straight out. With all the airport-hopping I had done, I was accustomed to landing with 15-20 knots of crosswind and thought I was pretty darn good. Besides, the workman had only paid me 75 cents and his time was up, so I decided to go ahead and land.

I centered the little Cessna on final with full cross control deflection. About this time, an instructor saw me approaching with the windsock pegged 90 degrees to the runway. He knew I was pretty good at crosswind landings, so he grabbed his new student, put him in the car and drove to the end of the runway. "Watch carefully," he told the student, "This is how a crosswind landing is properly done."

We continued down on final, controls crossed. I rounded out, then touched down. Piece of cake, no sweat. Slowing down to not more than 30 miles an hour, I eased up on the cross controls. Suddenly the plane veered into the wind, 90 degrees to the runway.

We heard the twisting snap of the gear shearing off. The wing dug into the asphalt. We slid off the side of the runway. The fuselage was bent, the propeller broken, the wing was crunched and the gear was gone. My passenger was having a great time. With a beer in his hand he shouted, "Hot damn! What a ride!"

The instructor sitting at the end of the runway sheepishly turned to the student and said, "That is *not* the way to make a crosswind landing!"

Sold the airplane for $500 as junk.

TOO BAD THEY DON'T MAKE
ADRENALINE FOR AIRPLANES

The first time I ever saw a surface-to-air missile (SAM), it was an adrenaline rush. I will never forget it.

We learned to spot SAMs where they were launched. First came dusty air forming a circle over the ground. Then, a thin pencil with its tail on fire emerged from the circle, heading right for you. SAMs were just like aircraft traffic, if it stayed at the same point on the canopy, it had your name on it. If it moved across the canopy, it was pointed somewhere else. Once you got used to observing them, they became easier to spot. However, you never totally got over the rush.

If you spotted a SAM coming right at you, you employed a basic escape maneuver. One of the many SAMs I saw in 1972 was launched on June 1. I watched it drilling a hole in our canopy. It was coming right at us. I started a pushover to fly under the SAM's path. I then turned the airplane into the missile and pushed forward on the stick as hard as I could.

The G-meter in the F-4 shows four negative and 8 1/2 positive. As I was in the negative G push, the SAM was tracking, staying on the windshield. I pushed harder and harder, the G-meter was pegged at four negative. Then John Madden called, "Steve, pull up, you've got another one right under you."

They had fired a second SAM from another site, one that I didn't see. In one pull, I took the airplane from more than four negative all the way to 8 1/2 positive, pegging the G-meter on the positive end. That's a net change of 12G or more on the airplane. Both SAMs missed us

There was so much adrenaline flowing from seeing the first SAM and missing the second, I don't remember feeling anything during the 12+G maneuver. But the Phantom didn't like it. A whole bunch of rivets popped, the wings buckled, and the engine mounts broke. Like most aircraft, the F-4 engine is fastened to the airframe on four mounts. All four snapped, dropping the engine into the engine bay. I flew home very carefully, and landed safely. We missed the SAMs, but the airplane was seriously damaged.

TANK JETTISON

The F-4 carried three external fuel tanks—a centerline tank and two wing tanks. The two forward missiles couldn't be fired with the centerline tank in position because the tank would rupture during the launch. There was a book procedure for jettisoning the centerline fuel tank. It required pulling up the nose to about 15 degrees, slowing to about 250 knots (which is not good over enemy territory), putting about a half G on the airplane, hitting the centerline tank switch, and hoping it didn't rip the underside of the airplane as it came off.

After topoff from the tanker, the route over the Gulf of Tonkin was a little shorter than our normal route from the west. Consequently, the centerline tanks didn't empty until we were pretty close to the target area, not far from Hanoi. We started the bureaucratic-inspired book maneuver. Everybody pulled up, we slowed down to about 250 knots, and knocked off the centerline tanks. All of a sudden, we heard calls that MiGs were about five miles out. There we were nose-high at low speed... not a good place to be.

I pushed the nose over and began to pick up air speed. Then we spotted MiG-21s about two miles at nine o'clock.

One MiG screamed by while I made a nose-low turn inside of him. Rolling out in a rear quarter position at about 15,000 feet AGL (above ground level), and a range of almost two miles, we achieved a radar lock-on. The Sparrow missiles are good in the rear quarter at distances up to about three miles. The MiG rolled left. I gained some angle by cutting off his left turn, and fired the first two missiles.

Standard procedure is to fire two missiles for a better chance of hitting the target. After radar lock-on, it's four seconds before trigger squeeze. Then, there is a second-and-a-half delay before the missile breaks away from the airplane. So, if everything is just right, it's five and a half seconds before the first missile launches. That is a very long time in an air battle!

We had a good shot, so I committed two missiles by squeezing the trigger twice. The MiG turned to the left. We followed. The first missile departed and corkscrewed to the right. As soon as I saw the errant missile, I committed the last two missiles (F-4's carry only four Sparrows). The second missile left the Phantom, guided, but detonated about halfway to the target. Then the third missile came off the aircraft. By this time the MiG's nose was well down. The third missile also guided, but detonated about 500 feet behind the MiG. Since the MiG's nose was so far down, I feared the fourth and final missile would lock on the ground and go ballistic.

The missile pulled way out in front of the MiG. It appeared as if the Sparrow was 30 to 40 degrees out in front of the target. But the AiM-7 was pulling lead! The almost 500 pound missile hit the MiG in the forward part of the fuselage, blowing the nose off the airplane. Half a MiG, from the wings back, was all that remained. As we flew over, what was left went into a flat spin. It didn't even burn, just smoked. By this time, the other MiG headed for home. As we were out of Sparrows, we did the same.

Biography

BRIGADIER GENERAL R. STEPHEN RITCHIE (RET.)

A command pilot with some 4,000 flying hours including 800 combat hours, General Ritchie is our last American Ace. He's the only Air Force Pilot Ace of the Vietnam conflict and the Air Force's first and only pilot ace since the Korean War as well as the only American pilot in history to down five MIG-21s. In 1968, General Ritchie served as an F-4 pilot at DaNang Air Base, Vietnam, where he flew the first F-4 Fast Forward Air Controller (FAC) mission in Southeast Asia. In 1969 he completed the F-4 Fighter Weapons School at Nellis AFB, Nevada, and became one of the youngest instructors in the history of the school. General Ritchie volunteered for a second tour in Southeast Asia in January

1972 and was assigned to the 432nd Tactical Fighter Reconnaissance Wing. He served as Wing Weapons Officer, and it was during this tour that General Ritchie scored five MIG-21 victories. As a winner of the Air Force Cross, four Silver Stars, 10 Distinguished Flying Crosses and 25 Air Medals, General Ritchie understands commitment to excellence. This commitment flavors his speaking programs including: *Why Not the Best?*, *The Battle of Ideas, Top Gun Performance* and *The Cutting Edge.*

DANNY MORTENSEN

MOON OVER SAN JOSE

My buddy Greg and I joined the FAA as air traffic controllers in 1973 and also became roommates. Shortly after we were checked out on all the cab positions, a vacancy came up at San Jose Tower across town and Greg was transferred from Reid-Hillview.

One of the San Jose supervisors had the annoying habit of coming up and snooping around the tower cab at 7 a.m. each morning, long before the shift change at 7:45. The night crew, who could be just as annoying when they put their minds to it, decided to put an end to their unwelcome visitor with a typical controller response.

One morning Greg and the other two male controllers on duty stripped stark naked, except for their headsets, and continued to work traffic. When the early bird supervisor came bounding up the stairs... well, you can imagine the look on his face. The controllers kept working. He hightailed it back down the stairs and never showed up early again.

TALES FROM SACRAMENTO METRO (SMF)

In 1976, before Hughes Air West merged with Republic, one of their yellow bananas (a yellow DC-9) used to depart around 10:30 p.m. every night to Klamath Falls. After pushback, they would pass the terminal on their way to the runway and a microphone would key to the sound of a long, lonesome train whistle as if passing through a railroad crossing. I never figured out if it was the Hughes Air pilot or one of the other aircrews making fun of the little banana. _____

In 1978, the first airliner into SMF, a United flight from San Francisco on its way to Denver, arrived around 7:15 a.m. every morning. One morning, Approach Control handed the United flight off to me earlier than usual, about 40 miles out. All I knew was the United was inbound. On initial contact, I asked the United pilot his position, to which he replied, "I'm just the copilot. Would you like to speak to the captain?" _____

PSA was a great airline. They flew like a bunch of cowboys and would do anything you asked of them. They had a great sense of humor, too. One day when I was working ground control, a PSA pilot asked me if I could see the cockpit while he taxied to the gate. I knew something was up so I picked up my binoculars and replied, "Yup." The captain's side window slid open and out came a 10 foot long white scarf. I'd swear he was wearing helmet and goggles, too. _____

In 1977, I used to commute from a dirt strip in the foothills of the Sierra Nevada to SMF in my little Smith Miniplane, a single seat, open cockpit biplane. The trip took only 15 minutes by air, but over an hour by car. Flying to work above the freeway congestion gave me such a natural high, no matter how busy it got at work, I could deal with it.

One day, while working traffic and chitchatting with my fellow controllers, the conversation drifted around to a favorite topic, how controllers got paid. Controllers were paid according to how much traffic their facility handled. The more traffic a facility worked, the more the controllers were paid. I had an idea of how I could raise SMF from a Level 10 to a Level 11 facility. I suggested to my fellow controllers that on breaks, I could do lots of touch-and-go's in my Miniplane. All they had to do was to pay for my fuel. At the time, the highest traffic count in one hour had been 40 operations (operations consisted of practice approaches by the military, Pan Am & TWA training crews and the usual commercial airline traffic). Nobody took me seriously, so on my next break, I left the cab and taxied out in the Miniplane to prove my point.

The Miniplane could take off in less than 400 feet and stop in 800. The runway is 8,600 feet long. On the first takeoff, I climbed to 50 feet and requested permission to land. The local controller cleared me to land and upon landing immediately cleared me again for takeoff. We repeated this procedure the length of the runway and increased the traffic by a count of 12: six takeoffs and six landings. At the end of the runway, if there was no traffic, I would reverse direction and go back up the runway for another count of 12. In one hour, we reached a total of 127 operations. That's a record that still stands today at SMF. The only problem was the controllers didn't want to pay for the gas.

Metro made Level 11 several years later.

BAKERSFIELD MEADOWS TOWER

In 1979 we were pretty well staffed at Bakersfield, so eight weeks in advance, I asked for time off to fly the San Marcos, Texas, Air Races. I was a regular contestant in the races. That year I was scheduled to fly a Mong Biplane. It was a lot faster than the Miniplane. The team supervisor, in his infinite wisdom, said "No," and it looked like I was to miss my first race in four years.

A short time later, a good friend, Stan, who was also a fellow racer and an attorney by profession, called to arrange our usual rendezvous enroute to the races. After an unlawyerly response to my bad news, he came up with a brilliant and very "lawyerly" solution.

My friend was handling an impending lawsuit in Reno, the result of an earlier midair collision between two T-6 aircraft on the racecourse. Since I was an elected official of the race association, he proposed to subpoena me to testify on the Friday of the upcoming race. This would require travel on Thursday to Reno.

A few days later, the tower chief received the court-issued subpoena ordering me to appear in Reno. My team supervisor had forgotten about my earlier request for time off, and the chief told me to honor the subpoena. On the appointed Thursday, I departed BFL heading north to Reno, and then promptly "got lost" five minutes later, landing the next day in San Marcos in time to qualify and race.

It wasn't until several weeks later I realized I might get caught. Every aviation trade paper in the country listed the names of the race winners and my name was on the list. Those publications frequently showed up in the tower ready room and lounge. Fortunately, the supervisors seldom took time to read the airplane magazines. In any case, each time one arrived, I was quick to dispose of the incriminating evidence.

Danny and his Rutan racer.

LOOMIS, CALIFORNIA

My dad, Ernie, a World War II aircraft mechanic, served on the battleship Mississippi and on several baby flattops. He contracted Parkinson's disease from a head injury he received while working on a five-inch anti-aircraft gun. Dad has shuffled, stumbled

For 16 years, Danny Mortensen has been the Master of Ceremonies at *An Evening With Champions* at the EAA Oshkosh Fly-In. Danny back stage with EAA President, Tom Poberezny (left) and co-chairman of evening programs, Steve Weaver (right) at the Theater in the Woods at Oshkosh, Wisconsin.

and fallen through life ever since. He gets around pretty well, but if you didn't know him, you would swear he was drunk by the way he walks.

In spite of all this, or because of all this, dad has a great sense of humor. For his last birthday, we had a special golf shirt made for him with the inscription on the back, "How is my walking? Call 1-800-824-4170." The number is my business number. The shirt gets a lot of comments from folks whenever he wears it. Best of all, I can keep track of him throughout the day while he is cruising the neighborhood. People really do call the number—just to see if it's legit.

Biography

DANNY MORTENSEN

Danny Mortensen began his aviation career in 1967 at Arizona State University learning to fly as a private pilot. He worked as an FAA air traffic controller for eight years until the PATCO strike in 1981. He has flown as a corporate pilot, raced at the

National Championship Air Races in Reno for 14 years, winning the Gold Trophy in 1990, and set several world speed records. At the 1983 Reno Air Races, with four aircraft making a squeeze play for the first pylon's tight turn, Danny caught another plane's wingtip vortices losing all control of his aircraft. Within two seconds he struck the ground, scattering airplane for 1,000 feet. He exited quickly, unscathed, even before the huge dust cloud could settle. His racing buddies now call him "Crash," but the nickname "Lucky" might be more appropriate. Dan now works for a major airline and is also President of Bill Phelps' Airline Ground Schools. He has served as the master of ceremonies for *An Evening with Champions* at the Oshkosh, Wisconsin EAA Theater in the Woods for many years.

Danny holds ATP and CFII tickets and is an FAA Dispatcher Examiner. He is the co-author of the *Airline Career & Interview Manual*.

JIM SLADE

Jim Slade has covered the American space program since it began.

On the afternoon of July 20, 1969, he broadcast these events from the Johnson Space Center, Houston to a worldwide radio audience over the Westinghouse Broadcasting System. He is very proud of this accomplishment.

MOON LANDING 25 YEARS LATER
[Originally printed in *Air Line Pilot* July/August 1994]

They couldn't feel it. They were 10 miles high, 192 miles from designated touchdown; they had just commanded final descent; and at first, they couldn't tell if the engine was working.

Neil Armstrong and Edwin "Buzz" Aldrin, Jr., caught their breaths and then, like puppets pulled by the same string, looked to the instruments for the reassurance that every nerve in their bodies screamed for.

The rocket beneath their feet was throttling up so smoothly in the lunar vacuum that no sound or sensation told them that, indeed, they were on their way to the surface of another world.

Yet.

It was just after 4 p.m. Eastern Daylight Time, on July 20, 1969. It was a Sunday, and the whole world was praying.

The tiny cockpit had no room for seats. Armstrong and Aldrin stood at the controls of lunar module, Eagle. Wires, fastened to the waist of their space suits, kept their feet on the floor in weightlessness. Mission Commander Armstrong was on the left, Aldrin was on the right. At this point, they were facing down, feet pointing in the direction of flight. When the astronauts had time to look out their triangular windscreens, they had an amazing view of the lunar surface crawling by.

The official flight plan tells about their flight in clinical terms: "A three-phase powered descent initiation (PDI) maneuver begins at pericynthion at 102:53:13 GET [ground elapsed time] using the LM [lunar module] descent engine to brake the vehicle out of the descent transfer orbit."

"The guidance-controlled PDI maneuver starts about 260 miles prior to touchdown and is in retrograde attitude to reduce velocity to essentially zero at the time vertical descent begins."

"Spacecraft attitudes range from *windows down* at the start of the PDI to *windows up* as the spacecraft reaches 45,000 feet above the lunar surface and LM landing radar data can be integrated by the LM guidance computer."

In other words, Armstrong and Aldrin were at the mercy of a machine.

The astronauts spent 15 seconds at a quiet 10 percent throttle before the first real jolt. On cue, the descent engine applied the brakes, buckling the astronauts' knees and viciously rocking the little spacecraft as it sought equilibrium in its controlled fall.

Until the ship started pitching over to a vertical attitude and radar could scan the ground, all Aldrin and Armstrong could do was hold tight and follow the checklist.

If things went absolutely crazy, the way out was an abort back to orbit, where Mike Collins could catch them with the command module, Columbia. But that would be an untested, last-ditch desperation maneuver, and they knew it.

Finally, rolled around and in vertical descent, they began to realize that things were not quite the way they should be.

First, at 6,000 feet, the computer began signaling an overload; too much information was coming at it, even though it was totally refreshed once every second.

Second, they appeared to have overshot the landing site. Nothing below them matched the panorama they had studied and memorized.

First things first.

Handling communications, Aldrin gave Houston a "whataboutit" call on the computer alarm.

In Mission Control, Guidance Officer Steven Bales had to make some quick decisions. Was his computer okay? And would it hold up for the return to orbit? He knew it had survived this kind of thing in simulations, and this situation matched. Still, was he risking the astronauts' lives?

Bales conferred briefly with another expert. Meanwhile, Armstrong made his own call: "Give us the reading on that 1202 alarm."

"Go," snapped Bales. "Just go."

Go it was, even though the computer cursed and screamed the whole way down. Bales said, "Go."

But problems were still piling up.

For the first time, Armstrong could see exactly where his spaceship was headed, and the prospect of an abort became very real to him.

They had overshot their intended landing zone by more than four miles. And now the error was compounded by a huge, boulder-rimmed crater directly beneath them. Eagle's landing program was taking them into it like a falling rock.

Suddenly, Armstrong the spaceman became Armstrong the airplane pilot, and his spaceship began moving like a helicopter.

The screens in Mission Control told the story: Eagle had about two minutes of fuel left and, without warning, was beginning to move laterally in its descent. What the hell was going on?

Calling the numbers for his pilot, Aldrin started chanting something new: "800 feet, down three and a half—47 forward—one and a half down—13 forward." The calls were mostly for Houston's benefit because Armstrong had his head (figuratively) out the window.

Eagle cleared the boulder field with "rocks as big as a house," sailing into a clear, relatively level zone that would not only provide a safe touchdown but would be a good platform for liftoff as well. But they couldn't see that back on Earth.

All they could hear was Aldrin's calm, steady recital, and no one was going to interrupt. Eagle was riding a tongue of flame, almost hovering before it eased to within a few feet of the alien surface.

Here was a machine made of Earth, about to settle onto the soil of another world. What would happen? Would it sink out of sight, swallowed by powdery dust? Would it tip over? Was something there that wouldn't tolerate the chemical fire? Would it explode? Less than 60 seconds of fuel was left.

"Light's on." (Low fuel light.)

"Seventy-five feet."

"Six forward."

It was too late to abort. They had no room or time; they were too close.

"Forty feet—down two and a half. Thirty feet. Two and a half down."

"Kicking up some dust."

Eagle's rocket was now blowing clouds of dust from the landing site. Nobody breathed.

"Faint shadow."

"Four forward—drifting to the right a little."

"Contact light!"

After a moment's silence, another voice came on the circuit, jolting listeners who had been hypnotized by Aldrin's almost sing-song calls: "Houston, Tranquillity Base here," Armstrong reported. "Eagle has landed."

And there it was, a moment dreamed about since imagination began: 4:17:42 p.m. Eastern Daylight Time, July 20, 1969. The human race had passed an evolutionary milestone.

At liftoff from Earth, the Apollo 11 transportation system stood 363 feet tall and weighed 6,484,280 pounds. Its first stage blasted against the ground with a force of 7,653,854 pounds of thrust.

As Apollo 11 climbed, it shed one stage after another. The third stage burned twice—once, to finish the climb to orbit, and the second time to accelerate the remaining stack enough to push it out to the moon.

Aerodynamic covers dropped off, and the lunar module, Eagle, was pulled from a nest atop the third stage to ride on to the moon on Columbia's nose.

Because the LM was never designed to fly in an atmosphere, it was simply a homely framework with aluminum skin covering parts that bulged out wherever they needed to be.

NASA had no plan for Eagle's return.

All that remains today of that great caravan is the Apollo 11 capsule, Columbia—about 11,000 pounds of living quarters and cockpit—now on display at the Smithsonian's National Air and Space Museum, as it should be.

Columbia's surface is charred, the admission fee for reentry to

Earth's atmosphere. And the cockpit has a sheen of ground-in dirt from another world.

But it has an air of nobility.

If you look inside, down past the footrest of the middle couch, you can see an oval navigation panel set in the far wall. Sometime during his lonely vigil in lunar orbit, CMP (command module pilot) Collins wrote on it:

"Spacecraft 107—alias Apollo 11—alias Columbia. The best ship to come down the line. God bless her. —Michael Collins, CMP"

That says it all.

ENOLA GAY

[Originally printed in *Air Line Pilot* February 1991]

A lot of them were always around, so nobody paid much attention to the stocky Army officer making his way along the assembly line. It was the spring of 1945, and Paul Tibbets had flown to the Martin plant in Omaha to pick out an airplane. What he liked most about the one he chose isn't clear, but he would name it after his mother.

Courtesy of BGen. Paul Tibbets

The Enola Gay

At the time of the Omaha trip, Tibbets was winding up a year-long secret operation that could end the Pacific War. In an interview, he told us he went to the Martin plant to get the most flawless B-29 the manufacturer could provide. First, he and a Martin supervisor pored over production records to find it. Then Tibbets went into the factory to see it for himself.

When he was satisfied, he requested a number of modifications to meet several special needs, without revealing what they were. By the time AAF serial number 44-83292 was accepted as a "special mission" airplane, it was bereft of guns and much of its armor plate, leaving it with smoother skin and 10,000 pounds lighter than the original Boeing design. To do what Tibbets intended, the aircraft would need all of the altitude and speed it could get.

Tibbets sent Capt. Robert A. Lewis to pick up the airplane on June 14, 1945. Lewis, who would later serve as Tibbet's copilot, flew it back to the 393rd Bombardment Squadron at Wendover, Utah that same day. On June 27, Lewis took it on to the island of Tinian, south of Japan, to join the 393rd at its new forward base. Soon after the B-29-45-MO arrived there, Tibbets named it Enola Gay.

It was flown on a few standard bombing runs, including one over Marcus Island on July 6, 1945, designed to familiarize the crews with combat operations. They were required to take part in as many as five to seven such missions before carrying out the job they had been specially trained to do.

Their time came on August 6, 1945.

To meet the requirements of Order Number 13, issued four days earlier, Enola Gay left Tinian at 2:45 a.m., carrying one five-ton bomb. After an extra long takeoff roll, Tibbets eased off the runway and out over the Pacific, radioing the cryptic phrase, "Judge going to work."

The primary target was Hiroshima, but the backups were Kokura and Nagasaki, depending on weather and visibility. Seven B-29s were involved. Three weather observers flew ahead to check each target. Two observers and one standby aircraft, all Top Secret, waited on Iwo Jima in case mechanical problems forced Tibbets to land and change planes.

There were 12 crewmen aboard Enola Gay instead of the normal 10-man complement, and only four knew exactly what was in the belly. Because of fear the plane might crash on takeoff, the device was not armed until they were three-and-a-half hours into the flight. At 6:30 a.m., Navy Capt. William Parsons and Lt. Morris Jeppson, nuclear experts, crawled into the B-29's bomb bay and armed the world's first atomic weapon destined for an enemy target. At that point, Tibbets went around the plane and personally confirmed each man's suspicions.

At 8:15:17 a.m., flying at 200 miles per hour on a heading of 264 degrees, Enola Gay dropped the bomb from an altitude of 31,060 feet.

At 8:16 a.m., the detonator fired at an altitude of 1,890 feet, about 800 feet from the Aioi Bridge, the bomb's intended target.

Tailgunner Bob Caron was assigned to take pictures because he would have the only clear view as the plane sped away. In an interview, he told me: "Coming up on the target, we were told to put on heavy, dense Polaroid goggles. When the bomb got away, the airplane leaped up, maybe 1,000 feet.

"Tibbets promptly threw it into a right-hand, pre-calculated, diving turn to get us furthest away from the explosion. That ride, as I have described it many times, was like being the last man on a giant crack-the-whip.

"About 45 seconds later came a tremendous flash that made me 'ah.' I thought I was blinded through the dense goggles; and Tibbets told me on the intercom, he said, 'Bob, describe what you see and start taking pictures when you get something.' (Another member of the crew was using a wire recorder to keep a record of what was said on the airplane.)"

"And [Tibbets] asked me if I had seen anything yet. And I said, 'Outside of a flash, nothing yet.' The turret was in the way... Then I saw the first shock wave come up. It was like an exploding bubble. I didn't know what it was. And it hit the plane very hard. In fact, so hard that Tibbets yelled 'Flak!' He thought we got hit by flak."

"The second one came up... from the ground, and I yelled 'Here comes another one.' And that hit the plane not quite as hard. And about that time I could see the mushroom starting to form over the turret, and started describing it over the intercom and taking pictures."

"The cloud climbed very rapidly. It had a... it was a dark purplish, blackish color with a fiery red core, with the familiar mushroom shape to it. I started taking pictures, and as we got a little further away, I was able to see the city. And the city was covered with a low, turbulent, bubbling mass of what looked like boiling molasses creeping out over the city and up into the foothills. The only thing I could see that was not covered by that was a big dock jutting out into the harbor. I remember saying 'With this thing, I think we have won the war'."

It's estimated that 80,000 people were killed instantly or wounded, and 62,000 buildings were destroyed. Looking back, copilot Robert Lewis wrote in his notes: "My God, what have we done?"

After the war ended, Enola Gay was flown on various test operations but did not stay in service very long. Placed in storage at Davis Monthan Air Force Base on August 30, 1946, it remained there until July 3, 1949, when Tibbets flew it to Park Ridge, Illinois, and turned it over to the Smithsonian. It was kept in storage until December 2, 1953, when it was delivered to Andrews Air Force Base, outside of Washington, D.C. Disassembly began in August 1960, and the plane was moved to the Smithsonian's storage and restoration facility in Silver Hill, Maryland, the next summer.

Enola Gay has always been a special problem for the Smithsonian because of the sensitive nature of its history. It has even been the target of bomb threats.

But now officials believe that the time and the public mood are right to display it as both memorial and reminder. Final restoration began in December 1984 and, according to Curator Robert Mikesh, is now being accelerated.

Today, Enola Gay is a fuselage in various parts. The rudder is on display at the main museum and the wings are stored at Silver Hill. The cockpit, where Tibbets and his crew steered us into a somber new era, and the tail position, where Bob Caron watched it emerge, have been restored faithfully to their appearance on August 6, 1945. Even the paint on the rudder pedals is scraped by aviator's boots.

It's hoped that Enola Gay will be displayed whole one day, but that will have to wait until the grand opening of a new National Air and Space Museum annex at Dulles Airport, Virginia. When the facility is in operation, large aircraft including the space shuttle Enterprise, a B-17, and Boeing's first B-707, will be displayed there intact.

Mikesh says the public continues to send things for Enola Gay. Three black boxes of the type used on the airplane have been received, and, most significantly, the plane's identification data plate was turned over to the museum by an anonymous benefactor who had kept it for years as a souvenir. All these things have been put in their original locations and locked inside, part of history.

IN THE SPIRIT

[Originally printed in *Air Line Pilot* May 1992]

When Charles Lindbergh titled his first book, *We*, he was referring to himself and to the little airplane that carried him safely across the Atlantic Ocean in May, 1927. Lindbergh felt akin to The Spirit of St. Louis and always referred to it in terms of a partnership.

It was named in honor of the men in St. Louis who financed his attempt to win the $25,000 Orteig prize, which was offered to anyone who would make the first nonstop flight between New York and Paris. Most of the entrants were teams of fliers who would "spell" each other on the long ride. Lindbergh chose to go alone.

To do that, he needed an exceptionally sturdy airplane and an even more exceptionally reliable engine. For the airplane, he

Spirit of St. Louis

chose a high-wing monoplane built as a mail carrier by Ryan
Airlines of San Diego, California. The engine he selected was a big
Wright Whirlwind J5C, capable of turning out 223 horsepower,
probably the most dependable engine of the day.

In the airplane's normal configuration, it would have had a
windshield and cockpit right up there behind the mighty engine.
But Lindbergh had distance in mind, which meant he had to feed
fuel to the Whirlwind much longer than normal tankage would
allow. He placed a large oil tank directly behind the engine, followed by a large gasoline tank, which was followed by an even
larger gasoline tank. In the final design, 200 of the plane's 450
gallons of available fuel rode where the pilot normally sat.

Lindbergh moved himself and the controls back so far that his
head was nearly even with the rear edge of the overhead wing.

He had no forward view so he installed a periscope that slid out of the side of the fuselage. To approach for landing, he slipped sideways so that one wing pointed toward the oncoming runway, letting him look out the side window at the ground. He flipped the nose around straight just before the wheels touched down.

To save weight and gain speed, Lindbergh installed a wicker chair instead of a standard pilot's seat—but he flew with the windows open, so wind whipping into the cabin probably slowed him down anyway.

I bring all this up to tell you that the Spirit is alive and very well, thank you. The 65-year-old airplane was lowered to the floor of the Smithsonian Air and Space Museum in early March 1992 so that workmen and curators could inspect it for signs of deterioration.

The curator, Bob van der Linden, said his crew lowered it for the first time in 15 years because they had seen a tear in the plane's fabric covering where one of the support cables was anchored and were concerned that it might break and fall. But in reality, there was no problem. The crew X-rayed the Spirit's steel-tube framework and found not one crack anywhere. The cloth fabric was aged but still presentable, and the plane sat on its own feet, proud and erect. The only concession made to age was that van der Linden and his crew put a set of automobile wheels (with radial tires) on the axles in place of the originals because they didn't trust the old rubber to hold the weight. The temporary wheel arrangement looked peculiar because the Spirit didn't need radial traction, but it wore them in good grace, anyway.

Most fascinating was the cockpit into which the tall, skinny Lindbergh folded himself for 33-and-a-half hours. We saw the marks Lindbergh made on the instrument panel to keep track of his fuel usage. We looked at the periscope and the little girl's compact mirror he stuck to the panel with chewing gum so he could see the compass slung from the ceiling behind his head. On the wall was a place where he'd marked "On" and "Off" for the carburetor heat. We could see the marks where his boots scraped paint off the rudder pedals. The color of the wood has softened to a lustrous reddish-brown.

The big surprise was the radioactive warning tag hanging from the instrument panel. I asked van der Linden if that was to scare off the tourists, and he said no. When the crew brought the plane down, they checked the interior and found traces of radioactivity from the instruments themselves. They'd been painted with radium to make the dials and numbers glow in the dark. Van der Linden and I both wondered how many of the old-time pilots eventually died of cancer.

I had a fascinating time—making friends with an icon. We were the first ones to see it so intimately for years upon years, and I believe we saw some things that most people have never seen. That includes the names of mechanics scratched into the airplane's metal. All those who serviced it and all those who built it seem to have left their names on The Spirit of St. Louis. In a way, they were partners, too.

LIFETIMES OF INVENTION

[Originally printed in *Air Line Pilot* December 1978]

The first successful airplane was not the product of random inspiration. It was the creation of two men who spent their lifetimes attacking problems with logic, exploring for themselves instead of accepting the word of others.

The Wright Brothers had a certain mechanical genius, which they applied from childhood to a partnership that yielded one mechanical contrivance after another. They were almost inseparable companions, knowing each other's thinking so well that one would begin a sentence and the other would finish. Often their exchange of ideas would come in such rapid-fire dialogue that one would say a few words and the other would be voicing an opinion or suggesting a change before the first thought was complete.

Neither man was formally schooled in engineering. Both completed high school courses, although neither took a diploma. Wilbur thought it too much trouble to return to school to pick up the sheepskin and Orville spent his senior year studying what he wanted to study, rather than finishing the specified curriculum. Their mechanical bent came naturally. Both parents, Bishop

Milton Wright and Susan Koerner Wright, were skilled tinkerers who encouraged the boys to experiment. As a result, the family kitchen was often a laboratory. By the time Orville was old enough to see the advantage of a dollar, the boys were collecting bones and junk to sell. Farmers bought the bones to grind up and use in fertilizer, glue and chicken feed. Later, the boys started building toys to peddle to their friends. To make their factory viable, they went to the scrap pile for parts to build a practical eight-foot turning lathe, powered by a foot treadle.

Orville was hired by his father to work on the religious weekly edited by the elder Wright for the United Brethren Church. Orville was to fold the papers for delivery. Before too much time had passed, the young inventor had lashed together a folding machine which allowed one boy to do the work of as many as five and to pocket the extra profits.

The boys soon went into publishing on their own, grinding out a neighborhood news sheet, printed, of course, on a press of their own manufacture. Printing stayed with them as one of many sidelines until the airplane started taking all their spare time in 1903.

Cycling was a big sport in the late 1800's. The Wrights gravitated to it pretty much the same as their friends, except they recognized opportunity in the fad. By 1892 they opened their first small bicycle shop where they sold, repaired and even built their own two-wheeler designs. The first Wright cycle was the Van Cleve, which went on the market in 1896 complete with the Wright brothers' special coaster brake and a hub with a reserve set of bearings. Business was good. They had to move to larger quarters twice, settling finally in a two-story building on West Third Street, which was to become the birthplace of the modern airplane.

The entrepreneurs toyed constantly with new ideas. Just before the turn of the century, the automobile was drawing speculative attention from a number of dabblers and Orville suggested they might consider inventing and marketing a practical car. Wilbur ridiculed the idea, saying, "You'd be tackling the impossible. Why, it would be easier to build a flying machine."

Studying problems of control

Otto Lilienthal's death during glider experiments in 1896 seemed to stir in the Wrights what had been a latent interest since childhood. Reading of the Lilienthal tragedy, the Wrights wrote to the Smithsonian Institution to inquire about literature in the aeronautical field. They were forwarded a meager list of five books and a series of pamphlets. That sparse library made the men realize how little attention was paid to positive control of the flying apparatus. Lilienthal, for instance, had relied on body movements through a low center of gravity, not much of a system for a load-carrying vehicle. The brothers were convinced that the key element missing was control.

Early experimenters tried to design machines whose aerodynamic properties would balance them more or less automatically. The Wrights thought that was backward. They felt balance and control should be in the hands of the operator, allowing him to deal with the changing forces attacking the airplane while it moved through the air. To satisfy themselves, they set out to test their theory.

Three years' study led Orville to suggest a shaft and cog mechanism, which would tilt or twist the wingtips, increasing lift on one side or the other. The idea looked good in principle, but the brothers were worried over structural weaknesses the device would build into a machine. It would amount to separating the wing into three parts held together by a turning shaft.

Then in midsummer 1899, weeks into the problem and with other things on his mind, Wilbur Wright stood in his shop, idly twisting a long cardboard box between his hands. Turning one fist one way and the other opposite caused one end of the carton's top to go forward while the other pulled back.

His answer was there in his hands: if the top wing of an airplane could be made to twist forward it would change the angle presented to the wind, gaining more lift. The other end would act opposingly. There would be no need to "section" the wing, structural integrity would be maintained and the operator would be in control.

The Wrights began testing a small working biplane, which was flown as a kite. Two control cables ran to each wing tip. The system worked handsomely enough to spur them on. They asked for and received advice from the Weather Bureau about locations where there was a good, stiff breeze to furnish lift, preferably somewhere that also had soft sand in case of accidents. They finally settled on Kitty Hawk, North Carolina, where the first summer's work with an unmanned glider-kite proved their control theories. It bolstered the conclusion that most previous aeronautical data were useless. But that meant if they were to realize anything more of their dream, they would need to produce whole new tables on air pressure and drag, and that seemed beyond them. They nearly gave up in frustration, but an invitation spurred them on.

The first wind tunnel

They had been corresponding for some time with leading aeronautical theorist Octave Chanute. After reading Wilbur's letters about their summer series of tests, Chanute asked them to address the September 1901 meeting of the Western Society of Engineers in Chicago. Wilbur, the older of the two, was to make the speech. He decided he would go ahead and "drop his bombs" about the previously mistaken data concerning air pressure and control.

The very idea of a speech to such a learned and prestigious society tied Orville into knots. He retreated to the laboratory where, under that kind of pressure, he devised the first crude wind tunnel to check his brother's facts.

The machine was built from an 18-inch starch box. Wind was furnished by a fan mounted on the shaft of an old grinding wheel. Through a glass window in the top, the brothers would watch the angles at which a curved surface and a plane surface produced equal pressures. A balance, built partly from old hacksaw blades, served as the technical mount for their test articles.

By the time the Wrights finished their studies with this and another, larger tunnel in late 1901, they had data runs on more than 200 types of wing surfaces. For Christmas that year, they presented themselves a new, revised set of tables on air pressure and drag. And work on the airplane resumed.

The next summer, the Wrights went back to Kitty Hawk with an aircraft having twice the dynamic efficiency of any ever built. To add control, they changed its fixed rear fins to a moveable "tail." Manned-glider runs off Kill Devil Hill were so successful that summer they felt they could go ahead with plans for "power assist." All they had to do was find the right engine.

Adding an engine

It wasn't as easy as they thought it would be. Most commercial engines were too heavy and manufacturers had no apparent interest in trying to build a single engine to their specifications. In fact, some companies let it be known that they did not want their name associated with anybody crazy enough to think they could fly. So, with the help of their employee, Charles Taylor, Orville and Wilbur Wright built an engine of their own. As usual, it had some of the charm of a scrap box, with at least one important part made from a tomato can.

The brothers left propellers for last, thinking all they had to do was to read up on marine propellers, which had been in use for some 65 years. As it turned out, technical data in that area was as deficient as it was in aeronautics, so it was back to the lab. They were the first to realize that a propeller was a rotating airfoil. In the end, they produced a propeller which was one-third more efficient than any propeller on the market. In doing so, they once again produced an original table of engineering figures for designers yet to come.

All this culminated in the first aircraft capable of lifting from one spot under its own power, flying under control of an operator and landing at another spot located at the same altitude as the point of takeoff.

The patent on their flying machine was requested on March 23, 1903, nine months before the first flight. It was granted on May 22, 1906.

The period between application and grant was rather grim. The Wrights found themselves in the ludicrous position of having to convince a lethargic public that they had indeed accomplished their goal. It was many months before the American press would take their claims seriously enough to assign reporters to the story. The U.S. government showed no interest, either. So, with Chanute's help, the Wrights turned to the British and French. Contract negotiations began but were fruitless, although several imitators cropped up, leading the Wrights into a series of bitter and exhausting lawsuits over patent rights. Court battles continued for the Wright Company until well after World War I.

In the years just after the first flight the brothers kept working. Constant improvements were being made to the airplane. The focus of their testing programs shifted from Kitty Hawk to Dayton and a pasture on the outskirts called Huffman Prairie. A catapult arrangement was devised to assist the airplane on take-off from the prairie, where winds were rarely ideal. The location added some amusement to their fight for recognition. Since the prairie was located next to the Dayton trolley line, riders were sometimes startled to see the strange contraption lift above the trees. Even at that, the official world paid little attention with the exception of a few newspaper editors who claimed the Wrights were "secretive" about their work, "whatever it amounted to."

Refining method and machine

The Wrights later said they really learned to fly at Huffman, rather than Kitty Hawk, because refined piloting techniques began to evolve at the Dayton location during the 1904 season. A more sophisticated airplane and engine were developed and 100 flights were conducted that year, including the first complete circle, a very real accomplishment for their control system.

In 1905, rudder and wing-warping were made independent operations and the wing camber was changed. The brothers also developed and patented what they called "blinkers"—tabs placed between the surfaces of the front elevator. The device helped the rear rudder to make a turn, preventing a tailspin. By the end of that season, the Wrights felt they had a machine good enough to offer to whatever market might develop.

Independent builder contracts were established in France, Germany and finally in the United States after the patent was granted. You could buy an airplane then for around $5,000. The Wrights incorporated in 1909, with most of the enterprise's big money coming from New York. For their part, the brothers received stock, cash and 10% royalties on every airplane sold.

Going it alone

Exhausted and worried over the patent rights litigation, which had fallen under his supervision, Wilbur died of typhoid fever in 1912. Grieving for his brother and feeling he could not function as well without Wilbur's thinking to balance his own, Orville sold his shares in the Wright Company in 1915, hoping to divorce himself from business affairs and devote all his energy to research. To do so, he set up his own laboratory and became a consulting engineer.

The next year, Orville won the Collier Trophy for developing an automatic stabilization system for his airplane, a device, which astonished the judges as Orville flew past them "hands off" through turns, as well as straight and level flight. Ironically, he had to be coaxed into entering the device in the competition by his staff and by publisher Robert J. Collier himself. Collier, a long-time friend and business associate, was the first civilian to buy an airplane in the United States.

Later, Orville devised the split wing-flaps which were eventually used by fighter planes in World War II. And, perturbed about the number of Army pilots being killed in stall-spin accidents aboard the early Wright flyers, he spent long hours in flight and even longer ones in his laboratory, working out procedures of stall recovery and building an angle-of-incidence meter. It was typical of the responsibility he felt for his brainchild.

Now going it alone, and relatively well off, the reticent Orville pulled his world tightly around himself at the laboratory, at his summer camp in Canada, and at the gracious home in Dayton that he and Wilbur had designed shortly before Wilbur died.

In these homes the tinkerer's spirit overtook the commercial inventor. One biographer wrote that "everywhere in his home and his summer camp in Canada, one finds what he [Orville] calls some 'crazy contrivance' which he has never bothered to patent."

The Canadian camp, Lambert Island on Georgian Bay, was pretty raw when Orville bought it before World War I. To a man who enjoyed gadgets as a way of making life simpler, things cried out for doing.

The large "main house" was on a hilltop overlooking the bay. Kitchen and dining room were on the lower floor, the upstairs was a large sitting room, exposed to the breezes by moveable shutters. The shutters could be adjusted from the inside and could be maneuvered to siphon whatever amount of sunshine or wind Mr. Wright desired.

Like his late brother, Orville was a doting uncle and surrounded himself as much as possible with a large selection of nephews and nieces. Summertime vacations at Lambert were made even more fun by an uncle who invented things like a motor-powered railcar for hauling things up the hill from the dock. The children were eager passengers. They called it the Bayshore-Lambert Island Railway. There was also a motorboat powered by an old airplane engine, which Orville could adjust to run on one, two, three or six cylinders as he chose.

A lively cook, Orville Wright made candy to his own recipe and hurried to make sure his own sweet tooth got its share. He was also a toy inventor, which led to formation of the Miami Wood Products Company, a family business. But the camp was a personal thing. When relatives visited there after his death, they found among Orville's effects a special toaster which browned bread just the way he liked it and an old felt hat with holes for ventilation and screens over the holes to keep out the bugs.

It was probably in his Dayton home, however, where Orville's penchant for gadgeteering reached its peak.

Sister Katharine lived with the brothers for many years, continuing to be Orville's official hostess until she married at age 52. It was Katharine who saw to entertaining the constant stream of people, famous and otherwise, who came to pay homage to the inventor of the airplane. Orville made his appearances, but preferred a quiet, private life, sparked by those "contrivances" which helped everything along.

For instance, Wright did not like running to the basement to adjust the furnace during the long Midwestern winters. It seemed only logical to him to stretch a wire through the hardwood floor of the living room down to the furnace so adjustments could be made without the long walk.

Actually, the basement was the focus of a variety of innovations. Orville devised a central-vacuuming system connected by pipes to every room in the house. All his housekeeper had to do was plug in the cleaning apparatus wherever she was and flail away at the dust. The container in the basement had to be emptied just once a year. To the inventor's dismay, the woman rarely used the gadget, calling it "just too cumbersome."

There was also a tank down there to collect and hold rainwater from the roof. The forerunner of the modern water softener, it was actually two cisterns connected through a filtration system, which kept out minerals. Lashed to this was a back-feed pump so that the flow could be reversed, cleaning the filter.

Scouting upstairs for something to do, Orville decided it was unnecessary to allow the iceman into the kitchen for deliveries when a door in the outside wall would do just as well. That, and a door in the back of the icebox made outside delivery quick and easy.

Since he did all the electrical and plumbing work himself, it is likely that Orville strung up the shower which one visitor later said was "like an automatic car wash." The shower surrounded the bather with sprays striking from several different angles. Incidentally, Orville's shower curtain was a weather-beaten tarpaulin, which had once covered the original airplane.

Because of the accident which broke his leg during the 1908 Army demonstration flights, Orville suffered from hip and leg pain most of his life. That not only led to things like specially designed air-oil shocks for his heavy automobiles (he was known as a "rapid driver") but also to a certain tilt in his easy chair. Located in the library, the chair also had a built-in device to hold a book for hands-off reading. A student all his life, Orville spent long hours in the book-lined room. Worn spots on the chair gave clear evidence of his voracious reading habits.

After Orville Wright died in 1948, the house was sold to the National Cash Register Company of Dayton to be preserved as a historic site and used by the company as a VIP guest facility.

With their inventions, Wilbur and Orville Wright challenged the thinking of men whose minds were far more schooled in the formal sciences. Yet they set for themselves, from some innate grasp of the scientific method, the most exacting standards of research. Their lives prove their genius, which was always less a talent than a way of life, always accompanied by insatiable curiosity and, in their case and perhaps to their true advantage, unfettered by dogma.

The plaque accompanying the original Flyer at the Smithsonian's National Air and Space Museum may tell the Wright brothers' story more clearly than any other tribute. It reads, in part:

"By original scientific research the Wright Brothers discovered the principles of human flight. As Inventors, Builders and Flyers they further developed the airplane, taught men to fly, and opened the era of aviation."

ONE STARTLING MOMENT
[Originally printed in *Air Line Pilot* December 1985]

When the S. N. Brown Company of Dayton, Ohio, sold four pieces of bent wood to Orville and Wilbur Wright in November 1902, the salesman probably thought the brothers were building a buggy. The company's product was normally used for carriage wheels or buggy roof supports, but the brothers had other ideas.

The Brown Company's name came to light in late March 1985 when craftsmen at the National Air and Space Museum began stripping away the fabric from the Wright Flyer's wings. They were starting to restore a machine that leaped into history a little over a year after the wood was purchased. A stencil advertising Brown's Wheel and Bow Manufacturing Company was found on the inside of the bows, which the Wrights used for their airplane's wingtips. Searches of the Wright brothers' records show they paid $5 for the four pieces.

That wasn't the only writing found as the fabric came away. The Wrights had put their bicycle company's address on the outside of the wing's spars—they put one sentence per spar so when the wings were stacked for shipping, the stack was properly labeled. The word "new" was found on some wing ribs that Orville replaced in the late 1920s. And someone's name was found scribbled on the fuel tank. No sentimental messages or significant dates appeared, just those few things in places no one ever looked before.

Brown's buggy bows are especially interesting, though, because they symbolize the simple solutions the Wrights applied to complex problems. The museum's director, Walter Boyne, says the more he looks at the airplane, the more he is convinced that the Wrights were "out-and-out geniuses."

The museum's decision to refurbish the Wright Flyer, commonly called the "Kitty Hawk" Flyer, was made over a number of months. Intense discussions took place over what would be the proper thing to do. Some museum conservatives believed nothing should be done at all, saying the plane ought to be left just as it came to the Smithsonian after World War Two. One faction favored encasing it in a Plexiglas box filled with nitrogen, a sort of displayable mummification.

The other side argued that the Flyer had been through a number of evolutions since the Kitty Hawk flights and therefore was not exactly as it had been in 1903. Besides, the grime and stains that had collected on the airplane had not been put there by the Wright brothers; time and circumstances had been responsible for that, so why hesitate to clean it?

In truth, a lot of things really did happen while the plane was in the brothers' possession. It was heavily damaged shortly after completing the fourth flight, when a gust of wind rolled it over. The brothers disassembled it and shipped it back to Dayton, where it was stored in barrels on properties near their bicycle shop. Occasionally, it was cannibalized for parts as new airplanes grew. A flood in Dayton once kept the Flyer under water for three days.

Nothing much was done to protect the Flyer until Alexander Graham Bell came for a visit. The inventor, himself a serious aeronautical experimenter, urged the brothers to preserve the plane as a historic artifact. Seeing the logic in Bell's arguments, the plane was assigned to workmen in the Wright shops for "fix up."

Around 1927, after an argument with the Smithsonian over whether the plane deserved a place in the museum, an angry Orville Wright covered the plane with new fabric and replaced some of its wooden ribs so he could send it to the Science Museum of London on indefinite loan. These changes mean the fabric removed during the Smithsonian restoration was not the original, another point in favor of the group who felt it was time to do something about the Flyer's appearance and, if necessary, its physical condition as well.

Appearance turned out to be the only place where improvement was necessary. In spite of all the plane had been through, including being in London during World War II, the Wrights' engineering and the materials they used made the museum people raise their eyebrows and whistle.

Craftsman Richard Horrigan pursed his lips as he looked around at the pieces stacked in his shop. "There's an airplane in here someplace," he reckoned. Studying the parts as he helped disassemble the machine, Horrigan estimated the Wrights needed no more than three or four days to uncrate the parts and put the Flyer together at Kitty Hawk. The job could probably have been done with nothing more sophisticated than an adjustable wrench and a screwdriver.

The Wrights built the Flyer in prefabricated sections. The wingtip bows were strapped to leading and trailing edge spars, which fit into a center section containing the pilot's position and engine components. The propeller drive came through chains similar to those used to turn truck wheels; the chain's edges were rounded to move smoothly through tubular guides. The 76 prebuilt ribs fit into pockets in the fabric and slid down the wing spars with the fabric, which was pulled over the frame like a sock. About a thousand carpet tacks held the fabric in place. Vertical spars had hooks on each end, fitting into metal eyes on the wings so the assembly was flexible for wing warping. Flying wires were heavy, single strands fastened through the vertical spars and attached to the wings with eyes made by simply doubling the wire back and soldering it under a tin sheath.

Horrigan and his friends were impressed. In the workshop, the craftsmen would pick up pieces to show their construction to visitors, marveling over the straightforward, clean work done by the inventors.

Carl Heinzel brought out the hip cradle, used to control wing warping. It was a wide, U-shaped affair lined with burlap padding. The cradle slid from side to side to pull the control wires. Heinzel said test flights with an exact replica proved it took 45 pounds of pressure to swing the cradle. A pilot who tried it on the replica said, at the end of a day's flying, his hips and thighs were very sore.

According to Boyne, modern pilots would have their hands full with the machine. The Wrights may have been outright geniuses, but stability was not a strong suit their first time out. The airplane's short-coupled controls make it "squirrelly." That was demonstrated the night the workmen lifted the manikin that represents Orville Wright back into place on the wing. Until the figure's hand was placed on the elevator control, jamming it to a nearly neutral position, the elevator simply rested "full up." Its pivot point was too close to center, probably accounting for the erratic over-control Orville reported during that first 12-second flight.

The museum was closed on the night in mid-June when the plane was to be returned to its display position. About 15 of the "faithful"—museum officials, writers and reporters, family members and friends—gathered in the workshop to watch and to form an escort. Chief among the group was the Wright brothers' niece, Ivonette Miller, and her husband, Harold, of Dayton. The Millers had come to Washington on this special evening to see what had been done to the machine that brings to the minds of millions of people the time and events through which the couple had lived.

Mrs. Miller was one of the first women to fly in the United States. She was in the second grade when word came from Kitty Hawk that her uncles had been successful. She says the family wasn't surprised; they expected nothing less from the brothers. Mrs. Miller's memory of the airplane as it was being put together in the Dayton bicycle shop had caused her to point out a few summers ago how badly the Flyer needed cleaning. Asked whether it now meets her expectations, she said, "This is perfect." Then she looked again and laughed, saying, "as a matter of fact, it probably never looked that good before." Her uncles had not seen it as a showpiece. It was a tool.

She may have been right. Sitting in the workshop on a specially built dolly, the plane was waiting to be rolled down the hall. Overhead lights shone on snow-white fabric sewn on the same old Kenwood sewing machine the brothers used, and on wooden parts that had been cleansed of an ugly brown coat of dirt collected since the Flyer was originally built. The wood was returned to its original honey color and was coated with wax. In short, the old airplane simply glowed.

The faithful gathered around as the workmen started to push it sideways down the hall. The old Flyer rolled sedately past its silent grandchildren: to the right was the Apollo Lunar Module. Straight ahead was the Apollo Command Module, and then Skylab. The Flyer rolled near Wiley Post's Winnie Mae, past a copy of the picture taken at the moment of the Flyer's first liftoff from Kitty Hawk, and into the giant center hall where The Spirit of St. Louis, Glamorous Glennis, and the X-15 are placed, all pointing their noses toward the spot reserved for their common ancestor.

A pin dropping in that place at that time would have shattered eardrums.

No one left the room as Horrigan climbed aboard the platform of a forklift, ready to stand guard as the lift raised the venerable machine back to its place of honor. Horrigan fussed, fiddled, and fumed until he was satisfied the supporting wires were exactly right. Then, he signaled the operator below to take down the supporting platform. There was an audible intake of breath in the room as the old Flyer first swayed and then steadied down—hanging free again.

After that one, heart-stopping, silent moment, cheers tumbled through the museum and champagne corks began to pop. In a new suit of clothes, cleaned and waxed, its metalwork polished, the 82-year-old Flyer simply dominated the room. The next time you come to see it, you will find your eye drawn to it the instant you come through the front door; and unless you are far less conscious of aviation's history than most, you will find its presence compelling.

As we were standing there, reluctant to let the moment go, I chatted with Harold Miller, Ivonette's husband. Mr. Miller was executor of Orville Wright's will and was largely responsible for bringing the airplane back from England after World War II so it could be turned over to the Smithsonian as Orville stipulated.

Looking at the machine, which represents one truly startling moment in time, Miller was flooded with memories. "Because the will wasn't signed," he mused, "I had to take the heirs to court to declare my intentions of selling the airplane to the Smithsonian for a dollar. Of course, they all agreed without hesitation, so there it is, and I got a dollar for it." Thinking again of the two brothers, he grinned and looked a little wistful. "They really started something with that thing, didn't they?"

They really did, Mr. Miller.

They really did.

Biography

JIM SLADE

Audiences say he's: enlightening, inspirational, humorous... powerful. And they're right. As a journalist, Jim Slade has witnessed some of the truly pivotal events of this century. His coverage of the American space program began with Alan Shepherd's launch in 1961 and continues today with the space shuttle. He has broadcast his space chronicles to millions around the world on ABC-TV and Radio, CNN, NBC Radio, Mutual, the Westinghouse Broadcasting system and the Voice of America.

Slade prides himself on seeing both the woods and the trees at the same time. A pilot and journalist who has always dealt personally with the astronauts, engineers and scientists who made it happen, he describes the Apollo moon-landing program as a 'prime-turn' in human evolution and he shows you why. In other fields he was there at the birth of the 747, and later watched engineers design the 777 on computers. He can talk about personal experiences in the search for Amelia Earhart, can tell you things about the Wright Brothers that you've never heard before, and show you Lindbergh's Spirit of St. Louis from a first-hand point of view.

Together Jim Slade and John Alexander authored *Firestorm at Gettysburg, Civilian Voices,* an incredible history book with 160 photos and illustrations and with eyewitness accounts from 1863.

For six years, Peter Jennings on the World News Tonight would cut to Jim Slade for an on-location report on aviation, space and science. Jim is also the narrator and host of a number of educational television documentaries.

CLIFF ROBERTSON

AIRPORT

It's your 14th summer, school is out and you are looking at three months of joy—90 days of freedom. Freedom to escape with that new Iver Johnson bicycle. That prize collected with 10,000 Brownie Coupons. Accumulated over three years of selling Saturday Evening Post and Liberty magazines in that sleepy little Southern California town. *Free* to mount that blue Iver Johnson and head southward along Coast Boulevard, past Bird Rock and Pacific and Mission Beach.

Pedaling madly across the causeway—the cool Pacific air whipping your face and stinging your teeth as you smile with exaltation—expectation. An extra burst of speed to catch that passing trolley and save your tired legs for a precious block or two, or until the motorman noticed. There was little danger. The motorman seldom noticed—or pretended not to. At the track intersection you peel off and pedal that 12th and last mile with an ecstatic fury. One mile to go—one mile left—one tantalizing mile that separates you from your goal. Your sanctuary from school—from routine—from earth. A sanctuary that will cocoon your day and transport you with your dreams to another firmament.

Suddenly your legs stop. Your body rests—there is a stillness: The Iver Johnson coasts on. Its tires humming an unwinding song as they carry you off the asphalt and to the sandy path. Still—so very still. The blue bicycle coasts slowly to a reverent stop—like a worshipper entering church. Your foot supports the two of you—you and blue steed have arrived—you taste the moment—you drink it—its simple structure a cathedral to your 14-year-old eyes. A cathedral of dreams. Lourdes never looked more magnificent than this simple, small proud place. This home for boyhood dreams. This......... Airport.

WHERE HAVE ALL THE OLD PLANES GONE?

Where have all the old planes gone?
Where have all their pilots gone?
They have flown to God knows where—
They have vanished in the air.

They have vanished so it seems
flown away with childhood dreams.

Where have all the old planes gone?
Where have all their pilots gone?
Left their memories warm and tall
left those memories with us all.

Where have all the old planes gone?
I must fly one ere I go
I must fly one high and low.

I will fly one last flight
unafraid of dark of night.
I will fly, but not alone—
I will fly with friends from home.
I will fly until dawn
in formation—with old planes gone.

Biography

CLIFF ROBERTSON

After a brief journalistic career, Cliff Robertson began acting on Broadway in the mid-fifties. Singled out for his promising work on the stage, the young actor was chosen to appear in his first motion picture, *Picnic*. He has starred in 57 major motion pictures including, *The Pilot*, and numerous television programs and Broadway plays. An Academy Award winning actor (*Charly*)

Robertson is also a writer, director, and producer. The late President Kennedy personally chose Mr. Robertson to portray him as a naval Lieutenant in the movie *PT-109*. He was commended for his brave stand against corporate corruption in the infamous "Hollywood-gate" scandal. A reporter once asked if the biggest thrill in his life was winning an Emmy or an Oscar. "Neither; it was going above 26,000 feet in a glider." The reporter said, "What?" Cliff responded, "You would not understand!" A licensed commercial pilot with instrument, multi-engine and glider ratings, he owns a Spitfire, a Stampe, an ME-108, a Grob Aster, and a B-58 Baron. All the airplanes are for fun except the Baron, which he uses to fly to Hollywood. Active in his support of aviation, he helped launch and promote the Experimental Aircraft Association's Young Eagles program.

DAVE GWINN

THE QUICK THINKING PILOT

An airline pilot keeps his days off only if Scheduling can't find him in a time of need. At three in the morning, jolted from a peaceful sleep, a pilot answered his own phone. (Gasp!) The sound of the scheduler's voice on the other end quickly restored the pilot's wits. He calmly handed his wife the phone and whispered loudly, "It's your husband's employer trying to reach him!"

THE AIRLINE CAPTAIN OBSERVED...

"Ground instructors understand flying like astrologers understand astronomy."

"A good captain and a good first officer go hand-in-hand... EXCEPT through the terminal building."

CAPTAINS AND THE PA SYSTEM

Some captains are skilled with the public address system. Others can drive you nuts. They have nothing to say, and say it endlessly. At midnight, with everyone asleep, they will point out a thunderstorm and explain its meteorology.

One captain's repertoire was amazingly good. "Well, ladies and gentlemen, we are about to take off on Runway 18, southbound, which should excite you southbound takeoff fans! Now sit back and relax, because there's just no sense in all of us being edgy and nervous."

CAPTAIN DAN, THE UNPREDICTABLE CAPTAIN

When I met Captain Dan, the Unpredictable Captain, for the first time, he turned to me, tapped his naked shoulder straps, and asked, "Do you know why I don't wear four stripes on my shoulders?"

"No, sir," I replied.

"Because *I* know who the captain is, that's why!"

Later in the month, at SFO before our flight, I saw Captain Dan in Scheduling. He was wearing a uniform overcoat, buttoned to the top, and hat in place. Since I was wearing my light tropical uniform, I figured he must know something about our destination that I didn't. Surely I was going to be cold, but it was too late to go back and change.

Once on the plane, Captain Dan removed his overcoat. Underneath, he was sporting a snappy red and blue tie, a gray sport coat over dark blue slacks, and a button down light blue shirt. He explained, "I've got a date waiting for me in New York, and won't have time to change. Don't open that cockpit door for anyone!"

On another occasion, Captain Dan arrived for his checkride carrying the world's smallest flight kit. It contained only his Jeppesen binder with his approach charts. The check captain, of course, was accustomed to seeing flight kits with the required equipment: the aircraft's flight handbook, the Federal Air Regulations, the Flight Operations Policy Manual, and the usual array of other equipment most pilots carry in their flight kits.

"I'm greatly disappointed in your flight kit and equipment. Why don't you have the required items?"

Captain Dan always had an answer. He turned to the First Officer and asked, "Have you got the Flight Ops Policy Manual?"

The First Officer nodded. He turned to the Flight Engineer, "Have you got a tool kit and the Flight Handbook?" Yes, he did.

Captain Dan turned to the check captain and said, "I think we have every piece of required equipment in the cockpit, according to regulations." Captain Dan was a master of regulations. He never followed them, but he knew them well enough to know precisely to what limit they could be violated.

"That may be so, Captain," retorted the check captain, "but the NEXT time I see you, you'd better have a flight kit like everyone else. Got it?" Captain Dan nodded. The flight engineer, who had flown with Captain Dan before, mumbled, "Oh-oh!"

The very next week, Captain Dan ran into the check captain in Scheduling. Captain Dan carried the most sumptuous, gleaming, extra-large flight kit that money could buy. It even had Captain Dan in gold letters on top. "That's better." complimented the check captain. "I'm glad to see you cooperated."

Captain Dan set the case down, popped open its snaps, reached in and extracted his tiny flight bag.

———

Month after month, Captain Dan flew the same trip from Los Angeles, via St. Louis, and on to JFK. Then the airline changed the schedule. It now went nonstop from LAX to JFK.

The next time out, at about 41,000 feet, some 100 miles north of St. Louis, Captain Dan dialed in the STL ramp frequency and announced, "Flight 444 is on the ground. What gate do you want us at?"

"You're where?" stuttered the ramp agent.

"We're on the ground. What gate?"

"But you don't land here anymore," wailed the agent.

"Whatta ya mean, I don't land here. I've been landing here every week for months," replied Captain Dan.

"But we've had a schedule change, and you don't land here anymore," the obviously frustrated agent added.

"Well... I wondered why we had all this fuel left. Tell ya what. I'm gonna taxi on out and take off again. Don't tell anyone about this. Okay?"

Utter silence on the frequency. Perhaps the agent was concentrating on oxygen intake. Captain Dan added, "Well, that's not fair to you. Go ahead and log us in the computer as a touch-and-go at St. Louis."

Upon arrival at JFK the chief pilot, the duty captain, security, public relations, and an array of impressive titles met the flight. To their questions, the captain snapped impatiently, "Are you nuts? Touch-and-go in St. Louis? I'm here nine minutes early, with the correct fuel, and you people think we descended and landed in St. Louis? What the heck are you talking about?" The Unpredictable Captain exited his airplane and stormed out.

SPACE SHUTTLE, WHERE ARE YOU?

The planet Venus is a beautiful sight. It is so brilliantly lit by the sun, when it sits low on the horizon it's often mistaken for oncoming aircraft. Many a pilot has called Air Traffic Control asking, "Are you talking to the aircraft at 12 o'clock?" When it sits high in the sky, it's a beautiful star.

When the Space Shuttle was first launched, it commanded a great deal of public interest and publicity. One night an innocent, young flight attendant entered the cockpit. The Captain remarked, pointing to the bright light over the horizon, "Yeah, you're right. You *can* actually see the Space Shuttle tonight."

The flight attendant gasped, "Can I see it too?"

"Not only could you see it," volunteered the Captain, "but would you like to talk to them?" Her eyes lit up as he handed her the microphone and said, "Just say, 'Space Shuttle, this is Flight 444. Over.'"

The Flight Attendant dutifully repeated, "Space Shuttle, this is Flight 444. Over."

Well, unknown to the flight attendant, the captain can select any one of a number of transmitters, including the cockpit interphone.

"Well, hello! Where are you?" replied the flight engineer, hovering over his own microphone as he leaned to the back of the cockpit.

"Just tell them you're down here, at about 37,000 feet, over Pittsburgh," advised the Captain. She did.

"Well, turn on your landing lights and let's see if we can see you," answered the Space Shuttle. "Yeah! Hey, we can see you down there. Thanks a lot for calling."

The flight attendant left enchanted and all smiles. I'm confident that passenger after passenger heard about her private talk with the astronauts, and no doubt her children's children will some day repeat the story.

A ROSE BY ANY OTHER NAME

Most companies complete a "Welcome Aboard" poster for the passengers, including the crew's names, route of flight, time enroute, cruise altitude and destination weather. Sometimes the pilots help complete it.

One day I arrived at the airplane first, hiding the "Dave" on the end of my flight bag. When I shook hands with the very senior flight attendant, I introduced myself, "My name is Justin" and handed her the "Welcome Aboard" poster.

To reinforce the myth further, my co-conspirator, the captain, arrived, introduced himself, and asked, "Is Justin here yet?"

"Yes, Justin is in the cockpit," answered the flight attendant. Now we have a psychological fix.

For three days we perpetuated the hoax, and for three days she dutifully announced, "In command of your flight is Captain John Brown, assisted by First Officer Justin Case."

Sometimes, for variety, we use Justin Credible. And on two-man crews, the nonexistent flight engineer, Ben Deleted, is introduced as well.

JUST ONE OF GOD'S CREATURES

Many years ago, in Phoenix, back in the Constellation days, when it was customary to keep the cargo bin door open due to the high temperature, the ramp agent took pity on the large dog panting in the heat. The ramp agent, with great difficulty, unlatched the crate, and wrapped his belt around the dog's neck to assure he could control him. The agent then took the pooch for a walk. It appeared to be an unusually large Siberian Husky or German Shepherd.

The animal was well behaved, performed his duties, and sniffed everything in sight. They say a man who has the time to give kindness to an animal gives God a smile.

When it was time to "reboard" the critter, the agent obviously needed help due to the height of the cage and the weight of the animal. So another agent climbed into the cargo bin and began to open the crate for reentry, and suddenly gasped, "OH MY GOD!"

On top of the cage was a label, "DANGER....WOLF....PROPERTY OF THE CHICAGO ZOO."

Committed, and because the puppy fellow was behaving, they did manage nervously to re-cage him.

TWO SHIPS PASSING IN THE NIGHT

In the old days at TWA, a harassed local scheduler could simply call one of the local pilots and say, "I'm in a jam. Take this trip and I owe you one." It always seemed to work out for both parties. Today, thanks to computers, things have changed.

In San Diego (SAN) one day, a well intentioned but extremely ill first officer reported for his trip. Finally concluding, despite his good intentions, he could not fly, he called crew scheduling, "Terribly sorry to create a problem, but I'm too sick to take the trip."

Crew scheduling's computer elected to remove a first officer from a Los Angeles (LAX) flight and deadhead him to SAN, now delaying the LAX flight two hours to await a reserve first officer. (By contract the reserve or standby must accommodate only two hours availability.)

Get this: The LAX first officer was flown to SAN to protect the now delayed flight disabled by the sick pilot. The LAX flight, as mentioned, awaited his replacement for two hours.

In the meantime (as these sagas go), the standby first officer was enroute to LAX... on America West... from... you guessed it... SAN. They passed each other on the way. Two delays, two conveniently located problem solvers transported to opposing locations. Ah, computers.

THE AVIATION LEGEND

A local aviation legend and masterful mechanic lost his medical after a relatively minor heart attack. He did not, however, lose his need to transport himself via his Bonanza. I was managing a flight school of about 420 students, and when the need arose, the legend would call me and summon a pilot to fly *with* him. (Of course, he wanted "a license in the cockpit" if the Feds should ask.)

On a hectic, March day, the Legend called. I replied, "All right, I'll see what I can do. I'm really pressured today. Yes, I know you're in a hurry, you always are! I'll do my best."

When I got off the phone and walked into the hallway, I saw a good-looking youngster who looked familiar to me. "Would you like to fly with Mr. Legend in his Bonanza down to St. Louis and back?" The youngster was absolutely elated and ran next door.

Sometime later I was looked out on the ramp from our lounge and noted the Bonanza rotating and leaping airborne. I muttered, "Wonder who that kid was? Shoot, I know him. I know he's enrolled here, and yet I just can't place him." Then I remembered! I enrolled him the day before yesterday in the PRIVATE PILOT COURSE!

The aviation legend and master mechanic was not only illegal, he was carrying a passenger!

Too late to correct that one, I thought, let's hope for the best.

Much later that day, the youngster stood in my office doorway, and said, "That mechanic is sure strange."

"Why?" I asked, not knowing what to expect.

"Well, we got up to altitude and he asked if I'd ever flown a Bonanza before. When I said 'no,' he unclipped the single yoke, flipped it over, and told me to enjoy myself. We got in a spiral pretty fast. He got excited, but pulled it out, and told me to calm down and try again. Another spiral. He REALLY got impatient then. In fact, he snapped at me, "MY GOD, son, how many hours do you have?"

"I told him about an hour-and-a-half total flying time. He didn't speak to me again all day."

The Legend didn't speak to ME for a year. Every time I saw him I found a way to escape somehow. In the years to come, though, he never mentioned it.

WHAT TIME IS IT?

"We have a very upset passenger and he wants to see the captain!" This exceptionally disturbed man wanted to know how we possibly believed we could fly over the Rocky Mountains at 7,000 feet! "Don't you know the Rockies extend up to 15,000 feet?" We were cruising comfortably at 35,000 feet, but his Casio altimeter watch told him we were at 7,000. Some people don't understand the concept of the "pressurized cabin."

NOT ME!

I've heard of it being done, although I certainly couldn't prove it. On long, boring, pitch-black all night flights, they tell me that seven clicks on a unicom frequency at 35,000 feet causes uncontrolled airports to sparkle at awesome distances.

IT'S ALL A MATTER OF PERSPECTIVE

Battered by turbulence, the DC-9 descended to FL280, then FL260 and finally FL240. The Captain's complaints never ceased. A corporate Learjet pilot smugly injected, "Well, it's smooth at Flight Level 450!" The airline captain snapped, "Yeah? Well, how's the pay up there?"

ROLE MODEL

Recently a little lad of a passenger told me, "When I grow up I wanna be an airline pilot." With solemnity and honesty, I had to tell the boy, "Son, you can't do both."

SIMULATORS

Computers govern simulators. Sometimes they get crazy. In a recurrent training session, the computer-stricken simulator pitched about 60 degrees nose up, rolled violently sideways, shuddered and all the lights went out. Before the computer finally went "tilt," it slammed the simulator into the jacks supporting the machine. We were all stunned and in pain. Out of the dark came the first officer's voice, "Man, I've had that happen in the airplane a lot, but never in the simulator!"

A COUPLE OF DECADES OF THANKS TO ATC!

Some ATC professionals have a hotline to Eddie Murphy, I'm sure. When asked for my heading, I replied, "3-8-0."

Without hesitation, ATC replied, "Turn right 4-1-0 and cleared to Wilkes Barre."

When asked to *stand by*, I said, "Roger, standby. That's the second best thing I do."

He was baited. "TWA, what's the best thing you do?"

I replied, "Well, I really excel at *disregard*."

Biography

DAVE GWINN

Dave Gwinn is a retired airline captain, aviation journalist, speaker and educator with 30 years of experience, fifteen pilot ratings and over 13,000 hours aloft. *Skytalk Humor* is his memorable and quick-witted keynote presentation. His humorous tales and airborne pranks are selected from three decades as an instigator, witness, recipient and rarely innocent bystander within the aviation community. Dave's *Weather Radar Seminars* are internationally respected and simply the best. He simplifies weather and all avoidance devices with practical, fast-moving presentations. He has appeared as an expert witness in federal courts, *always* in defense of the pilot. For eleven years, TWA assigned him to the pilot training center instructing and developing courses for the B707, B727, B767, L1011 and the MD-80 programs. Pilots enjoy reading Dave's monthly column in *Plane & Pilot* magazine and listening to him on *Pilot's Audio Update*.

ROD LEWIN

ME AND MY BIG MOUTH!

I was a brand new first officer on the very sophisticated E-120 Brasilia turboprop. This airplane looks fast even when it's standing still, with its long, pointed snout and sharp, elongated features and T-tail. It has a fully integrated "glass" cockpit and the ram's horn-style control yoke has so many buttons on it, it almost takes a checkride on this feature alone!

We had just left the ramp at our DFW terminal area, and we were taxiing north on the inner taxiway for takeoff on Runway 17L. Heading north on the inner taxiway, we were obliged to pass the entire American Airlines complex and their numerous exit ramps. As we approached one particular exit, the ground controller, who had just seconds previously issued a taxi clearance to a stationary American jet, saw that we were too close to his exit and would have to brake hard if he told us to give way.

Instead, he instructed us to continue taxiing, and in the same breath instructed the American jet to hold short and give way to us. Notwithstanding their status as the "number one airline at DFW," sometimes these guys got carried away with their own importance. This particular gentleman chose to ignore—or act as if he did not hear—the revised instruction to hold short. Since he was already spooled up and moving beyond the hold line, he powered up and cut right across our bow. We braked hard, no doubt throwing our flight attendant right off her feet.

As both the captain and I were applying maximum braking and screeching to a sudden stop, I hit the mic button and let loose a stream of blasphemy, intending to vent my feelings to my captain. "What the *@# does that #@* think he's doing?"

As previously alluded to, I was not yet totally familiar with the operation of all those buttons on the yoke. The radio transmit button and the hot mike button are one and the same. Push it one way and you are talking to your partner via the intercom. Instead, I pushed the button the other way and transmitted on the ground frequency for all listening controllers and aircraft to hear.

A stunned silence followed on ground frequency for a full 30 seconds. The next transmission was a chuckling voice remarking, "Sounds like American has done it again!"

My unique Aussie accent did not go unnoticed on the frequency. When I walked into the crew lounge on our return from the trip, I was invited by the chief pilot into his office for a lengthy discourse on decorum and the peculiarities of FARs relating to use of obscene language on FAA frequencies.

THE INDISCREET JUMPSEATER

One night when I was riding rear jumpseat on a Lockheed L-1011, I was both amazed and amused by the quick wit of one of the flight attendants. A very loudmouthed and overbearing check captain sat in the forward jumpseat immediately behind the operating line captain. He was making no bones about his superiority, general station in life and his seniority with the airline. He apparently felt his position also entitled him to make coarse comments about the flight attendants.

I felt embarrassed and awkward in the close quarters of the cockpit, and was about to request permission from the operating captain to leave the flight deck and find a seat aft. We were just leveling out at initial cruising altitude when the cockpit door buzzer rang. The captain pressed the door release and a very attractive female African-American flight attendant entered and began to take beverage orders from the crew.

The captain, first officer and flight engineer were asked first, in accordance with custom, to give their respective coffee orders. The flight attendant then politely asked the jumpseat-riding check captain if he would like coffee. He responded in the affirmative and with a poor attempt at inappropriate humor, he added with a leering wink "and I like my coffee just like my women."

Without a second's hesitation, the quick-witted lady in question looked him right in the eye and replied, "I'm sorry, captain, we don't serve stupid coffee."

THE WINDBAG

I had been flying with the same captain all month. Both the flight attendant and I dreaded each of his in-flight "welcome aboard" PAs as he was so long-winded he sometimes took a good five minutes or more to give his spiel. He would go on and on about weather trivia in both the northern and southern hemispheres, the landforms we were passing over (even if there was total cloud cover), the possibility of turbulence, the necessity to wear seatbelts at all times and the weather (even if there was not a cloud in the sky).

One day I discovered that novice first officers aren't the only pilots who can manage to mishandle the audio and microphone buttons. It was my turn to fly, which meant that it was the windbag captain's turn to do the PAs and handle the radio calls. We had leveled out at cruising altitude when the captain picked up the hand mic, pressed what he thought was the PA selector on the audio panel, and began his lengthy discourse. Four or five minutes had gone by and I thought nothing of it until I sensed something amiss. I realized that I could hear the flight attendant in the back giving a PA, which should have been impossible if the captain was using it, as his button overrides the cabin PA.

Then I realized I was hearing his voice in my headset, instead of a muffled PA in the cabin, and the transmit light was illuminated on the number one Comm—the one tuned to the current ATC Center frequency. I grabbed his arm and pointed to the light on the audio panel, but he waved me off and frowned that he wanted me to answer what he assumed was a call from Center.

He continued blathering on for a while longer. When he finally replaced the mic and was about to reset the audio panel button, he realized, almost at the same instant as the incoming transmission from Center, his grossly embarrassing error of keying the wrong button. The Center controller came on in an acerbic, high-pitched voice which was masking either barely suppressed laughter or extreme disapprobation, and remarked, "Why, thank you 659. You have managed to single-handedly block my entire frequency and my ability to communicate with 23 IFR and 37 VFR aircraft for precisely nine minutes and 35 seconds. And if that were not bad enough, while trying to follow your lengthy instructions on how to fasten my seatbelt, I fell off my damn stool."

DON'T TRY THIS ONE AT HOME

Back in my halcyon days of living and flying seaplanes in that paradise on Australia's Great Barrier Reef, we had to improvise a lot to create our own entertainment.

We flew out of a small grass and dirt airstrip way up on the northeast coast outside a little town called Airlie Beach. Airlie's primary source of income came from tourists passing through enroute to the several island resorts in the Whitsunday Passage. The white, sandy beach fronting onto the crystal clear waters of the Passage invited the usual plethora of Aussie outdoor activities, such as flying low over the beaches on departure and arrival to "perve" on the naked women below—though we did also enjoy genuine, healthy, physical water sports as well.

Our "job" consisted of flying tourists out to the Reef, and then playing tour guides when we alighted in the coral lagoons where we took them snorkeling and scuba diving. We probably had the best flying job in the world, albeit poorly paid. And though we were a team of about a dozen pilots, not one among us owned any kind of respectable boat for water skiing.

We operated a fleet of six Lake Buccaneers, two Grumman Mallards and two Beavers on floats. A few of us were sitting in the little bar/bistro by the flightline on a typical hot, clear blue day, complaining about the lack of a suitable skiboat. One bright lad made what was intended as a facetious comment. "Aw, whadda we need with a skiboat? Look out there. We've got a couple of perfectly good Lakes sitting there doing nothing!"

The rest of us sat up, looked at each other as if we had been complete morons not to think of this before, and immediately set off in different directions. "I'll gas up one of the Buccaneers," said one.

"I'll race home and get my skis," said another.

"I'll stop at the marine shop and buy some line and some kind of handle on the way back."

"And I shall call the ambulance and have them standing by," I quipped.

Ten minutes later, the Buccaneer took off with Pete and I at the controls. We climbed to 50 feet to clear the palm trees, coasted over their tops, then chopped the throttle and glided in over the beach to alight in the slight swell. We turned her downwind, dropped the landing gear into the water, taxied up onto the beach, and waited amid a growing circle of tanned and sandy beach bunnies for our friend to arrive with the skis. He did so shortly and we quickly hitched up the rope to the rear tiedown point conveniently located on the keel just forward of the main air/water rudder.

"Aw'right, who's first?" he asked, expectantly holding the rope firmly in hand.

"You go first, Paul," I said. "After all, it was your brilliant idea. I'll stay here and entertain the lovelies. Maybe sign some of 'em up for a tow. We might make some money at this."

"O.K. Good idea. You want to tow first, Pete? Be careful! No smartass maneuvers."

"Who me?" Pete replied with the hurt tone that only he could muster, despite his bending more planes than the rest of us put together.

Paul strapped on a single ski as Pete jumped into his mount and started the engine with a roar, blasting fine sand into all our faces. He rolled the few feet into the water, sucked up the gear and motored out until the line was almost taut. He looked back in time to see Paul drop his arm in signal to "hit it," then he closed the canopy and shoved up the throttle.

The engine bellowed, white spray plumed through the prop, the plane leaped forward and instantly up onto the "step," jerking Paul off the sand into the water. Amazingly, Paul managed to stay upright and moments later, with the Buccaneer step-taxiing in a wide turn at about 40 knots, he was slaloming all over the bay to the cheers of the now-large audience on the beach.

Things were going quite swimmingly for five minutes or so. Then, just as our intrepid team had come round for a run fairly close in and parallel to the beach, I saw something I didn't like at all. Way out on a long final, straight into the beach was a tiny dot, which quickly materialized into one of our white Beavers. The wind was light and variable and the slight swell was parallel to the beach, so he was coming straight in. I knew he was landing in the water because he was too low to make it over the trees if he was aiming for the strip behind them.

He touched down lightly across the swell, bounced over a couple of them, then was running in a high-speed taxi directly towards the beach and at right angles to the Buccaneer and Paul on his ski. He obviously had his eyes focused on the Buccaneer, as he turned slightly away to pass well aft of his wake. He apparently did not see our brave skier. Moments later, before he realized what was happening, his forward float struts fouled the towline at a forward speed of about 50 knots!

In an instant, to our horror, Paul was whipped around closely behind the Beaver, still clinging frantically to the towbar. Then everything seemed to happen at once. The Beaver decelerated and came off the step into displacement about 20 feet off the beach. Paul finally succumbed to the influence of momentum, gravity and sheer terror and released his death grip on the towbar. Now free from its recalcitrant skier, the towbar became a hurtling missile behind the almost airborne Buccaneer, slamming into the Beaver's float support structure but somehow missing its prop. Paul had let go just as the combined forces of nature acting upon him had literally dragged him underwater close behind the Beaver.

For a moment I thought he was gone, but just as the Beaver beached, a human torpedo sliced up onto the sand, missing the right float by about four feet. The skier turned frogman lay awash and motionless for several seconds, and then gratefully allowed himself to be assisted upright on wobbly legs amidst a hearty cheer from the crowd of spectators who had gathered around. Apart from the top layer of skin on his forehead and face being surgically removed by first impacting the sea and then the sand, he was remarkably unharmed.

He became the hero of the day, and he managed to get several gallons of free beer past his skinned and broken lips before passing out. However, when the boss found out about the incident, he cut off Paul's supply of free beer for quite some time, despite the fact that our scenic flights that day numbered an all-time high.

Biography

ROD LEWIN

Rod Lewin thought, "I must still be alive, I can't be in this much pain if I'm dead." A near-fatal airplane crash the day before his commercial checkride had destroyed his lower spine. Rod was left a paraplegic. He tells with candor his success story of winning back his walk, contrary to all of the medical experts. He then continued on to win his commercial ticket with calipers on his legs. More obstacles were met as he limped into various pilot job interviews. Rod's delightful Aussie accent and plucky humor accent his incredible story of beating the odds. Pilots also enjoy his post-recovery stories of adventure and high-jinx, flying seaplanes in the beautiful but treacherous waters of the Great Barrier Reef. He has flown many types of seaplanes including Lake Buccaneers and Grumman Mallards and his ratings include B-737, DC-3 and E-120. Rod's inspiring book, *Steel Spine, Iron Will*, tells how he overcame not only paralysis, but bitterness and deep depression. Rod's story is an inspiration to anyone facing a problem, looking to achieve a goal, or wanting to overcome obstacles in their lives.

BILL LISHMAN

GEESE OVER MANHATTAN

Jacques Perrin is a world-renowned French filmmaker and actor best known for *Microcosmos*, an acclaimed artistic special on the rarely-seen world of miniature creatures. In the fall of 1996, Jacques came to see me to discuss his latest project—a film on the world as seen from a migratory bird perspective. Jacques explained that he had been inspired by my original 1988 film entitled *C'mon Geese*, a documentary of my pioneering flights with Canada geese. After that film, I led three more flights of geese south by homebuilt ultralight aircraft. In 1995, I acted as Jeff Daniel's double in Columbia Pictures' *Fly Away Home*—a fictionalized Hollywood version of what I had been doing; a kind of twisted windows look at my life.

My research asked the question: Is it possible to develop a technique to establish new migration routes for endangered birds? Joe Duff, my partner and fellow pilot in these experiments, and I had always felt limited in sharing this virtually unseen perspective with the earthbound human world. *Fly Away Home* had captured some great imagery, but we felt there was potential for more. Subsequently, Jacques produced a fine promotional piece, raising megafrancs. He and his crew then set out on a three-year global bird filming odyssey.

Shooting progressed as planned on location in Europe, Iceland, and Africa. While I felt honored to be a part of the project's initial inspiration, only the occasional little story of the film's progress filtered through. I felt left out. Then in the late fall of 1999, there came a phone call. One of Jacques' film crews was in northern New York with a flock of aircraft-imprinted Canada geese and two special ultralight aircraft. They were having a few problems and needed help.

Their plan was to bring the geese to New York City and film them against the backdrop of the Manhattan skyline, particularly France's gift to America, the Statue of Liberty. Location Manager Vincent Steiger was charged with getting the appropriate clearances for the Manhattan flights. In the end, he had a stack of 19 different permits from a variety of government agencies.

operationmigration.durham.net

Ultralight aircraft are not certified in the U.S. by the Federal Aviation Agency (FAA), so it is unlawful to use them to carry passengers. Vincent found the appropriate channels and had both the Cosmos trikes thoroughly checked and re-registered as U.S. experimental aircraft. Once deemed experimental, the French pilots, who had only ultralight licenses (which are not recognized in the U.S.), could not legally fly the planes.

Isn't bureaucracy wonderful? The Cosmos trikes could now be flown only by a pilot holding a minimum of a U.S. private pilot's license. The requirement then was for a pilot current on trike type ultralights with float experience. Moreover, a private pilot may not fly for hire, so the pilot had to be willing to fly without remuneration. Thus, the phone call. Vincent asked me to be a consultant for the Manhattan shoot and to fly for free. My relatively painless task: to have my Canadian private license converted to a U.S. license.

Monday, November 8, 6:30 a.m., I find myself slowly rocking back and forth in the front seat of a highly modified Cosmos trike. I am dressed in a sawed-off windsurfing dry suit, scuba diver boots, a snowmobile floater jacket, and an inflatable life jacket. In the back seat is Jacques Perrin's son, still photographer Mathieu, who is equally attired and encumbered with two long lens Nikons. For those of you unfamiliar with trike flying, saying that the two-place arrangement is cozy is a major understatement. The passenger is virtually piggybacked; their knees are your armrest. With all the gear on—helmets, headsets, mitts, intercom cables, and radio interface push to talk cable—one feels just slightly entangled.

We are tied to the dock at the boat launch ramp at Liberty State Park in New Jersey. Off to the east in the pre-dawn gray is the distinctive silhouette of the lady of Liberty. Behind her stand the equally distinctive towers of lower Manhattan. The other trike is also a Cosmos, though barely recognizable as such. In front of the pilot, a fiberglass plank spans the floats. Cameraman Thierry Machado and his Aaton 35 mm movie camera rest and ready themselves on this flying ledge.

Photo by Mathieu Simonet

The area in which we are to fly is located between JFK, La Guardia, and Newark Airports. We will be in the dead center of three of the busiest airport control zones in the world. The plan is to lead a flock of French-raised Canada geese around the Statue of Liberty and then across the Hudson and up the East River. The goal is to capture Manhattan and the Statue of Liberty from a bird perspective with flying geese in the immediate foreground. Two boats will shadow us in case of a problem.

The 19 permits aside, Vincent must call Newark control tower prior to each flight. Edgar, whose English is limited, is piloting the camera ship. He will have enough to keep him busy, so I am to manage the radio work for both craft. As soon as I'm airborne, I'm to alert Newark tower. Then, as I pass the Statue, I'm to call La Guardia. Then, I'm to switch immediately to Hudson River frequency, calling our position every few minutes. Once past the Battery, I'm to switch to East River frequency and again announce our position every few minutes. It's cold. I'm wearing snowmobile mitts. Changing through four frequencies on a tiny hand held radio within a distance of less than four miles is going to be challenging.

My French is limited to what I remember from high school 45 years ago. Thankfully, Mathieu's English is considerably better than my French. Between the two of us, we work out an arrangement for Mathieu to hang on to my right mitt while I change frequencies.

The trike has a pusher prop situated about three feet behind us. Although it has a protective guard, anything dropped in flight gets sucked back. A dropped mitt could conceivably cause the propeller to explode. To avoid a major disaster, great care must be taken

Firing up a pull-start ultralight on wheels is normally a non-event, but encumbered with all our gear while on floats, it proves to be impossible. A person on the dock, free of flight gear, and preferably acrobatic, can do the job. If the aircraft is not tied to the dock, it departs immediately. Or, if pointed toward the dock, the aircraft will bump around like a berserk water bug.

Chief Pilot Jean Michel comes to the rescue. He is grounded because of a broken elbow acquired in a non-flying accident five weeks earlier. Jean Michel is a tall, athletic man with a sense of humor that forever flows through his broken English. Five pulls later, with his plaster encased elbow, he manages to start us out from the dock and push us far enough to taxi into the small bay for takeoff. The helmet intercom/radio system seems to work while taxiing.

The takeoff will be to the west. Edgar is in position in the camera ship. The geese, already ferried out on one of the boats, are released. Away we go.

Photo by Mathieu Simonet

We do a parallel take off and then a 180 toward the statue. The geese break from the camera ship and, for a few moments, form up on my craft. We slide gently toward the camera ship. By slipping beneath, I am able to pass off the geese and get distant enough so

Photo by Mathieu Simonet

that the birds stay formed on Edgar and Thierry. I attempt to call Newark tower, but there is so much background noise I cannot make out a confirmation. Switching to our communication channel, I attempt to call Edgar. His transmission in broken English filters through.

Alex, the American boat driver monitoring the frequencies on his aviation radio, is able to take over the radio work—a good thing, as the headsets are useless. Passing my mitt back to Mathieu, I fool with the radio. My attempts are futile save for holding the earpiece tight to my ear. I can hear Alex *self-announcing* for us. There are several helicopters in the air. In order not to distract the geese, I stay clear of the camera ship while it heads toward the Battery.

I sit back, take a breath, and look around. The Statue of Liberty, lit with the golden dawn sun, stands out—brilliant against a dark gray sky to the west. Our altitude is about shoulder high to the Lady. I ease the trike into a gradual right hand turn. The air is so stable that the whole panorama becomes a turntable—the statue at its center. I hear the click-zip click-zip of Mathieu's Nikon. How appropriate, I think, that a Frenchman is capturing the images of this giant figure that was hand formed by his countrymen in the last century.

Breaking away, I climb to the northeast toward the Battery and pass over the Staten Island ferry. Edgar and Thierry are now almost at the mouth of the East River. The geese string off their left in close formation. Pulling the bar into my chest, we make haste so as not to lose sight of them. The morning sun breaks through the layers of cloud flashing golden off the towers.

Halfway across the river, at about 300 feet, we come across a flight of 50 or so wild geese. They are unperturbed as I gradually close in on them. Like most New Yorkers, they are quite blasé about our presence. We are just another kind of bird. I hold a position about 30 feet off the flock while Mathew fires off a few more frames. The towers, dominated by the World Trade Center twins, form the background.

When I look down at the jam-up of traffic on the Manhattan streets, I cannot help but feel that even this—the busiest of air traffic areas—is so uncluttered. A helicopter on its final descent to the Wall Street Heliport is below us. A news helicopter stands off to the south. Every few minutes, a jet passes a few thousand feet above us. The air is a vast ocean, as open and clear, by comparison, as it would be if there were only three cars in all of lower Manhattan. How privileged I feel to have bird freedom around this outcrop of architectural wonders.

Photo by Mathieu Simonet

My experiences in New York stretch back 40 years. For a few moments, as we round the Battery and head up the East River, I find the memories. It dawned on me that each time I had visited New York it was unique and marked a turning point in my life.

In 1959, while still a teenager, I took an overnight bus from Toronto to New York. Quite scary for an Ontario boy just off the farm. Once there, I bought a one-way ticket to England on the old Queen Mary (she now rests as a hotel in Long Beach). The Queen was berthed at the end of 50th street. I recall standing on the dock, bowled over by her immense size. She was the largest passenger ship in the world, befitting her place in New York. Everything in the city was grand. A blast from her great whistle made my heart nearly stop as she was nudged into the Hudson by a bevy of tugs. It was from her foredeck that I had my first view of the Statue of Liberty.

I remember the spring of '63, riding my '59 Triumph motorcycle through upper New York State, New England, and finally through the canyons of Manhattan. I was visiting my sister who lived on the Lower East Side, in a five-story walk up. The apartment was just wide enough for the bathtub that doubled as the base for the dining room table. I spent a couple of weeks touring the haunts of the village, listening to guys like Bob Dylan who were, at that time, little-known weird sounding troubadours playing the coffee houses that populated that stretch of the city.

Six years later in the late fall, just freshly married, my wife Paula and I crewed a 40 foot ketch from Lake Ontario through the Erie Canal to Albany. From Albany we rode the current down the Hudson to tie up for a week around 40th Street. In 1983, after selling a major piece of my art in Washington, I took the train to Manhattan to rendezvous with Paula who had coincidentally achieved a major coup in her fashion business. We celebrated with a bottle of champagne in our funky suite at the Algonquin. The result was conception of our daughter Carmen.

In '96, I flew to Manhattan for the premiere of *Fly Away Home*. I was chauffeured around "Hollywood style" in a limousine. I was able to break away for a few afternoon hours and have the gritty experience of accompanying a detective friend on his rounds in

Manhattan's midtown south precinct—only to learn that crime was at an all time low. Forty-second Street was being restored to its old glory.

And now, here I am, over the East River, almost at the Brooklyn Bridge. We orbit for a few turns while the camera ship heads south. Our featherweight craft begins to buck and roll in the slight northwest wind, which has been twisted by its struggles through the great wall of structures off our wing.

It gives me pause to absorb the image of lower Manhattan. At this altitude, with some of the floors of buildings at a higher altitude than our passage, I am awestruck by the shards of glass layered upon one another, each erupting from the elongated flat iron barge that is Manhattan. What keeps this collection of skyscrapers afloat? I do not know. It is invisible. It appears an elongated tray overloaded with thousands of polished sculptures, each a unique concretized-midnight dream of some inspired architect, each a trophy of power attempting to outstretch each other to the sky. They stand seemingly arrogant, arranged on a gridwork flowing yellow with taxis—the blood cells of this creature. The whole protrusion seems precariously top-heavy, anchored in the current of reality only by the most minimal filigree of bridges. The river is like a large intestine that has become rudely distended to allow for Manhattan's being. Compacted into this geometry of outsized crystalline forms are millions of beings each with unique dreams and aspirations. I grope for the reality of it all as we buzz its periphery like a mosquito in a world of surreal wedding cakes.

We are off the 17th street pier as the camera ship rounds the Battery and heads north up the Hudson. The geese are still a fine line in the camera ship's wake. All the while, Thierry hangs off the right float attempting to get that definitive goose-over-Manhattan shot. The helicopter still sits beneath us, its rotors at idle, on the Wall Street Heliport. The two boats, in hot pursuit of the geese, skip past. Earlier, I had met the grizzled, crusty guy in charge of the boats. I had the impression that he had been the captain of a barge on the Seine. Later, I found out that he is Bernard deGuy, a retired admiral from the French Navy, also a

Photo by Mathieu Simonet

captain of one of Jacques Cousteau's ships during an around-the-world undersea exploration.

Heading back westward, across the Hudson, and still at 300 feet, we rendezvous with Edgar, Thierry and the geese. Just north of Ellis Island, it appears that the geese break away from the camera ship and are heading straight back toward Liberty Park. Edgar is too far east to recover them so we position ourselves along the west shore and are able to intercept. The geese form on our craft. I throttle back and push the bar forward, slowing in an attempt to let Edgar reposition. The birds string across and surf on the leading edge of my wing. Their slowed wing beats transfer back to create a pulsing of the control bar. Mathieu, having rarely seen the birds in this tight, presses against my shoulder to shoot a few more frames on one of his Nikons.

Meanwhile, Edgar pulls a tight 360 to the left, his wing becoming almost vertical and for a moment blocking the view of most of the World Trade Center towers. Thierry, gripping his camera, is held sitting horizontal by centrifugal force in the middle of his perch. He should be a candidate for the Legion of Honor for bravery, I think to myself. Edgar, now level, maneuvers the trike up on my left wing and again they are able to *scrape* the birds off while

I dive clear and distance myself. Edgar, Thierry and the geese circle the statue twice and then head back for a landing on the bay to the south of the park. I cannot resist rounding the statue a couple more times.

I notice a Channel Two News 'copter shadowing us off to the south. We skim on to the now choppy water of the bay south of Liberty Park and taxi up to the dock behind the camera ship. The news helicopter hovers to the north as the geese nonchalantly swim in and walk out on the boat ramp to *mama de oei* and their breakfast of dried wheat.

Photo by Mathieu Simonet

It isn't eight a.m. yet and the winds have picked up, making further flights impractical.

"Did ya get it?" I inquire.

The answer is "no" from Theirry.

"The light eez not good and the air is too..." His body language mimics the rock and roll of the turbulence we had felt over the East River. With only four minutes of film per flight, he could not waste it on a shaky shot.

The winds don't subside for a few days. Our next attempt is on a Friday, but the day turns into a series of mixups. Sitting again at the dock, now with a new headset and communications system, Jean Michel attempts to speak to me. I take off my headset to hear him, but I only hear the plunk of my glasses plopping into the Hudson. Oh well, I think. I only need them to read the instruments, of which there are none.

Then the engine, which had been previously warmed up, won't start. It wears out the production manager, the location manager, and Jean Michel before we get it going again. The camera ship waits for us out in the bay. Late, I taxi out and hastily advance the throttle, attempting to get the floats planing for a fast taxi. Just as I am transitioning from full splash mode to smooth plane, the engine balks and loses power. Throttle back. We sit a moment. The engine is idling fine. Again, I ease the throttle forward. Again, it almost gets up and goes. But this time, the engine quits completely.

At least the radio works.

"Bernard de Beel," I call on the radio (unconsciously mimicking how they pronounce my name.)

"Beel de Bernard," Bernard calls back

"Le moteur est arret," I announce.

Bernard maneuvers the boat and throws us a line. As we approach the dock, I misjudge the offshore wind and release the line too soon. We begin to get blown away from the dock. Bernard yells, "You only let go when I say!" His English is perfect (up to this point, I had only heard him speak French). With some difficulty, he repositions and tows us in again. The command comes in an admiral fashion. I release. Whoops, just as bad as last time, and we're blown back again. I don't feel so badly now. The third try is successful, but as we approach the dock, Jean Michel leans out to grab the rigging. Both his aviation radio and cell phone slip from his pocket to join my glasses in the sludge at the bottom of the Hudson.

On the weekend, with my glasses dredged up and the technical glitch solved (a pinched off fuel tank vent), we fly twice more around the statue and up the East River. Each time, I am afforded a unique experience.

On one flight, the north wind picks up and I am able to slow my craft to a speed that almost matches the Staten Island ferry. Passengers look at us and we look at passengers in the early morning golden light. Further up the Hudson, we circle a sloop flying a Swedish flag. They are heading out towards the Verrazano straits and from there... Who knows? The Islands? Rio de Janeiro? The middle-aged couple stop their sailing chores for a moment and wave as we pass. On our return, I do a low-level orbit around Ellis Island, the welcoming spot for so many immigrants in the last century. What stories must be contained in its old stone walls, a vacant relic of so many past emotions.

The next day, the weather closes down our activity. My contract is complete and Phillipe Gautier, the production manager in charge of the shoot, is satisfied that the valuable geese won't become lost somewhere between Hoboken and Brooklyn. I am no longer needed.

I have seen the Big Apple from the goose's eye. I will wait to see the shots that Thierry finally laid down on film. With all the effort, I am sure it will capture that breath-taking bird view wonder of the Great City. Two New York minutes in a great winged migration.

Photo by Mathieu Simonet

Bill has conducted several studies with Canada geese, leading them on southerly migrations. These aircraft-led migrations proved successful in that the birds returned unaided to their northerly home the following spring. This technique, initially developed with geese, will now be used in an attempt to establish a new migratory flock of the highly endangered Whooping Crane.

Biography

WILLIAM LISHMAN

Bill is a pilot, artist, sculptor, filmmaker, author, inventor, naturalist and entrepreneur.

In 1988, Bill raised a flock of Canada geese, imprinted them to an ultralight aircraft he designed and built, and flew with the birds around southern Ontario. The success of this work led to conducting a migration experiment by leading flocks of Canada geese on their journey south by acting as surrogate parents. This was documented by ABC's *20/20* and captured the attention of biologists around the world. Bill documented his first flights in the award winning video, *C'mon Geese*. His first book about his work with the geese is in the curriculum of U.S. public schools. For *Fly Away Home*, the feature film inspired by his career, Bill consulted and was the stunt double for the lead actor, Jeff Daniels—who was playing Bill. His autobiography, *Father Goose*, is on the best seller list. Bill is president of Operation Migration (http://operationmigration.durham.net) a non-profit organization dedicated to the survival of endangered birds. In 1995, the Canadian Owners and Pilots Association's highest honor, the prestigious COPA Award, was presented to Bill. In 1996, he received Odyssey of The Mind's prestigious Creativity Award (previous recipients were Walt Disney, Chuck Jones, and NASA). Bill's 21st century earth-integrated domed home has been featured in magazines for its innovative design. His sculptures are displayed in television commercials, IMAX films (*The Last Buffalo* and *Titanica)*, the Oklahoma Aviation and Space Hall of Fame, Canada's Wonderland and EXPO '86.

CAPTAIN AL HAYNES

Editor's note. On July 19, 1989, United Airlines Flight 232 departed Denver at about 2:09 p.m. and climbed uneventfully to a cruise altitude of 37,000 feet. At approximately 3:16 p.m. the crew notified ATC the #2 engine had failed and that the aircraft was only marginally stable. What followed was one of the most compelling dramas in aviation history as the crew fought to control and eventually land the huge jet, which was effectively without flight controls due to loss of its entire hydraulic system.

Although 112 people died in the landing, the wonder is that 184 survived. Many of the lessons learned that day continue to be taught to successive generations of pilots and emergency personnel.

The captain of Flight 232, Al Haynes, was one of the survivors. He continues to present the story of Flight 232 and its lessons so that others can continue to learn from the experience. The following is excerpted and edited from one of his presentations, made at NASA's Ames Research Center, Edwards, California.

ATC: *232 heavy, say souls on board and fuel remaining.*

UAL 232: *We have 376, [unreadable].*

ATC: *United 232 heavy, Sioux City.*

UAL 232: *Confirm we have no hydraulic fluid, which means we have no elevator control, almost none, and very little aileron control. I have serious doubts about making the airport. Have you got someplace near there that we might be able to ditch? Unless we get control of this airplane, we're going to put it down wherever it happens to be.*

ATC: *United 232 heavy, say again? 232 heavy, think you'll be able to hold about a 240 heading?*

UAL 232: *We're going to turn into it about right now.*

ATC: *When you turn to that 240 heading, sir, the airport will be about oh, 12 o'clock and 38 miles.*

UAL 232: *Okay, we're trying to control it just by power alone. We have no hydraulics at all, sir. We're doing our best here.*

[portion omitted]

UAL 232: *United 232. We're starting a left turn back to the airport. Since we have no hydraulics, braking is going to really be a problem. I would suggest the equipment be [placed] toward the far end of the runway. And I think under the circumstances, regardless of the condition of the airplane when we stop, we're going to evacuate, so you might notify the ground crew that we're going to do that.*

ATC: *United 232 heavy, wilco, sir, and if you can continue that left turn to about a 220 heading, sir, that'll take you right to the airport.*

United 232 heavy, you're going to have to widen out just slightly to your left sir, to make the turn to final, and also to take you away from the city.

UAL 232: *Whatever you do, keep us away from the city.*

ATC did keep us away from the city, and we did land the airplane, though I feel that "land" is a rather loose term for what actually happened. In the final analysis, though, we were successful in preserving the lives of 184 people.

I think there were five factors that contributed to the degree of success that we had at Sioux City: luck, communications, preparation, execution and cooperation.

LUCK

We all have our own personal beliefs and convictions and I would never intrude on yours, so for the sake of discussion, we'll call our first factor "luck." You may call it whatever you wish. But what did luck have to do with it?

Well, before we talk about luck, how did we get the airplane to Sioux City? When the number two engine blew, it took out the number two accessory drive section, which took out the hydraulics for the number two system. Some 70 pieces of shrapnel penetrated the horizontal stabilizer, severing the number one and number three lines. The net result? We ended up with no hydraulics.

The DC-10, like a lot of other aircraft today and many of those that will be made in the future, has no cables going to the controls. There is no manual reversion in the airplane at all. The cables go to the servos and then hydraulic pressure does the work.

In order to protect against the loss of all fluid, a lot of redundancies are built into the system. The DC-10, for instance, has three completely independent hydraulic systems. It has two engine-driven pumps per system, each with its own hydraulic reservoir, its own supply lines and its own return lines. These systems are not interconnected fluid-wise in any way to one another. They are connected mechanically, so that if we shut down say, the number one engine, the fluid in the number three system runs a motor which operates a pump in the number one system. The pressure's built right back up. That's all automatic, you don't do anything about it. Should you lose the fluid in the number one system due to a leak in one of the components, you won't lose the number two and three systems, because they are not all connected together.

All the major component flight controls are powered by at least two, and sometimes three, of these independent hydraulic systems. As the last resort, there is an air-driven generator that drops out of the bottom of the fuselage and runs a motor in the tail that will provide hydraulic pressure to one of the systems.

Enough redundancy was built into the system to where the odds were placed at a billion-to-one that complete hydraulic failure would occur. On July 19th, Murphy's Law caught up with us. We lost all three systems.

As a result, we had no ailerons to bank the airplane, no rudder to turn it, no elevators to control the pitch, no leading-edge flaps or slats to slow the airplane down and no trailing-edge flaps for landing. We had no spoilers on the wing to help us get down, or help us slow down once we were on the ground. On the ground, we had no steering (nosewheel or tail) and no brakes.

All we had to control the airplane were the throttles on the number one and number three engines. By manipulating those throttles and skidding the airplane into a turn, we were able to control the heading somewhat. Controlling pitch was just about out of the question. We kept saying we thought we had the elevators under control. Unfortunately, we never had them under control. We thought we did, but we didn't.

Working with just the throttles on those two engines, we managed to get the airplane on the ground. It was a tremendous piece of luck because the same scenario had been tried in a simulator, and, we've been told, it can't be done. Everything had to work in the right sequence and it did. That's how we got the airplane to an airport.

Another piece of luck involved our location. We could have been halfway to Honolulu or over the Rockies or we could have just departed JFK. We were over the relatively flatlands of Iowa. In the back of our minds, all of us had serious doubts about making the airport. But we knew that if we had to ditch, we could probably find some fairly flat terrain and we might have a chance of survival. Knowing this relieved a lot of the pressure on us.

The weather was another amazing piece of luck. If we had to control that DC-10 under any kind of turbulence, we would never have made it. If you are familiar with the Midwest in the summer time, from the Canadian border to the Gulf of Mexico, there is usually a line of thunderstorms that are doozies. We had one little buildup, which we went around. The rest was clear skies.

We had scattered clouds at 4,500 feet and about 10 miles visibility. A year to the day later, when we went back for a memorial service, there was a huge thunderstorm at Sioux City resting directly over the airport. Had that been there a year prior, we would never have made the airport.

The time of day was also very advantageous. It was day, which meant we could see the airport. Finding an unfamiliar airport in unfamiliar terrain at night would be very difficult. We were able to spot the airport four or five miles out, permitting us to approach it visually. We landed on a closed runway—Runway 22. It has no lights. At night, I'm sure we would never have found that runway.

But the greatest stroke of good luck in terms of time of day was that it was right at shift-change time for the hospitals. Marion Health Center, which happens to be a regional trauma center and St. Luke's, which happens to be a regional burn center, are both located in Sioux City. They were just changing their shifts, so they were double-shifted for our arrival. Additionally, all the clinics and health centers around town were releasing their workers from work. With about 30 minutes notice that we were going to Sioux City (as broadcast on the radio), all these emergency personnel were able to head to the hospitals. So many volunteers showed up that some had to be turned away.

The last piece of luck involved the Air National Guard stationed at Sioux City. There were 285 trained National Guardsmen on duty at the airport waiting for us when we got there.

You can see how the luck factor was exceptionally high for us. Our luck ran out about 50 feet in the air, but it lasted for a long time, nevertheless. Luck played a very important part in getting the airplane to Sioux City and having the survival rate we had.

COMMUNICATION

The second biggest factor was communications. We had quick response by ATC. Minneapolis Center quickly turned us over to an extremely calm young controller, Kevin Bockman. I met Kevin in person at the White House about a month later. When I finally could talk to him—we couldn't say much the first time we met—I learned he had moved to Sioux City because he found his previous duty station too stressful! He was looking for something a little quieter. I haven't the foggiest idea where he is now—he's not in Sioux City.

The communication with him was outstanding. The DME did not work at Sioux City that day. The cockpit voice recorder shows numerous times when we were asking where we were in relation to the airport and how far out. Kevin was right there every second, giving us every bit of information. He picked out airports we could go to as well as runways and highways we could land on. The Highway Patrol even blocked one of the freeways going out to the airport and kept it open for us as a landing option.

Communication in the air was tremendous. Probably what helped us the most was the second officer, Dudley Dvorak. I asked him to get hold of San Francisco area maintenance. Like all major airlines, United keeps a crew of maintenance experts on call for each type of equipment they fly. They have all the computers, all the logbook history, all the aircraft history as well as other information that they can draw on to help a crew with a problem. And we definitely had a problem. Unfortunately, they had no answer to our problem even though they desperately tried to find one. Every time they tried to find something we could do, we had either already done it, or couldn't do it because we had no hydraulics.

The hardest problem Dudley had was convincing them that we didn't have any hydraulics. "Oh, you lost number two," they'd say.

"No, we lost all three."

"Oh, you lost number three."

"No, we've lost all of them."

"Well, number one and two work."

"No." We went on like this for quite a while, before Dudley finally convinced them we didn't have any hydraulics. I was a little upset with them at first. At least I was a little ticked until I realized how frustrating it must have been for these four or five people, with all those computers and all that information and there wasn't a thing they could do to help us. I have not yet had a chance to go down and see them and apologize for what I was thinking, but at least I didn't say it out loud.

Dudley's communications with them did two things: it alerted our crisis center in Chicago and it alerted our dispatch center in Chicago. Those two facilities, knowing that we were now headed to Sioux City, were able to prepare for our arrival. It just so happened that there was a meeting between our union, the company and some other people in the United executive offices that day. United pulled a 727 out of the hangar in Chicago, loaded it with people that would normally be involved in handling aviation accidents and flew them to Sioux City. In fact, these folks were in Sioux City before I was admitted to my room at the hospital. Dudley's communication made for a very quick response at the company.

When we declared an emergency (Bill, the copilot did this), everything stopped on the ground. The focus was now on us. ATC cleared the frequency and gave us all the help they could.

Lightplane pilots are often afraid to declare an emergency. They're afraid they're going to cause problems or somehow disrupt the system. Private pilots say to me, "Well, you have all these resources of United Airlines at your disposal as well as ATC resources." But, so does *any* pilot. With four words: *I'm declaring an emergency,* a pilot has all the help he or she wants. You've got American Airline's maintenance facility, United's maintenance facility. If you stay in the air long enough, they'll patch you through to them. You can talk to them. So you've got all kinds of help, if you just ask for it.

If you declare an emergency and nothing happens, you've got a lot of reports to fill out when you land and you're going to have a lot of airline pilots upset with you, especially at a place like Chicago. They're out holding while ATC is helping you get down.

Sure, some of the pilots may complain but they're really glad you made it and they're very happy you're able to use the services available to you. Communicate with the ground, tell them your problem and they'll help you.

There was really very little communication between the cockpit and the cabin. I called the "A" flight attendant—the senior flight attendant on board—up front. She said later that she took one look at the cockpit and she knew we didn't just have an emergency—we had an enormous crisis. Her thought was, "We're at altitude, we've got some time, he told me to go back and prepare the cabin. I'll do that and I won't bother them. I'm sure he'll communicate with me again."

That's what happened. The flight attendants didn't call us—it wasn't necessary—and this was very helpful. Training allowed each of us to focus on our respective tasks.

While we were headed for the airport, a lot was happening on the ground. Here, too, communication was excellent, much to our eventual benefit. There was a lot of ground communication between emergency response units and the hospital, excellent communications in that respect. The 20-minute warning time we gave them was a great help. If any of you serve on emergency rescue staff, or are volunteer firefighters, you know that if you're in station and ready to go, it's a lot better than being home and having to respond. In the 20 minutes we gave them, they were able to put their disaster plan into effect.

In fact, I believe it was 15 minutes before we crashed that the tower changed the alert status from Alert 2, which is "an aircraft is on its way with problems," to Alert 3, which means "an airplane has crashed." That's how much confidence they had in us. All the systems were set into motion for responding to an airplane crash. The hospital was notified. They called Des Moines and said they were going to need more medical supplies. They were actually loading another Air National Guard plane in Des Moines which departed shortly after we crashed, heading to the airport with supplies. Communications and advance notice were very, very important.

PREPARATION

How do you prepare for something like this? I gave a talk in Anchorage to the Alaska Air Safety Foundation and they subtitled my talk, "Disaster in the air, are you ready?" No, you're never ready. But you might be prepared. That's one of the reasons I go around the country talking about what happened. I want to increase the awareness of just how much it means to be prepared.

The preparation for the ground crew, for the emergency rescue unit, was a drill in 1987. They pretended a B-727 narrowbody aircraft crashed on a closed runway at Sioux City and they had 150 survivors. When they ran the drill, they identified some shortcomings (which most drills do). They have FAA-mandated live drills once every three years and a paper drill every year. It was part of our luck that 1987 was their year for a live drill and they decided to have a plane crash. They'd had a bus crash the time before.

In this disaster drill of airplane crash, they found a lot of things to improve, all of which eventually benefited us. One thing they found was that their resource net wasn't cast far enough. If you're going to have 150 survivors, you're going to need more equipment than an airport the class of Sioux City has. Sioux City is not classified for wide-bodied aircraft, so they aren't required to have quite the emergency response units that larger airports would have. They have to rely on outlying communities. Gary Brown, the director of emergency services, brought the community people in and made them a part of his plan. They attended the meetings, they attended the practices and everybody contributed their thoughts and efforts to creating a plan.

Gary also brought in a very important unit, the Post-Traumatic Stress (PTS) Unit. I was never one to believe much in post-traumatic stress. I had heard it a lot in WWII and from

Korean and Vietnam veterans. I thought, well, okay, if they say such a thing exists, I'll let it go but I don't really believe it.

I believe it now and I'm asking you to believe it. It may never happen to you. I'm fortunate enough not to have suffered PTS—yet (I've been very fortunate). But it can happen tomorrow and not just to victims of the crash. The 185th Air National Guard suffered a tremendous amount of PTS. So did the people of Sioux City. So did the staff of the hospital.

Fortunately, Sioux City was prepared. They had already practiced for the crash of a narrow-bodied aircraft at their airport. On July 19, we put a wide-bodied aircraft on the very same runway they'd used for practice and we gave them 200 survivors instead of the 150 they originally practiced with. So having a drill, having a plan, taking it seriously and practicing it, is very, very important for any community, no matter what size you are, or which airline serves you.

Up in Alaska, a lot of the pilots said, "We're up here in the bush and we don't have these things [facilities, equipment, etc.]." Alaska is the main transcontinental stop for aircraft going to Japan. It's unlikely that any accident happening in these parts will occur over or near a major airport. Accidents can happen anywhere, even in isolated areas. Nevertheless, we need to be as prepared as we can possibly be, just like they were on the ground at Sioux City.

In Sioux City they had a plan that they worked on and they left some flexibility in it so it could be changed. I'll talk about that too.

The flight attendants were prepared by their recurrent training. Once a year they go back to our training facilities in San Francisco, Denver or Chicago to review all their emergency drills: how to open the doors, how to prepare the cabin, how to prepare the passengers, etc. For example, we have a 767 simulator in Denver that has about 40 seats. We'd sit in the simulator for one of the training sessions while several of the flight attendants performed their normal duties. Somewhere during or shortly after takeoff we'd have a crash.

The simulator tips over on its side, it fills up with smoke and it darkens, just like it would on an actual airplane. There are fires outside some of the doors. It's very realistic and it paid off. Each one of the cabin attendants, in a tape they made later, said, "The training that we had! The training that we had!" They kept saying it. So training is very very important. Sometimes it's boring, sometimes it's repetitious, but it's very important.

As for the crew, there was no training procedure for total hydraulic failure. We've all been through one failure or double failures, but never a complete hydraulic failure. But the preparation that paid off for the crew was something that United started in 1980 called Cockpit Resource Management, or Command Leadership Resource Training. I think we called it CLR to start with. All the other airlines are now using it.

Up until 1980, we kind of worked on the traditional concept that the captain is THE authority on the aircraft. What he says goes and his decisions were not to be questioned. We lost a few airplanes because of that. Sometimes the captain isn't as smart as we like to think he is.

We had 103 years of flying experience there in the cockpit, trying to get that airplane on the ground. Between us, we had not one minute of practicing or experiencing a total hydraulic failure, so why would I know more about getting that airplane on the ground under those conditions than the other three? If I hadn't used CLR, if we had not let everybody contribute their knowledge and ideas, it's a cinch that we wouldn't have made it.

I don't know if any of you remember the old movie, *Marty*. In that movie, Ernest Borgnine (who played Marty) and a group of his cronies, try to find something to do on a Saturday night. The dialog is classic. They said to Marty, "What do you want to do Marty?" And Marty says, "I don't know, what do you want to do Joe?"

That's kind of the way we flew the airplane. "What do you want to do?"

"I don't know," and "Let's try this," and "You think that'll work?"

"Beats me." That's about the way it went, really. If you read the cockpit voice recorder transcript, there's a lot of that on there: *When are we going to put the gear down? I don't know. How are we going to put it down? Well, we have two ways to get it down. Which one are we going to use?* That type of thing. So CLR really paid off. CLR is being taken out into other areas.

If you recall the zip-top Aloha 737 in Hawaii, Bob and Mimi used CLR to its utmost. Without it, they could not communicate with each other. They used hand signals to point to the things they wanted to do. That's how they got that airplane on the ground. Flight 811, the 747 out of Honolulu enroute to Sydney, blew the cargo door and lost two engines on the right side and did damage to the flaps and hydraulics. They used CLR to get the airplane back to Honolulu. They had a grossly overweight airplane that couldn't maintain altitude with two engines out on one side and by using CLR and the crew working together and everybody thinking together, they got the airplane back. The days of the captain being the autocratic authority are gone. He may sign the papers and all that, but you fly together as a team.

I think Sister Margaret from Sioux City said it the best, "When you've got a crisis like this and there are so many diverse things going on, let those in charge take charge. Don't let one individual try to run the whole show. Let those who know how to do their specialties handle those things and you'll get things done." That's exactly what happened.

EXECUTION

How did we execute? Well, first of all, how did we do it in the air? Not having any experience at all in flying an airplane under those conditions, our basic problem was keeping the airplane in the sky and trying to find an airport. Besides losing all of our hydraulics, which rendered our flight controls useless, we had two other problems. One of which is best described by the engineering term "phugoid." Phugoid means an airplane that wants to fly its trim speed.

As soon as you cut power on one engine, you lose speed, the nose drops, airspeed starts to build, you'll go through that speed, the nose will come back up, you'll go through the speed again on the slow side and you'll continue oscillating like that. Maybe you can stop it, maybe you can't.

We found that in order to stop a phugoid, you have to do the opposite of what you would normally do. When the aircraft reached its apex and started down, you had to add power. As the speed built up, you'd have to actually add power to create lift in the wings, which got the nose to pitch up. The hardest thing to do, though, was as the nose starts up and the plane slows down and you're approaching a stall, you'd have to close the throttles. That's very difficult to do. We found out, though, that this was what we *had* to do.

Adding to our problem was the fact that the aircraft constantly wanted to roll to the right, due to tail damage. If we left the power alone, the aircraft would roll over.

When the engine failed, Bill immediately took hold of the aircraft. Bill (the co-pilot) had 26 years of flying experience. He'd been with National and Pan Am, then came over to United when we acquired another airline. He's a very competent pilot. I'd flown with him a month before and had no qualms at all about his flying ability. When he grabbed hold of the yoke, he demonstrated step one in any emergency procedure. Fly the airplane.

We've lost several airplanes because everybody was working on the problem and nobody was flying the airplane. One of those situations was down in the Everglades. Everybody was working on the problem while the airplane flew into the ground. Not to criticize the pilots, because everybody wants to do their share to get the problem solved, but somebody has got to fly the airplane. Bill immediately took hold of the airplane, called ATC, told them that we'd lost an engine and needed to get a lower altitude, turned off the airway—all those things you're supposed to do.

So my attention now is focused on helping Dudley shut the engine down. At United we don't use many memory items in emergency procedures, we use mostly checklists and severe engine failure in flight is all textbook. Dudley got out his book and the first thing it said was, close the throttle. When I tried to pull the throttle back, it wouldn't come back. Now, I've never shut an engine down in flight on a jet, so I didn't know that when you pulled the throttle back, it didn't come back. In the simulator, when you do it, it always came back. This one wouldn't come back. Then Dudley says to try the fuel—the next step is to shut the fuel off. I tried shutting it off but the fuel lever wouldn't move. Something was binding these controls.

We now know there's damage to the tail other than just the engine failing. We did get the fuel shut off by pulling down on the firewall shutoff, which shut off all the electrics and hydraulics to the engine. And then the fuel went off. Whether it was coincidental or our actions actually helped, I don't know, but about that time, the fuel flow was cut.

Now we were about 15 or 20 seconds into our problem. Bill says to me, "Al, I can't control the airplane." Now I divert my attention from shutting down the engine to the instrument panel. The first thing I noticed was that Bill had full left aileron deflection, which calls for a full left turn. You'd never see that deflection anywhere on a DC-10, much less at 35,000 feet. He's also got the yoke pulled back in his lap. The only time you're likely to see that is when someone wants to embarrass the captain on the ground by hitting him in his fat stomach before he can push the yoke out of the way. That catches my attention quickly. But even with a full left aileron and full nose-up elevator, the thing that really got my attention was that we were in a *descending right* turn!

I tell all pilots around that this is when I said the dumbest thing I've ever said in my life: "I've got it." I didn't have it very long.

We immediately determined that we could not control the airplane; it wouldn't respond to the inputs of the crew. At this time, we were in a right bank and the bank was increasing. We were up to 38 degrees of bank. We closed the number one throttle completely and firewalled the number three throttle. Very slowly, the wing came back up. Three times on our attempt to get to the ground, we got to 38 degrees of bank. An airplane about to roll onto its back at 35,000 feet is pretty scary, so you just do anything you can to make it stop. We were overpowering the airplane—overcontrolling. Concern was one reason and not knowing what we were facing or doing was another.

By manipulating the throttles this way, we kept the wings fairly level—for a while. Then we had to start down. Like everyone else, we felt that this couldn't be happening. You can't lose *all* the hydraulics in a DC-10.

We were reasonably sure we weren't accomplishing anything with the yoke, but we kept using it to fly the airplane. The problem is, it took both of us to fly the yoke. Just one of us couldn't do it. But we also had to operate the throttles. We'd let go of the yoke, move a throttle, let go of the yoke, move a throttle and so forth. Even if we had known then what we know now, I don't know if we would have or could have let go of the yoke. To let go of the yoke is extremely difficult. After almost 40 years of flying airplanes and holding onto something, not having something to hold on to isn't natural—I don't know if we could do that.

We found out that it was very difficult to move the throttles. I was about to have Dudley turn around and take over the throttles—and I'm glad we didn't because we would have lost all that communication. We were told there was a DC-10 captain in the back who was an instructor. We like to think instructors know more than we do, so I figured maybe he knew something that we didn't and we asked Captain (Denny) Fitch to come up. Well, he took one look at the cockpit and that was the end of his resource. It was sort of funny reading the transcript, because he's about 15 minutes behind us and trying to catch up. Everything he says to do, we've already done. After about five minutes he says, "We're in trouble!"

We thought, "That's an amazing observation, Denny." We kid him about it, but he's just trying to catch up with our thinking. When he found out that he didn't have any knowledge for us, he said, "Now, what can I do?" I said, "Here, you can take these throttles and try to help us. He stood between us—not kneeling on the floor, as the news media said—with one throttle in each hand so he could manipulate them together. Since the number two throttle was frozen, we couldn't get ahold of the number one and number three engine throttles together. Now he could. We say things like: *give us a right bank, bring the wing up, that's too much bank, try to stop the altitude* and he'd try to respond. After a few minutes of doing this, everything we'd do with the yoke, he would correspond with movement of the throttles. So it was a synchronized thing between the three of us, with Dudley still being able to do all his communications. That's how we operated the airplane and that's how we got it on the ground.

After Denny came up, we began to descend and determined we were going to Sioux City. They wanted us to go to Des Moines, but that was over 170 miles away. There was no way we were going to keep the airplane in the air that long. When we declared an emergency, they gave us the nearest suitable airport. It was only 70 miles away, so now we had to get down. We accomplished this through a series of right turns. Some of these we did; others, the airplane did on its own. All we did was keep it from doing any more.

When the NTSB came in to talk to us, they asked why we made a left turn. All four of us said we never made a left turn. Even though I said we were starting a left turn back to the airport, we all four swore we never made a left turn. We finally determined that there was a cloud buildup, which we had to get around. We didn't want to go through any buildups.

When I asked how long the runway was, the controller told us it was 6,600 feet with a wide-open field at the end of the runway. So, the scenario was to land and hopefully stay on our gear, go off the end of the runway, shear the gear and go on our belly. We did have a left quartering tailwind that might cause us to go into the field since we couldn't steer. Either way, the gear would probably shear enroute. We kind of hoped it would happen like this.

We got the right wingtip in the center of the runway and the right main gear off to the side. We touched down on the right wing tip, the wing flap fairing, the number three engine (the one on the right side), the right main gear and the nose wheel, all pretty much simultaneously.

The right wing broke off, which caused fuel to spill, thus the reason for the ensuing fire. The right main gear separated from the airplane. The left gear stayed on. The airplane slammed onto the ground. We did not hit and cartwheel like all the news reports said. We hit and slid on the ground, on the left main gear and the right wing stub. We slid along sideways for about 2,000 feet or so when the left wing came up. Also, on impact, the tail broke off. The entire tail section of the aircraft broke off, so there's no weight in the tail at all. When the left wing came up—probably because of our speed—the tail came up. The aircraft went up on its nose, bounced three times and left radome marks on the runway. We went upside down and were, once again, airborne. Fortunately for us and unfortunately for the first-class cabin, the cockpit broke off. Then the aircraft went over on its back and skidded to a halt.

At our point of impact, where the right main gear touched down, the concrete is 12 inches thick and the hole we left was 18 inches deep. You normally land the DC-10 at approximately 120 knots. We were doing 225 knots (ground speed, 215 knots plus a 10-knot tailwind) and accelerating. You normally touch down at a descent rate of about 200-300 feet per minute at the most. We were doing 1,850 feet per minute and accelerating. You normally like to go straight down the runway. We were drifting left and right because of the 10 knot quartering tailwind.

You can survive an airplane crash. We had survivors even in the piece of wreckage that was once the first-class cabin. We actually had one of our deadheading pilots sitting at the back of the first-class cabin. He went out a window. I later said to him, "You can't go out a window." He said, "Yes you can. When you realize you're upside down and the thing's on fire, you can get out a window."

Sadly, we did lose many of the first-class cabin passengers, but some did survive.

The tail broke off and went straight down the runway, while most of the aircraft curved off to the right. I've always been concerned about a DC-10. Specifically, I was concerned about the engine sitting on top of the tail. If that engine blew, you might lose the whole tail. Well, despite all that happened to this airplane, the engine housing is still sitting there. So Douglas put that tail on to stay.

The main portion of the aircraft wound up upside-down and it burned. This is where most of our survivors came from. Unfortunately, 34 were trapped back there and died due to smoke inhalation.

There was no metal, no glass, nothing to indicate that one piece of the wreckage was in fact the cockpit. They're guessing that for 35 minutes after the crash, we were ignored. They felt the cockpit was an uninhabitable part of the avionics compartment, because wires were the only thing holding the remains of the cockpit together.

In the rescue operation, they tried the Jaws of Life. They applied it to Bill's side and, when they did, it put pressure on my side. I happened to be conscious at the time and I strongly recommended they stop doing that! So they came on to my side and tried it there. Then Bill said the same thing. The back of Bill's seat had collapsed with him inside it. He had eight broken ribs and a broken pelvis. He was in considerably more than a little bit of pain. They came up with the idea to bring a forklift over and use chains to lift the cockpit straight up. By doing this they raised the cockpit and pulled us all out of the bottom. That's how they got us out of the airplane.

All four of the cockpit seats stayed together. All four of the seat-belts and harnesses also stayed intact—they had to cut us out to get us out. What saved our lives, I'm sure, was the fact that those belts held.

How did the ground people react? Well, the ground crew did exactly what they had been trained to do. By having advance notice, they were in a position to put all the emergency vehicles in a designated area, then dispatch them as they were needed.

We only gave them two minutes to line up for Runway 22. They were all set up for Runway 31. When I told Kevin that we saw this runway ahead of us and that's where we were going to land, he had two minutes to get the equipment off the runway. The ground people were actually positioned on that runway.

Videos taken of the final moments are deceiving. It looks like we had everything pretty much in control. We were starting a "down phugoid," accompanied by a right bank at 300 feet in the air. That's when our luck ran out. Without altitude, we were unable to make a correction. We were just too close to the ground. In an attempt to stop the phugoid and the turn, Dennis added power and unfortunately the left engine spooled up faster than the right—the first time in the day we noticed that this happened—and the bank increased. In four seconds, we went from four degrees of right bank to 20 degrees of right bank, then we hit the ground. Safety experts say the tumbling of the aircraft probably saved a lot of lives. It took up most of the inertia, most of the shock and allowed people to get out of the airplane.

The emergency crews responded as they were trained to do. Preparation was the main factor in their reaction time. The tower, switching to the Alert 3 way ahead of time, really set the wheels in motion. They knew that this was going to be bad and they reacted appropriately.

There were so many doctors and nurses at the hospital that the director was trying to figure out what to do with them. He formed a line consisting of a doctor, a nurse and a tech. Then lines formed behind them. The doctor's line contained psychiatrists, obstetricians, pediatricians. They had all kinds of specialists in this line. When an ambulance rolled up and a gurney was pulled out, the survivor had already been through triage at the airport. He already had EMT care all the way in to the hospital. Now he had a doctor, a nurse and a tech on him immediately. They stayed with him through the ordeal until he was either sent to a room or released. The medical care was instantaneous and continuous, thanks to the preparation and flexibility of the emergency plan.

As people were released from the hospital, another issue arose. Where was everybody going to stay? I usually get in trouble with the media for saying this, but when the notice came out that we were going into Sioux City, the news media reserved all the rooms in all the hotels in Sioux City. So when the survivors finished with their immediate medical needs and were being discharged several hours later, there was no place to put them. One of the doctors at St. Lukes looked up at Briar Cliff College, which sits up on a hill overlooking Sioux City, and called Sister Margaret Wicks to see if she could do anything. It was summer and they had a skeleton crew there consisting of a small summer staff. Yeah, she did something. By nightfall, she had 250 people in her dormitory.

The reaction of everybody was just fantastic.

COOPERATION

Which brings us to the fifth crucial element, cooperation. The cooperation that took place was outstanding, just unbelievable.

First of all, there was the cockpit crew. The team effort with the four of us was extraordinary. As I said earlier, we had 103 years of experience between us. It showed in the way we reacted to the problem, the way we cooperated with each other in getting things done.

When it came time to put the gear down, we had to make a choice and the way it was made is instructive. There are two ways you can get the gear down on a DC-10 with hydraulic failure. You can put the gear handle down, which manually unlocks the doors. The doors fall open and the gear just falls out because it's resting on the doors. Or, there's an alternate method when you don't use flaps. There are four ailerons on the DC-10. You fly with the inboard ailerons at high speed and then you unlock the outboard ailerons for landing when you lower the flaps.

Well, we didn't have any flaps, so we couldn't unlock the outboard ailerons. That's what the alternate gear method is for. We talked about this. How do we put the gear down? It was suggested that we unlock it with the outboard ailerons using this alternate gear extension method, since there might be some fluid trapped out there. So, we discussed this thoroughly. The one thing we all agreed upon was that the gear was going down. We had to have a shock absorber. If we had touched down as we did, but without the gear, I think we would have just exploded. Having the gear down helped enormously. It was the efficacy of CLR that got us down.

The cooperation between the cabin and the cockpit crew was very very good, too. We had a few communication gaps because flying the airplane commanded all of our attention. I never turned around to look at the flight attendant while I talked. In fact, the second day after the accident, I asked to go see the rest of the crew and they put me in a wheelchair and wheeled me down to intensive care where Bill and Dennis were. As they were taking me to Dennis Fitch's room this captain came up and offered his assistance. Suddenly I thought, "If there is more than one person in Dennis' room, I won't know what he looks like." It seems that Dennis had stood right there in the cockpit for 30 minutes and worked the throttles for us during the landing. I didn't have the foggiest idea what the man looked like because I never looked back at him. As it turned out, Dennis was the only one in the room so I didn't embarrass myself.

That's the way our communication was—we had to communicate without looking at each other. The attendant came up, did her thing and went back. The cooperation among her group was outstanding. The procedure for United is, when you're going to have an emergency preparation, you call all the flight attendants together and the senior flight attendant briefs them. Then they proceed to their duty stations and demonstrate, ensuring that the passengers know what they want done.

When the engine blew, it was so loud and so violent—they even heard it on the ground—that everyone in the aircraft knew something was wrong. Besides that, I had channel 9 on and everyone with a headset tuned to channel 9 and listening to ATC knew we'd lost an engine. Fortunately, I turned this channel off before we got to the really bad stuff.

One of the survivors even commented, "We were listening until the captain turned us off." They didn't know how bad off we really were until we told them later. But, Jan (the flight attendant) decided to go back there and brief each station individually. Bringing everyone together for the briefing, she thought, would upset the passengers. By doing this, there remained a high level of outstanding cooperation between the flight attendants and the passengers.

Unfortunately, it was children's day on United. We had some 30 children on the airplane, a lot of them traveling by themselves. What the flight attendants did was ask the adults to move, so that there was at least one adult sitting next to every child. The passengers cooperated without hesitation. When they selected people to sit by the emergency exits, they all responded very quickly. Great cooperation. After the crash, several of the flight attendants were assisted getting out of their harnesses by passengers. Because they were upside down in their harnesses as well as their belts, they were unable to loosen the belts by themselves.

There was an infant who was separated from her parents. One of our survivors was just leaving the airplane, getting out of that thing, full of smoke and fire and he heard the baby crying. He went back into the airplane, searching for the baby and found her in an overhead bin, where she'd been thrown by the force of the impact. That's the way the passengers responded and cooperated with everybody.

I've talked about what ATC did. I've talked about the 185th and how they helped. When we said that we might might make the airport, they went so far as to call cities outlying the airport, informing them that there was a DC-10 headed their way. Trucks were dispatched onto the highway to look for us just in case we didn't make the airport.

I'm not all that familiar with mutual aid, but I know it exists. I've seen pictures of a fire truck sitting on a county line while a house across the street burns because they don't have a mutual aid pact. In this case, they threw all the rules out the window. That was part of their plan and they wouldn't worry about the financial details dictated by mutual aid. Respond now, then worry about who's going to get paid for it later. That's exactly what they did and it worked.

I was asked, "Did you get any therapy while you were in the hospital?"

I said, "No, I don't think so."

They said, "No psychiatrists or psychologists came?"

I said, "Oh yeah, but all they did was come to the room and talk." Then it dawned on me just exactly what therapy is.

When I woke up in the hospital and began to remember what was going on, there was a gentleman holding my hand. Of course, the next thing I saw was the security guard with my wallet. He had it in his hand. But this guy was holding my hand and he said, "I'm the staff psychologist." He was with me when I woke up and he was the last person I saw when I left the hospital. So I had therapy from day one. All of us had guilt complexes—severe guilt complexes. As captain of the flight, I felt a responsibility for the accident. They had to convince us that there wasn't a lot more we could have done.

We all had the "Why me?" syndrome. Why did 112 people die and 184 survive? How do we decide who lives and who dies? Why me? Why did I survive? And that's another thing. That's one of the biggest problems of post-traumatic stress. That's what the mental health professionals worked on.

The people of Sioux City headed to the airport immediately. They didn't go out there to see what was going on. They brought food, blankets and clothes. They were ultimately directed to Briar Cliff. A lot of people opened their homes to the survivors. It was just a tremendous, warm response. They offered their cars. They took clothes made filthy by the crash, washed them and brought them back to the hospital. They just did everything. More than 400 people lined up at the blood bank to give blood and that was *without* a call for blood.

The cooperation of the United Airlines people was very impressive. A lot of people were upset at first, saying there weren't enough people from United to take care of survivors. We have about a five or six person staff at Sioux City. When United knew this plane was going to crash, they pulled ticket agents, passenger agents and reservations clerks off their jobs at San Francisco, Seattle, wherever they could and, without even giving an opportunity to go home, threw them on the first available airplane to Sioux City. By the next morning, or the middle of the next day, they had at least one United employee for every family that was there.

I think any airline does that. I'm not saying that's just United's doing. But the cooperation demonstrated to all of us by United was good. To a certain extent, they turned us over to the union. The Airline Pilots Association and the Association of Flight Attendants handled us, relieving the company of any responsibility there. One of the biggest responsibilities is the press. We were not in any condition to talk to them. We were the survivors of this spectacular crash and the press wanted to talk to us. ALPA hired a policeman. They stationed him at my door. They put one at Dudley's door. They didn't need anyone for Bill and Denny. They were in intensive care. You couldn't get down there anyway. But I often wondered if that policeman was at my door to keep me in or keep the press out. Whatever the reason, it worked.

At the end of five days, we had to hold a press conference, because we had held the press at bay. They were entitled to an interview.

I've talked about how well the passengers did. But the best help, I think, came later from our families and friends. This is where you can help someone who has experienced a crisis or trauma in their life. I had a lot of people say, "I didn't call you, because I felt you were going to be so busy that I didn't want to bother you." You're not bothering anybody. If somebody has a crisis or trauma, try and help them. Call them, tell them you're there. Maybe they won't talk to you. Maybe someone else will answer the phone. That's all right. At least give them a call. Let them know you're thinking about them. Let them know you're concerned about them, because that's part of the healing process.

Talking about it is part of the healing process. This is my 52nd speech on 232 [as of May 24th, 1991]. Every time I give it—I've talked to the doctors about this and have asked the psychiatrists about it—I think I convince myself just a little bit more that there was nothing else I could do. It's part of my healing process. To not talk about it, to bury your head in the sand and pretend it didn't happen will surely cause you to explode someday. If somebody wants to talk about a trauma, listen to them. If they want you to talk about it, then talk about it. Make sure you listen to them. Be there for them and help them. That's very important.

Having a response program is very important. Preparation for a disaster is very important. You're not going to stop all disasters, no matter how hard you try. There are all kinds of disasters—train crashes, hurricanes, tornadoes, earthquakes—not just airplane crashes. Each can spread disaster over a wide area, each requiring communication and emergency effort. So having a good, workable emergency plan is very important.

On July 18, 1989, 112 of us—passengers and crew of 232—did not survive. I hope you will remember them and think of them whenever you have occasion to recall the events of Flight 232. But 184 of us did survive. I think that's due largely to the fact that Sioux City Gateway Airport and the surrounding communities were prepared to respond with a practiced, organized, updated emergency plan. What I ask of you, although you're probably familiar with it now, is to look into your community's emergency plans. Check with the people who make those plans. Determine if, should such a disaster befall your community, you will be as prepared to help as Sioux City was. If not, why not?

Biography

CAPTAIN ALFRED C. HAYNES

Captain Al Haynes is one of the most in-demand speakers today. He has selflessly spoken to over 1,000 audiences, with no compensation to himself. Nor will he accept compensation for publication. Now retired from the airlines, his travel schedule for speaking is possibly more grueling than that of an airline pilot. Captain Haynes generously donates his time so that other pilots, controllers, flight attendants, emergency crews and emergency planners may learn from this experience. His narrative of the July 18, 1989, *Against All Odds* crash landing is a tremendous teaching tool. There were 184 survivors, but we will never know how many more lives will be saved in the future by this valuable information being tirelessly disseminated.

Captain Al Haynes is a Texas A&M graduate, a Marine Corps flight instructor and a 35-year veteran of United Airlines.

Editor's Note. If you've had the opportunity to meet Captain Haynes, we think you'll agree that his fellow pilots must have enjoyed flying with him. He is capable, but unassuming. He is generous and has a wonderful sense of humor. A good cockpit atmosphere is conducive to excellence in teamwork, also known as Crew Resource Management. When Captain Haynes speaks about their luck on July 18, there was an omission. Luck also brought the flight a highly skilled, cool-under-fire, respected captain. Captain Haynes wouldn't want us to use the word *hero*. Perhaps he won't mind if we say that he is a gentleman who is admired by pilots and nonpilots alike.

RALPH HOOD

ME, CLYDE AND LINDBERGH

It wasn't just a trip. It was more in the line of an adventure.

Back in the '80s, friend Clyde owned a small Piper Seminole, and he came up with the idea of flying from New Orleans across the Gulf to Mexico's Yucatan Peninsula. He invited me to go along.

I opened my mouth to say no, but glorious visions of Lindbergh and Amelia Earhart rose before my eyes, blocking out all reason. I said yes before I remembered that Amelia's last overwater flight hadn't worked out all that well.

It's about 700 miles across the Gulf, and a trip like that requires a lot of planning about such dismal things as life rafts, emergency rations, flares, and other items useful in the event of a forced landing at sea. Early on, we discovered a basic difference in our attitudes. Clyde believed we could last for days in a raft, so he wanted plenty of survival equipment. Having no such faith in survival, I wanted emergency radios, so we could scream for an early rescue. Clyde worried about sharks. I was more afraid of sunburn. After all, I had been sunburned before but never bitten by a shark. We finally agreed that Clyde would carry survival gear and shark repellent, while I toted sunscreen and radios.

We departed New Orleans looking like drug smugglers in spacesuits. We wore life vests, and our pockets were crammed with our own ideas of what the well-dressed pilot wore in a life raft at sea.

The airplane was filled with various and sundry gear, all tied together so we could get it out of the airplane quickly in the event of a ditching. In reality, we would probably have become entangled in the strings and gone down with the airplane.

During most of the trip we could receive neither navigation nor voice radio. Far from the sight of land, we were back in the days of Lindbergh, holding a heading while watching the clock and fuel gauge.

One exciting moment was passing the point of no return. Beyond that point, we didn't have enough fuel to return to any U.S. airport. Regardless of weather, we *had* to continue on to Mexico. Another high point was the sighting of a coral reef about 100 miles off the coast of Mexico. That was the first proof we were on course, and we shouted aloud in delight.

We spent two days in Mexico, looking at ruins and trying to speak Spanish, then flew back by way of Key West, Florida. We flew just north of Cuba, talking to Havana air traffic controllers and wondering if Cuba shoots down airplanes that wander off course.

All in all, it was a great experience. Later, Clyde flew a single engine airplane the *long* way across the Gulf, from Brownsville, Texas to Key West, and once again he invited me along. That's almost a thousand miles over water on a single engine.

There was only one reason I didn't go. I was chicken.

AVIATION EMERGENCY

Most people think that pilots live from one emergency to the next, constantly avoiding death through a combination of steel nerves and superhuman skills. Actually, it's not true, but please don't tell everybody. We sort of like the image.

Every now and then, of course, a real aviation emergency does arrive, and I remember my last one vividly. Bees.

Friend Jack wanted to fly on a Friday afternoon, but the hangar door was covered with swarming bees. Jack made other plans. I wanted to fly on Saturday, but the bees were still there. I believe in getting expert advice, so I called a beekeeper. He assured me, "Bees won't sting when they're swarming. Just ignore them."

I'd probably have been okay if he had stopped at that, but he went on. "Now if a few of 'em do sting you, whatever you do, don't swat at 'em, and don't run. That'll upset 'em."

Listen, if a "few" bees sting me, I'm going to be upset. I could care less how they feel about it.

I left the airplane in the hangar. I still believe in expert advice, but there's a limit.

On Tuesday, I needed to fly, but the bees were still around. By this time we were beginning to take them seriously. I mean, just how long can you allow an airplane to be held hostage by a swarm of bees, anyway? Jack and I discussed several alternatives, including the "ignore them" idea proposed by the beekeeper. We both liked that theory. I was in favor of Jack trying it. He wanted me to try it. Neither of us could convince the other, so we took up a different tack. Obviously, we decided, this problem came under the heading of the airport maintenance department. At first I couldn't quite see the connection, but Jack explained it to me.

"Look," he said, "they're supposed to keep the hangar doors operable, right?" I agreed. "Well," he said, "I can't open them, can you?"

Once I saw the wisdom of his logic, I quickly agreed, and we set off to fuss at airport maintenance. Somehow, Jack convinced them that bees are a maintenance problem, and they agreed to send somebody right around. Jack should hire out as a door-to-door salesman.

We waited at the hangar, wondering out loud what newfangled technology the maintenance folks would use to eliminate the bees. Maybe, we thought, they might have a newfangled spray or some sort of smoke bomb. Maybe they had a blowtorch. Maybe they had some sort of ultrasound machine.

About that time, a pickup truck came along, braked to a stop, and Bill Gault got out. Bill is a long, tall, slow-talking fellow. He got out of the truck, opened the hangar, and pulled the airplane out while bees flew all about.

He then asked, "Is that all you wanted?" We shakily answered yes. He got back in the truck and left.

Bill wasn't much on technology, but he sure was high on guts.

THE PILOT: BUBBA PART I

This is the story of Bubba, the cropduster pilot. Bubba and I worked for the same Mississippi aviation firm back in the mid-seventies. He sprayed cotton. I sold cropduster airplanes. If you sell new airplanes, you have to pick them up at the factory and deliver them to the customer, and that's where Bubba and I worked together.

Bubba and I, when he wasn't spraying crops, picked up new cropdusters at the Cessna factory in Kansas and delivered them to customers from Texas to Florida. We covered a lot of territory together.

Bubba was one good cropduster pilot. He could spray cotton, fertilize rice, and poison fire ants, all from an airplane. He was good.

But Bubba could not—repeat *not*—navigate. He could get an overweight cropduster off of a short strip. He could fly under power lines, around trees, and keep the wheels six inches above the cotton, but he could not navigate.

Bubba couldn't dependably find his way from one town to another in an airplane unless there was an interstate running between them, and even then he was subject to confusion. He was once 30 miles from home, following a railroad track that went straight to the home airport. We still don't know how, but he ended up 90 miles from home and 90 degrees off course.

The boy just couldn't navigate.

But he could flat follow.

I flew many thousands of miles with Bubba following right along behind me. He didn't even take a map, he just followed.

It got to be a game. I tried to lose Bubba. I'd fly low, high, fast, and slow. I'd turn complete circles and duck behind clouds. It never worked. No matter what I tried, Bubba would end up right on my tail, grinning like an idiot.

Eventually, Bubba got to know the territory pretty well, and he could find his way home from a few places he had already been before. If, for example, he could find the Mississippi River anywhere between Memphis and Natchez, he could find his way home. Usually.

Bubba wasn't all that big on geography, but he did try to improve his knowledge. One day I said, "Come on Bubba, we're going to Texas."

"Texas," said Bubba, "ain't that someplace near Arkansas?"

"Yeah," I answered. "Why?"

"Well," he said, "I've been to Arkansas." You could tell he was right proud of himself.

Well, that's the story of Bubba. If I was Paul Harvey, here's where I'd say, "Now, for the rest of the story."

I ran into a Mississippi cropduster pilot the other day and we got to talking about old friends, where they are and what they're doing. "What about Bubba," I asked. "Where is he?"

"Bubba," the guy answered, "is now an airline captain."

I have been reading the paper ever since, looking for a story about the airline captain who is proud to know that Texas is near Arkansas.

TRUE STORY: BOBBY JOE

This is a true story that I have been sharing with audiences since the early seventies. It is usually a favorite. One name has been changed to protect me.

Bobby Joe Strickland (that's the changed name) was a Mississippi cropduster back in the days before cropdusters became civilized and started calling themselves aerial applicators.

Like many cropdusters of the era, Bobby Joe wasn't big on navigation. He was expert on the geography of his own county. He knew where every cotton patch was, who owned it, where the trees were, and how to fly under the power lines at the south end. But, he seldom left the county.

Then one day there was a bug infestation of some sort in Texas, and the story was that a cropduster could make big bucks there. Bobby Joe wanted that money, so he got out his maps and headed for Texas.

As Bobby Joe put it, "There's a whole heap of Texas, and it all looks just like Texas. I got lost quicker'n a boll weevil can eat cotton."

Well, there he was, totally lost, and nothing to see but miles and miles of miles and miles. But being lost wasn't the problem. "Heck," Bobby Joe said (That's not exactly what he said.), "I'd been lost before. That didn't bother me none. The real problem was that the fuel gauge was stuck on the letter 'E', and I knowed that didn't mean 'Excellent.'"

Bobby Joe finally found a narrow, blacktop road running straight across Texas. "I lined up on that road like a teenager headed for a hamburger joint. I figured sooner or later there'd be a filling station on that road, and I'd land on the road and fill up with car gasoline.

"Now, there's a lot of talk today about being goal oriented and focused on the job at hand. Let me tell you, there ain't never been nobody more focused on the job than I was on that blacktop road. I didn't look left or right, I just kept my eyes down the centerline of that road. Sure enough, after awhile here come a filling station on the side of that road."

Bobby Joe circled around, lined up and landed on that little road. He figured his troubles were over. "Well," he says, "I was one happy puppy. I knew at least I wasn't gonna die, and I got to feeling real good about the whole world."

"Then I got to thinking. This sure is gonna shake up the old boy at the filling station. I bet he ain't never seen no airplane coming up the road to his place."

Sure enough, the filling station attendant was standing out front, staring up the road at the noisy airplane. Bobby Joe whipped into the filling station, hopped out and waved to the attendant. "Fill it up," said Bobby Joe.

"I figured it'd shake the old boy up, but he didn't say a word. He filled that airplane up and I paid him. He never said a word about the airplane at his filling station."

Finally, Bobby Joe asked him, "Well, I reckon you kinda wondered why I come up to your filling station in an airplane, didn't you?"

He said, "Yep, I did. Most everybody else lands across the street at the airport."

Ralph, the airplane salesman, when he had hair!

SMALL GROUP METHODOLOGY

Most of my income is derived not from writing (I bet you had that figured out already) but from public speaking. Billed as *the Flying Humorist*, I travel about the country making people laugh.

One agent booked me in Menomonee, Wisconsin, for a group called TSEA. (The name has been changed to protect the guilty.) I didn't know anything about TSEA but knew written instructions would arrive telling me who, what, when and where.

Sure enough, six sheets of instructions came in the mail from TSEA. Scared me to death.

According to the instructions, I am a "presenter." Not a speaker, but a "presenter" for—get this now—*TSEA's International Leadership Development Symposium and Career Enhancement Conference.*

That didn't worry me. Lots of meetings have ridiculous names, and I've been called worse things than a presenter. The rest of the instructions terrified me.

In the first place, I learned the whole deal was to take place at a college. College always scares me. College and I have never really understood one another. I barely escaped from college back in the sixties, after cramming a four-year course into only five years, and I've avoided college as much as possible ever since.

It has been my experience that anything coming from a college is too complex to understand, and these instructions didn't do anything to contradict my experience.

My presentation should, they said, use "the latest in large and small group methodology."

Folks, if I ever saw a large or small group methodology, I swear I didn't recognize it. I can spot a small mouth bass when I see one, but I'm weak on methodologies. I knew I was in deep trouble.

I was instructed to send my "syllabus," including topics to be covered and supporting materials, so they could monitor the "total program to assure quality flow." Furthermore, my presentation should fit the theme of "The Joy of Leadership," and I should understand "transformational" leadership.

I understood no such thing. Is a supportive material something like a girdle? Is the Joy of Leadership any kin to Joy James, who married Ernest Cribb right after high school?

I was also advised to familiarize myself with "the enclosed Leadership Development Model" which would, I was assured, "clearly" drive home the theme.

I looked at the model and there was nothing clear about it. It said things like "shared expression" and "consistence culture."

I thought it was all over. I sent them a copy of the operation manual for a Cessna airplane and the warranty for my microwave oven. I figured they'd fire me and that would be the end of it.

They wrote back that they were pleased with my syllabus and were looking forward to my presentation.

I'm really in deep trouble now.

THE "EXPERT"

Back in the mid '70s, the federal government decided to eradicate fire ants in the South. (Today, 20 plus years later, fire ants still abound, but, no matter, the Feds are busily eradicating the boll weevil. Anyone want to bet against the boll weevil?)

The chosen means of fire ant annihilation was agricultural aircraft spreading crushed corncobs soaked in Mirex poison over hundreds of thousands of acres. Contracts to annihilate the fire ants were bid on by commercial aerial applicators (formerly known as crop dusters). Bidding was highly competitive, and huge contracts were won or lost by a few hundredths of a cent per acre.

I worked for a company that won one of those contracts and it was a lot like a war. We had 15 aircraft scattered around Mississippi, flown by pilots who had come in from all over the country. This was during one of the fuel crises that punctuated the '70s, and just supplying gas to each airplane was a battle. We owned a small fuel truck, and on any given day I never knew if I would be an airplane salesman that day, or an airplane insurance agent or the driver of that gas truck.

Of my three jobs, driving the gas truck was by far the most exciting. If you forgot to pump the brakes, the brakes forgot to stop the truck. With 1,500 gallons of avgas on board, I once sailed right through a red light on a busy highway, dodging semis, ignoring horn blasts, returning hand gestures, and trying to act like I wasn't terrified.

Most of the fire ant pilots had no idea what I did for the company. They just knew I had access to the boss, and could drive a fuel truck. I, ever seeking respect, tried to pretend that I was, indeed, far more important than they could possibly understand. (It is quite difficult to pretend importance while driving a fuel truck with bad brakes.)

One day I drove the truck to the Starkville, Mississippi airport, where four of our airplanes were based. One of those airplanes was pulled up onto the FBO ramp with the cowling removed, and our pilot and the local aircraft mechanic studied the airplane engine with furrowed brows. Just to make conversation, I asked, "What's wrong?" The pilot took me seriously. He told me the engine wasn't running right, describing the symptoms in great detail.

Now I didn't understand the first thing about engines. Still don't. However, wishing to appear intelligent, I said wisely as I tapped on a fuel injector, "The last time I heard those symptoms, that fuel injector right there was clogged." Then I went into the FBO to use the telephone. (Actually, I wasn't exactly lying. I had been standing around one day when a mechanic discovered a clogged injector.)

About 20 minutes later, as I left the FBO, I noticed the pilot and mechanic putting the cowling back over the engine. "Did you find the problem?" I asked.

"Yep," the mechanic answered. "You were right. That injector was clogged." Dumbstruck, I nodded and climbed into my fuel truck. For the rest of that contract, the pilots sought me out for mechanical advice. I sadly told each of them, as I climbed into the fuel truck, that I'd love to help but unfortunately, I had weightier duties pressing. As far as I know, I kept them fooled.

A LIVING LEGEND

I recently attended two parties, both held at airports. The first, held at a grass airstrip called Moontown, was in honor of recently chosen astronaut Jan Dozier. We all fully expect Jan to blaze new trails in aviation. The other party was held at the home and airstrip of George and Dottie Epps. Glenn Messer, who has already blazed trails in aviation, was at the Epps' party.

What shall I tell you about the late, great Glenn Messer? If I tell all of it, you'll never believe me.

For starters, when you leave the expressway at the airport exit in Birmingham, you are on Glenn Messer Boulevard. He invented the automobile headlight dimmer switch. He defeated Charles Atlas in a contest of strength—pulling railroad cars with his teeth!

But those were just his sidelines. His real field was aviation. He first flew in 1911, in a Wright Model B. When he retired from aviation he owned a company that made instruments for the space shuttle. He flew, as a pilot, every single year from 1911 to 1982. That's more consecutive years than anyone in aviation—and you can look it up in the Guinness Book of World Records.

His flying license is signed by Orville Wright.

I first met the man in the mid 70's. I wanted his help on a project and I called him on the phone. The conversation went something like this:

RALPH: "Mr. Messer, I understand you knew most everybody in aviation."

GLENN: "Well, I knew a few of 'em."

RALPH: "Let me see, did you know Amelia Earhart?"

GLENN: "Oh yes, she stayed at our house when she was in this area."

RALPH: "How about Billy Mitchell?"

GLENN: "Yes. It's a shame what they did to that young man."

RALPH: "Did you know Lindbergh?"

GLENN: "Well, according to his book, I was the person who checked him out for his first solo, over in Georgia."

I don't mind telling you that I was somewhat excited by this point. But I asked him one more question.

RALPH: "You didn't know the Wright brothers, did you?"

GLENN: "Well, to tell you the truth, Wilbur and I never were all that close. Orville, I knew pretty well, but Wilbur and I never were all that close."

Glenn Messer's life and career covered almost the entirety of aviation history. He is truly a living legend, and, as always, I enjoyed visiting with him and his lovely wife Tommie.

AIRPORT CARS

From 1972 'til 1985 I worked at airports and went through a succession of memorable airport cars.

The first criterion of an airport car is that it be cheap enough that you are not afraid to lend it to visiting pilot friends. It helps if it is ugly enough and beat up enough that nobody really wants to borrow it.

You should never insure an airport car for collision. As you hand the keys to your friends, tell them "It's not insured, so if you wreck it just pay me for it." This, too, discourages borrowing.

It also helps if the car has a few quirks so you can say, "If it quits running in traffic, just let it sit for an hour. It'll crank right up."

Any pilot within 1,000 miles will tell you that I have owned some of the all-time champion airport cars. My first grand champion was a 1960 Impala. We retired the tag number when the car quit. The Impala had no alternator. I charged it every night and it would—usually—get me back to the airport the next day.

The ignition on the Impala was a little messed up. To crank it, you twisted two wires together, then held the resulting tangle against the blade of a screwdriver while you shoved the blade into a slot. This created a few sparks, but it did crank the car. This is the truth. There is no need to lie about any of my airport cars.

For years, my theory was simple. Buy an old car for $100. Drive it 'til it falls apart. Then buy another one. It was a good theory. It quit working when $100 cars went on the endangered list, then disappeared altogether.

For example, I bought a 1962 Impala for $120. I finally sold that car to Robert Hill for $20. He signed a paper swearing that I was under no obligation to take it back, no matter what.

My last grand champion was the airport car I created myself. We bought a 1973 Dodge Dart when it was brand new and just kept it until it *became* an airport car, somewhere around 1983. The Dart had various and sundry bumps and bruises. It remained fairly civilized, however, until some drunken hillbillies bashed in the windows and the windshield while son Brett and I were canoeing in Tennessee.

I never had it fixed. Half of the windshield was okay, but the other half was in place but smashed. Two windows were gone. In the winter I put plastic over the windows and drove on. It was cold.

The driver's door latch wore out so I rigged up some ropes to tie the door shut. Ken Hill's wife, Cookie, felt so sorry for me that she volunteered to buy a door latch and windows.

That shamed me. I sold the car to Richard Frank and got a decent car. Now, son Brett has an airport car, a 1978 Impala. But he calls it a paper route car.

As good as it gets—Kodiak, Alaska and a big-tired Super Cub.

A ROMANTIC, EXCITING CAREER

You've seen the ad: "YOU, TOO, CAN HAVE A ROMANTIC, EXCITING CAREER!" It advertises a motel/hotel school, auctioneering school, broadcast school or flight school. No matter, the words are the same, and the flight school ad always has a girl in a bikini.

In my favorite ad, a bikinied girl lolls on the hood of a convertible at the airport, waving goodbye to a departing jet, presumably piloted by her lover, who recently graduated from the flight school.

Be honest. Have you ever seen a bikini-clad girl on a car at the airport? Neither have I, but the ad would have you believe this is the norm, once you begin your romantic, exciting career in aviation.

Okay, let's say the girl is there, waving as you depart into the wild blue yonder. You are leaving, and there sits your girl in a bikini on a car (your car?) at the airport. Do you really believe she will be there when you come back? Come on, fella, any girl who wears a bikini to the airport is NOT gonna hang around waiting for you.

In another ad, the girl in the bikini is, again, at the airport, but this time she is guiding you to a parking place as you, flight school graduate, taxi up in the latest corporate jet. The implication is that you will be thus greeted at all airports as you fly in to spend a few days (and nights). Talk about a romantic, exciting career.

I have a friend who searched for that girl at airports all over the country. He never found her, but I did.

I really did. She was fiftyish and working in a parts department then. I asked her how long ago it was that she greeted airplanes in a bikini, and she said, "Oh, I never really did that. I just wore the bikini one day, long enough for them to take the picture." They're still using that picture today.

I had a career in aviation and often thought about that line, "YOU, TOO, CAN HAVE A ROMANTIC, EXCITING CAREER!"

I thought about it as I sat at country airports, eating stale crackers and drinking lukewarm water because the drink machine stole my last quarter and there was nobody there to make change. Uh-huh, I thought, you wanted a romantic, exciting career in aviation.

I really thought about it the night I slept on the concrete at the Hamilton, Alabama airport with a German Shepherd dog. The place was deserted, so I slept on the concrete, thinking to myself, "This is sure exciting and romantic." Even the dog didn't like it.

In my younger years, I had a short-lived romantic, exciting career in show business. Another fellow and I headed down the road in travel trailers with a show called *The Children's Magic Circus*. Oh, it was romantic and exciting!

A travel trailer will quickly teach you more than you ever wanted to know about the "waste disposal system." It breaks often, and repairs tend more toward odious and messy than romantic and exciting. Without getting into too much detail, let it be understood that I was once intimately involved—deeply involved, you might say—in just such a repair. I did not enjoy the job. It was made all the worse by my partner, who sat giving me instructions and singing, loudly, "There's No Business, Like Show Business."

I could go on about my romantic and exciting career in aviation, but there are some parts so romantic and exciting that I don't want my wife to know about them. (My wife just read that line. She snorted. She's big on snorting, particularly when I get to talking about romance and excitement.)

Some of these stories have been excerpted from
The Truth & Other Lies.

Biography

RALPH HOOD

Ralph Hood sold aircraft for a living until the demands for his speaking began to take all of his time. During the eighties, Ralph wrote an award-winning newspaper column and taught an aviation management course for Southern Illinois University. Now he travels from coast to coast sharing his insights on marketing, sales and service to aviation and non-aviation groups alike. Though Ralph has excellent programs to improve your business, he is probably best known for making us laugh and feel good with programs such as *It's Clear On Top* and *I Told*

The Flying Humorist

Wilbur and I Told Orville... and *Ground Clutter.* In these programs Ralph humorously weaves his experiences as a pilot into his motivational message. He writes a thought-provoking monthly column in *Airport Business Magazine* and his book *The Truth & Other Lies* is chock full of original Hood wit and wisdom. Ralph's ability to share his experiences, laugh at himself and deliver a message that inspires thought and hilarity makes him an ideal speaker and seminar leader. Ralph gives more serious programs on aircraft sales and service, of course, always laced with humor. *His Ethics of Flying Safely* is great for all pilots. His *Learn to Fly* program helps FBOs and CFIs build their student base.

MAJOR DEANNA BRASSEUR (RET.)

ROSA ONE-ONE

So far, it had been a terrific day. I was flying passenger in the back seat of the T-Bird, an old American Air Force jet trainer aircraft. The flight from Duluth, Minnesota to Portage La Prairie, Manitoba had taken only an hour. Flying was a welcome change from my Air Weapons Controller duties. Enroute I'd spend much of the time thinking about the future. My days of sitting inside a windowless concrete bunker, in front of a radar scope, directing fighter aircraft against training targets were soon to end.

Just a month before, I'd received word I'd been selected as one of the first four women in the history of the Canadian Armed Forces to undergo pilot training. I was on top of the world! Since then, I had flown in the old T-Bird several times during daily intercept missions. I had experienced the pilot's job first hand:

the constantly changing headings, altitudes and airspeeds; the extreme forces of gravity, both positive and negative; and the rapid changes in cockpit pressurization during high rate climbs and descents. Flying presented the ultimate physical and mental challenge, definitely the job for me, and I was getting a chance to be a military pilot. Today, the aircraft was running well, there wasn't a cloud in the sky and the forecast for our night flight was for more of the same.

Our dark moonless night mission had finally arrived! I was very excited and trying to absorb every minute detail for future use. Major Bob Patrick was at the controls. Back home he was my boss, a pilot doing one of those much-hated ground jobs. Working in the unfamiliar world of controllers, Bob often asked me for advice and assistance. We worked well together. I liked and respected him as my supervisor and as a friend. Here in the aircraft, where he'd spent thousands of hours, he was the expert, he was right at home. Knowing that I was on my way to pilot training, Bob patiently explained all the unfamiliar things happening around me, from the funny noises on startup to the flashing cockpit lights and the foreign sounding radio transmissions.

Bob sat in the front, I in the back. We were strapped comfortably in our individual spaces, which were, at best, three feet wide. I looked out over the rear cockpit instrument panel, but Bob's ejection equipped seat blocked most of my forward view. Bob's seat extended upward to within an inch of the Plexiglas bubble canopy. I felt like I was sitting in the back seat of a small sports car behind an oversized headrest.

The isolation was only physical. We were connected electronically via the aircraft intercom system. The headphones in our helmets and microphones in our oxygen masks enabled us to communicate with each other and the rest of the earthbound world. When neither of us was talking, we could hear the sounds of our breathing in our headsets.

Startup and taxi were routine. We sat at the hold position waiting to receive our takeoff clearance from the tower. The radio crackled, "Rosa One-One, Portage Tower. You are cleared for takeoff on Runway 31, contact Winnipeg Centre Departure Control when airborne."

"Tower, Rosa One-One roger. Cleared for takeoff." Bob rolled the T-Bird into position on the runway and stopped for his final checks. I could just see the top of his helmet over the instrument panel.

"You ready?" he asked.

"Yep," I replied confidently. The airplane started to roll as the engine spun up. The dials on the instrument panel sprang to life. Airspeed and engine RPM wound up. I glanced out the right side to look at the bright lights of the tower and the line of hangars. The runway distance markers ran towards me at increasing speed: 5,000, 4,000, 3,000. I could barely hear Bob's quiet breathing. I thought to myself, "Boy, it's taking a lot of runway to get airborne tonight." Just then, the aircraft broke ground. Slowly, ever so slowly, the aircraft reluctantly pulled away from the earth's grip. I looked out at the end of the runway passing below me. We were low, much lower than normal. Bob was now breathing very hard.

"Rosa One-One, this is Portage Tower. Switch to Winnipeg Centre climbing through 3,000 feet."

I heard the mike button click open. "Portage, Rosa One-One," said Bob, taking a quick deep breath, "I don't know if we'll make 3,000 feet." Bob took another deep breath. "I'm declaring an emergency." The mike clicked off. My heart stopped dead. I felt the T-Bird start to descend, then I heard Bob yell, "Dee, get on the stick!"

"What do you want me to do?" I asked.

"Just grab the stick and pull as hard as you can," he answered. I grabbed the stick with both hands and pulled with every ounce of strength I had. Slowly, ever so slowly, we brought the nose up and started climbing. My heart was racing.

I realized, at that instant, my life was in serious jeopardy. I started breathing hard and fast. The sound filled my helmet. I felt a bead of sweat trickle down my back. We continued climbing slowly through 3,000 feet and upwards. Bob explained that the elevator system had malfunctioned in the full nose down position, forcing us to descend. Neither the stick-mounted control nor the alternate backup control could budge the trim tab from full nose down. Only brute force was keeping us airborne.

As the plane passed through 6,000 feet Bob said, "I want to try something. Let go of the stick and let's see what happens." I did. The aircraft's nose snapped down, diving for the earth. Bob yelled, "Get back on!" I grabbed the stick. He said, "I can't hold it alone. We're in this together." Five minutes later, the muscles in my arms were starting to ache. Our combined physical effort was just enough to keep us airborne, but we had to land as soon as possible.

Easier said than done. The T-Bird's two wing tip mounted external fuel tanks, still full, made us too heavy for a safe landing. Bob asked the tower if there was a safe area where we could jettison the tanks. The controller suggested Lake Winnipeg. Bob quickly rejected the idea. The lake was too far north. "If something goes wrong," he said, "we don't want to be ejecting over the lake at night." I agreed totally. "What about on or near the airport," Bob asked the tower.

"You could make a pass at 500 feet and drop them between the parallel runways," replied tower.

"Are you nuts?"

We had only two options left. We could eject in the dark and run the risk of serious injury or we could try to hang on and fly the aircraft together, until we burned off the excess fuel. Neither one of us was keen on leaving the cockpit, so we resolved to stick it out.

We flew circle, after circle, after circle around the elusive comfort of the Portage airport below us. Thirty minutes had passed. I had been pulling on the stick for so long, my arms felt numb. They screamed at me to let go. Then they started shaking to get my attention. I was afraid I would lose control of them. If only I could get some leverage, if only I could put my feet up on the instrument panel. Impossible, of course, there wasn't enough room. If only we could get a break, if only the hand of God could reverse the levers so we had to push instead of pull.

Time passed slowly, my agony became excruciating. I fought a constant struggle of mind over matter. My arms now screamed relentlessly, "We hurt, we're tired, let go of that stick." My mind's will to survive was my only defense. Bob kept telling me if I weren't with him, he'd have to eject, he couldn't hold it alone. Bob had a family, a wife and five children whom he loved dearly. I couldn't let him down. We flew the aircraft together, almost as one pilot. "I'm hanging on, Bob. I'm not giving up," I assured him. Somehow, hearing my own voice speak those words helped. I became even more determined to see this through.

Forty-five minutes had seemed like an eternity, but the tanks were finally empty. We were ready to attempt an emergency landing. Bob explained the 360 degree circular descending turn we would start once we were overhead the runway. "If at any point things aren't going well, I'll say Eject, Eject, Eject and you go. Any questions?"

"Just one," I said. "If you go do I?"

"Yes," came the answer. I had no doubt I could pull the ejection handles if I had to. The assurance that I wouldn't be left behind was momentarily comforting.

Bob selected gear down. The gear started coming down. I watched the indicators change from up and locked to in-transit, and finally to down. The red gear warning lights turned green. The gear was safely down and locked for landing. We started the left descending 360 degree turn towards the runway at 6,000 feet. Halfway down, everything looked normal. Flaps selected to half. Our breathing could be heard steady in our helmets. At 90 degrees, flaps selected full down. We were over the end of the runway. Descending, descending, descending. Time passed in slow motion. Finally, bump, bump, bump. Three wheels touched ground. We're down! Bob slowed the aircraft with the brakes. The canopy opened letting in a rush of cool night air, a God-sent welcome relief.

My hands were still wrapped tightly around the stick. My arms were still frozen in place. Bob asked, "You still want to be a pilot?"

I heard a strange new, confident voice reply, "Sure do."

Biography

MAJOR DEANNA BRASSEUR (RET.)

Major Deanna Brasseur (Canadian Armed Forces, Senior Officer Retired) is one of the first two women pilots in the world to graduate as a military operational jet fighter pilot qualified to fly the CF18 Hornet and CF5 air-to-air and air-to-ground fighter interceptor aircraft. Additionally, she was the first Canadian Forces female pilot to hold the positions of Jet Flying Instructor, Instrument Check Pilot, Senior Course Designer, Flight Commander, Test Pilot and Aircraft Accident Investigator. Following retirement she was appointed to serve on the Minister of National Defense's Advisory Board. Dee is very charismatic and articulate and has been profiled on many Canadian national radio and television programs. Her presentations include The CF18—Flying Canada's Premier Fighter Aircraft, Human Factors in Aviation, Breaking Gender Barriers, Goal Setting and Overcoming Obstacles. Her book *Achieve It* (shown above) is a personal success journal.

MARK GRADY

EXIT... STAGE LEFT!

After years of speaking to practically every civic group I had ever heard of, for free, I was finally getting offers to pay me for speaking. Several years in radio had paid for me talking, but I wanted more of a direct contact with people.

In late 1990, I got booked for what was my highest paying talk to date. I was hired to be the keynote speaker for a large state association of secretaries and administrative assistants. The venue was to be one of the beautiful grand ballrooms of the Raleigh Marriott.

"This is the largest group yet. I sure hope I do okay. I want them to get their money's worth."

Those were thoughts from the nervous side of me as I drove into the Marriott parking lot. The other half was elated.

"Wow! Just think. Getting paid to talk and eat! That's just like the president, except the hours and stress are better," I thought.

The instructions from the program chairman of the evening's event clearly said they would find me in the lobby. I didn't know them, but they assured me they would find me. I guess they believed it would be pretty easy to find a guy built like Dudley Moore, with a face for radio, wearing a suit.

As I entered the lobby of the Marriott, a man approached me. As he smiled and came my way, I recognized him as a fellow who had dropped in on a couple of the live, remote broadcasts of the radio station I was working for at the time.

"Hi Mark! Good to see you again. Are you part of our big meeting tonight?" he asked.

"I guess that's me," I said.

He led the way back to one of the impressive ballrooms. As we entered, the huge group of attendees, all in their finest Christmas party attire, were just beginning to be served quite a spread by the Marriott wait staff. My host led me to his table and introduced me to his dinner neighbors where we all exchanged the "nice-to-meet-you" and "good-to-have-you-with-us" pleasantries.

It was hard not to really dig into the food. It was great! It was all I could do to keep from overdoing it before it was time to make my talk.

Before we could get a good start on the pecan pie, a man made his way to the speaker's platform and began to speak.

"I hope all of you have enjoyed this great dinner and service. How about a hand for the Marriott crew. I think they outdid themselves this year," he said.

As the applause subsided, he continued.

"It is my privilege to introduce our special guest speaker."

I cleared my throat and sat up straight, waiting for my cue.

"Our speaker is one of the most respected chiropractic physicians in America..."

My straight went to slouch and the cleared throat went to nearly choking.

"Chiropractic Physician! Most respected in America! Where in heaven's name am I?"

I had always wondered why God had made me so short. Now I knew. It was for this precise moment. I was able to stand up, quickly move towards the side ballroom entrance and into the hall, without interrupting the line of sight of the seated guests. My heart was pounding and my nerves were shot as I entered the hallway of the prestigious hotel. Just as I turned to head in the direction of the lobby, a frazzled-looking lady caught my eye and shouted.

"Mark! Thank goodness you're here! I almost thought you weren't going to make it. We're going to start the program in about five minutes. Do you need anything to eat?" she said, calming down as she spoke.

"Oh, no ma'am. That's okay. I already ate," I said, as she led me to the right ballroom.

I haven't run into that guy who took me in as a guest since then. I must admit, I'm kind of grateful.

REAL HEROES

My first recollection of aviation centers on an airshow. I believe it was in 1962 and I was six years old. The airshow was part of the North Carolina Azalea Festival and was held at what is now Wilmington International Airport, then known as Bluthenthal Field. The stars of the airshow were the U.S. Navy's Blue Angels.

When the Blue Angels started their act, I decided I didn't like airshows. The noise was a little more than this small-for-his-age boy could stand. I held my ears and waited for it to be over. Although I was impressed with the skilled maneuvers, the sound made it uncomfortable.

What a difference an hour makes.

My father was a very patient man. Deciding it was in our best interest not to be in a hurry to leave the airport and fight the traffic, he recommended we just walk around the airport a while.

This, of course, was before security forced metal detectors and barbed-wire fences around airfields.

As we walked against the tide of people leaving the show, we found ourselves on the ramp. Soon, we were around a corner and at an area in front of a hangar. My father caught my attention.

"Look. It's one of the Blue Angels' planes," he said.

I looked up. Sure enough, right in front of me was this remarkable looking flying machine. No noise, just a plane. I changed my mind about airshows. I liked the looks of this jet.

I tugged at my father and excitingly said, "Can I take a picture of it?"

My dad grabbed the Kodak Brownie camera hanging on his shoulder. Raised during an era of not being wasteful, he coached me through the process of taking the picture so that I would not "waste any film."

Just when I was about to hold my breath and push the shutter release, it happened. An event that would change my life. The pilot of this mag-nificent flying machine walked out beside his jet. He stopped and looked. Then, in what I now know is typical PR style for these pilots, he looked up

and saw this six-year-old-who-looked-like-four-year-old boy about to take a picture. He snapped to attention and saluted. I fired off the shot and thought to myself, "*Wow*." I knew then I wanted to fly someday.

While some of my flying friends talk of being born at the wrong time, dreaming of being a barnstormer in the 20s or 30s or a World War II fighter ace, I feel very fortunate to have lived at the time I have. I have had the privilege of knowing what our country considered as real heroes. I got to see John Glenn's first launch, and man walk on the moon, live on television. It has been an amazing time.

I guess it was only natural that I would eventually want to fly. The people I looked up to in my youth had names like Chuck Yeager, Neil Armstrong, Buzz Aldrin, Alan Shepherd, Jim Lovell and a Blue Angels pilot whose name I never knew. I saw these men as brave and the cream of the crop.

Last year, I flew to the same Wilmington airport which introduced me to aviation. This time I was going to pick up my father and fly him to the Raleigh-Durham International Airport, where my brother was waiting to drive my dad to Duke University Medical Center for tests. As we made the flight, I shared with my father the memories I had of taking that picture years before. He said he vaguely remembered it.

The tests turned into treatments at Duke. My father, who had never been seriously ill during my lifetime, now had a progressive cancer. The doctors did what they could and sent him back home to Wilmington.

On September 21, 1998, I was sitting at the foot of my father's bed in the Intensive Care Unit at New Hanover Memorial Hospital in Wilmington. He took one last breath and left me with a lifetime of memories and respect.

There were some real heroes in my childhood. Neil, Buzz, Chuck, John and Jim; they were real heroes. But, now I realize that the biggest hero was always there for me. The other guys may have supplied some inspiration, but it was the man who actually took me to that airshow who was the real hero. He never had a pilot's license and his military career was spent at below-sea-level altitudes, mostly aboard a submarine. And he liked trains more than planes. It doesn't matter now, his courage was enough to encourage me to eventually learn to fly. And being able to save him from a long uncomfortable car trip, when I flew him to Duke University Medical Center, was worth all the efforts of learning to be a pilot.

It's okay to have heroes. But is there a real hero that's right under your nose who has gone unnoticed for what they've meant to you? Maybe you better tell them how you feel. I can assure you of one thing. One day it will be too late.

Biography

MARK GRADY

Mark Grady is a writer, professional speaker, commercial pilot and CFI. His presentation skills were developed during 22 years in broadcasting and as a speaker and seminar presenter for aviation safety events. In 1998, the FAA named him North Carolina's Aviation Safety Counselor of the Year. Combining broadcasting with his love of flying, he worked 10 years as a traffic watch pilot, reporting for three radio stations. He is familiar to North Carolinians as a radio talk show host, TV telethon host, reporter and television commercial personality. He pokes fun at his height (or lack of it!). In his humorous keynote, *Flyin' Friendly*, Mark shares with you the perils of being a "vertically-challenged" pilot. How do you get the FAA to STC a phone book as a "pilot height extension device"? What Mark lacks in height, he makes up for in heart—tickling our funny bones. His other programs include *You're on the Air, Real World GPS, How to Make Money with Your Pilot's License, How to Make More Money As a CFI, U.S. Aviation & Space Accomplishments* and *Why Did I Do That?* His relaxed friendly way of speaking is also reflected in his writing for various publications including the *Southern Aviator, Weekend Flyer, Wilmington Star-News* and *Jacksonville Daily News.*

CAPTAIN GERALD COFFEE, U.S. NAVY (RET.)

I SURRENDER

[Excerpt from a chapter in *Beyond Survival*.]

This would be only my second flight over North Vietnam. Having joined the squadron in early January, 1966, I had flown all of my previous missions over South Vietnam or Laos. My missions over South Vietnam had been productive but uneventful. I had seen flak only twice but never felt threatened. At the prospect of actually meeting resistance on this mission, my adrenal glands were already pumping a little more than usual. I noted this while carefully taxiing the big sleek Vigilante onto the starboard bow catapult, making my last few checks, and saluting my readiness to the animated Catapult Officer on the deck below me.

I thrilled again at the near instantaneous surge and sharp kick of the cat shot propelling my thirty tons of warplane to 170 miles per hour in less than three seconds. It was never "routine."

"We're on our way, Robert," I had said to Bob (my backseater) rather rhetorically. I eased the nose up into a gradually climbing turn as the early afternoon sun slowly swept its patchwork of shadow and light from one side of the cockpit to the other.

"Roger, Boss. Take up heading three five zero. Our rendezvous with Lion Eleven is at three four zero degrees, twenty miles, angels eighteen."

God, it was a sparkler of a day. The deep shining blue of the Tonkin Gulf seemed to intensify the more ethereal blue of the Southeast Asian sky. At the western horizon, where the blues would otherwise have met, ran the variegated green and brown ribbon of the North Vietnam coast. With the exception of a few low puffy clouds far to the north near China, the sky was absolutely clear. It stretched on forever. Had the earth been flat, I mused, I could have seen beyond that seemingly benign coast-line to Laos, Thailand, Burma, India, perhaps across the Middle Eastern countries to the Red Sea and the eastern Mediterranean, where I had flown three or four years before on similar crystalline days and conjectured on my ability to see the Tonkin Gulf to the east... if the earth were flat.

I had established a left-turn, three-mile orbit at our ren-dezvous point. Scanning back over my shoulder toward the ship, I picked up our escort plane visually. The F-4 Phantom jet had been launched just after us and was now climbing toward the ren-dezvous point. All reconnaissance planes were escorted by an armed fighter in case it should be attacked from the air. (It was also operationally prudent to fly over enemy territory in flights of two or more so that one pilot could account for the fate of the other should trouble arise.)

Since the Phantom's wings were level, I knew the pilot was still heading for the prearranged electronic point in the sky.

"Lion Eleven, Green River Two. We're at your ten o'clock, slightly higher."

"Roger, Greenie Two... I've got you."

The instant the pilot of Lion Eleven made visual contact, he altered his course to turn inside my turn but adjusting his angle of bank to just a little less than my own standard thirty degrees of bank for rendezvous. This would make his turn radius slightly greater than mine, causing him to move closer and closer to me on the inside of the circle while adjusting his throttle in tiny increments to match his own airspeed to mine.

"Okay, Bob, he's as good as aboard. Let's check in on Strike Freq."

"Rog!"

The VHF radio clicked through several bands of static, a fraction of another airborne conversation, and then stabilized on the check-in report of a flight of A-6 Intruders from the *Hawk's* all-weather attack squadron. When they were finished, Bob checked us in.

"Master Strike, this is Green River Two with escort at rendezvous. Over!"

"Roger, Green River Two. Contact! You're cleared on course. Strangle!"

"Roger. Out!"

I noted on my instrument panel the termination of the tiny blinking red light denoting the pulse of our IFF (Identification Friend or Foe) radar beacon as Bob "strangled our parrot," a code phrase for securing the beacon. No use giving the Vietnamese search radar monitors a bigger and more defined blip on their scopes than necessary.

By now Lion Eleven had slid smoothly out of his own radius of turn, hesitated briefly just off my port wing, and crossed under to my starboard side. There he took up a comfortable cruise position on the outside of the turn and slightly aft.

As my compass pointer swung to a heading of two nine zero degrees, I eased my wings level. Lion Eleven matched me. Ahead, the tranquil coast stretched out on either side. At the Than Hoa River delta, the overall S-curve of the entire Vietnam coast ran close to true north and south. There, just a small course correction to my left and now at a slant range of about twenty-five miles lay our first reconnaissance target. I repositioned the folded map on my kneeboard to put west at the top, matching the scheme of the world ahead of me.

I noted the flight line drawn on the other map clipped below this one. There had been no time to brief my escort pilot on the additional last minute requirement. Mission security and radio discipline precluded informing him now. I knew he would wonder

what the hell was going on when I deviated from our prebriefed flight plan, but he'd stick with me. That was his mission. I'd explain later over a cup of coffee in the Ready Room. Hell, I had thought magnanimously, I'll buy him a drink at the Peninsula's bar our first afternoon in Hong Kong.

The mission went like clockwork. Since there had been hardly any cloud cover over the lower half of North Vietnam, I had bracketed the husky steel and concrete bridge the way I had taught so many others as a "recce" (reconnaissance) training instructor in Florida. The actual targets for the attack boys had been less distinct, but I had flown the line and was sure of the coverage from my panoramic horizon-to-horizon camera. Although I had seen no flak, I had jinked frequently during the entire time I was over land, changing directions slightly with high G-turns often enough to keep any gunners from tracking me. Then, heading back

toward the coast, my F-4 Phantom fighter escort spewing black smoke as he tried to catch up, I felt it. WHUMP! Hit!

It happened so fast—no flak or tracers, no warning! After the hit somewhere back in the aft part of the plane, I had felt a light vibration followed by the illumination of my master warning light. Uh-oh! Red hydraulic #1 light ON. Red hydraulic #2 light ON. Red hydraulic utility light ON. I pushed the throttles forward now to afterburner to get maximum speed toward the relative safety of the Gulf. Thu-thump. The burners lit off and, with a light fuel load remaining, the effect of their thrust was multiplied, pushing me back against the contour of my ejection seat as the Vigilante shot forward and slightly upward.

"Hit! I think we just took a hit!" I knew damn well we'd taken a hit, but years of being Top Gun-cool had tempered the alarm in my voice. Bob had heard my radio transmission and would be giving me a heading back toward the ship. The vibration had become heavier and the control stick sluggish. Still accelerating, the plane suddenly rolled to the left. Control stick stiff—no effect. Jammed right rudder pedal. Left roll stopped but then immediate right roll. Left rudder—no effect.

Instinctively I reached for the yellow T-handle protruding from the side panel of the console near my right knee. I yanked it out sharply and felt the clunk of the two-in-one emergency generator and hydraulic pump extending into the wind stream from the starboard side of the fuselage. The wind-driven turbine pump should have regained the hydraulic pressure to my essential flight controls. Still no effect. Whatever had hit us must have severed both flight-control hydraulic lines, spilling all the precious fluid. Even with the emergency pump extended, with no fluid, there was no pressure. Still rolling, I tried to muscle the control stick into effectiveness.

Nothing! No control! Sky–land–sky–land–ocean. The nose had dropped now and we had picked up more speed. "Mayday! Mayday! Mayday!" Rolling rapidly! Speed 680! Red lights flashing! No more sky ahead, only the shimmering blue gulf spinning in front like a propeller. Christ! "Eject, Bob! Eject! Eject! Eject!"

THE GOLDEN GECKO

The little yellow tropical lizard, the gecko, was every POW's cellmate. We followed the cycles of their lives, marveling at their infant fragility, cheering their exploits, and mourning their deaths. The geckos became our symbol and our mascot, for through them we saw ourselves more clearly.

REFLECTIONS OF HOME

One of the benefits of solitude is the opportunity to go within one's self and contemplate issues, ideas and feelings that often are left unexplored in everyday life. For American prisoners of war in North Vietnam, that journey within and the resulting exploration led to a deep appreciation for classic poetry. Soon we began to communicate our thoughts through original verse as well.

Historically, the poetry composed by men in prison has reflected all of the pathos of the most basic of human feelings: hope, despair, fear, anger and even joy. Ours was no exception. We recalled and composed the poetry from which we drew strength with no resources other than our minds. Without pen and paper—and without face to face verbal communication—we shared our thoughts by tedious and secret means. Our common language became "tap code," a system of taps on prison walls which identified letters of the alphabet. These taps became words, then sentences, and finally the poetry from which we gained insight, comfort, and pleasure.

Representations of this poetry follow. Our prison poetry speaks not only of loneliness and despair, but also duty and honor, love and faith, freedom and home. And, as airmen, our love of flight and adventure is also apparent.

This poetry reflects perhaps better than any other statement the soul journeys that took place within the prison walls of North Vietnam.

THE POW TAP CODE

POWs in North Vietnam were not allowed to communicate with each other, so we used the centuries old "prisoners' code"— a tap code. It was derived from five rows of five letters each, deleting the "K" because a "C" could usually be used when a "K" was called for. We communicated the individual letters by tapping first the row and then the column representing a particular letter.

We shared this poetry and all other information by using variations of this tap code matrix.

FRED

Little weevil in my bread
I think I just bit off your head.
I see the place where you have bled—
The dough around it is all red
But that's okay for now, instead,
I know for sure you're really dead.

I wonder if your name was Fred

TIGER LILY

When Daddy tucks me in at night
He calls me "Tiger Lily"
Or lemon drop or dandelion
Or something else that's silly.

He tells me I'm his ice-cream girl
His tea cup full of honey
His lady bug, his candy kiss
His cuddly baby bunny.

He says that I'm a sugarplum
His white marshmallow dove
His gingersnap, his little bag
Of jelly beans and love.

At last he says that I'm as sweet
As a hundred chocolate creams
And then he'll kiss my nose goodnight
And leave me to my dreams.

Ed note: Captain Coffee's daughter Kimberly was seven years old when his plane was shot down.

THE "COMMUNE" OF COMMUNICATING
[Excerpt from a chapter in *Beyond Survival*]

All that I learned about tap code those few days would become the heart of an incredibly effective system facilitating our mutual support and survival, to help each of us return with honor. By applying our communication system persistently and creatively, we would breach barriers of brick and concrete and vast spaces in between. We would console, encourage, sympathize with and even entertain one another. We would form close friendships through the walls of Hanoi's jails. I would come to know and love other men as my brothers, sharing feelings for families, hometowns, and hopes for our future, and still not even know what the other men looked like. We would not have the chance to meet shake hands or, more likely, hug one another for years.

Many times in the next several years I would be down and hurting, being punished with my ankles in the stocks on my slab and with wrists cuffed tightly behind me and my buddy in the next cell would be up on the wall with a "GB!" "God Bless!" But I knew it also meant, "Hang tough, Babe. I love you and I'm praying for you." And I knew he really was, and it helped so much. Then when he was being punished I'd be up on the wall for him as well: "GB!"

Each night before Render and I would go to sleep we would softly exchange on the wall. "GN," "Good night," and "GBA, " "God bless America." I never knew if we started that or not, but it became the custom—no, a ritual—for every man every single night throughout the entire system for as long as we would be there.

ONE MORE ROLL

We toast our faithful comrades
Now fallen from the sky
And gently caught by God's own hand
To be with Him on high.

To dwell among the soaring clouds
They knew so well before
From dawn patrol and victory roll
At heaven's very door

And as we fly among them there
We're sure to hear their plea—
"Take care my friend; watch your six,
And do one more roll... just for me."

Biography

CAPTAIN GERALD COFFEE, U.S. NAVY (RET.)

Gerald Coffee is an inspiring example of the power of the human spirit to survive and triumph over the most adverse circumstances. As a navy pilot flying reconnaissance missions over North Vietnam he was shot down over the Gulf of Tonkin on February 3, 1966. Parachuting to safety, he spent over seven years in the infamous Hanoi prison called Hoa Lo—the *fiery forge*. Jerry says, "When you're by yourself and can go deeply within yourself, you come to really understand just how much people need a spiritual dimension to their

lives. There's no way that ideology or materialism or indoctrination can snuff out that little spark that tells us there's more to life than human minds can begin to understand." Jerry draws not only from the insights derived from that incredible experience but also from the perspective of his unique experience since then. His military decorations include the Silver Star, Distinguished Flying Cross, Two Bronze Stars, Air Medal, two Purple Hearts and the Vietnam Service Medal with 13 stars. He has a masters degree in political science. His book, *Beyond Survival*, in the condensed version, was featured in Reader's Digest, Guideposts Magazine, and in audiocassette by Nightingale-Conant. In a national survey of corporate and association meeting planners, he was selected as one of America's top ten speakers. His inspirational and motivational presentations cover topics of change, overcoming adversity, teamwork, leadership and communication. *Beyond Survival* and *A Time for Heroes* are reaffirmations of the invincibility of the human spirit.

ROBERT J. GILLILAND

THE UNBEATABLE BLACKBIRD

Millions of pilots have probably flown the SR-71 Blackbird... in their dreams. Lucky for me, the dream came true when Kelly Johnson entrusted me with flight testing duties for his ultimate aeronautical masterpiece.

Johnson, founder of the famous Lockheed Skunk Works, was arguably the greatest aeronautical designer of all time, and the Blackbird is arguably the greatest airplane ever built. To be given the controls of the prototype was certainly the high point of my flying career.

How did it happen that Kelly Johnson chose to entrust me with the prototype of the billion dollar SR-71 program? Ultimately, it was because I asked. Kelly knew of me from the F-104, the A11/A12, the CIA-funded Mach 3+ reconnaissance program, and the YF12A USAF-funded interceptor program. When I heard of the new SR-71 program I went to Kelly and asked him if I could be the main test pilot on that program. "I was hoping you'd say that," Kelly replied.

As a fighter pilot who is slightly over the standard height and weight specifications, I've spent a lot of uncomfortable hours in fighter cockpits. I am six feet, three inches and 195 pounds, and had to be squeezed into places designed for men who were no bigger than six feet and 180. It was thus a particular pleasure to assist in the development of the SR-71 cockpit so it was both functional and comfortable for a person of my size.

I have often been asked how I felt before the first flight of the SR-71, with its experimental airframe and engines. There is a mild amount of apprehension, but that is more than offset by the high honor of being the one to do it. Any pilot at Edwards AFB would have given his right arm to be in my position. I once told James Stuart, a fellow test pilot, that I would have done the SR-71 program for nothing, even if I thought the chances were pretty good I'd get killed. Stuart was a short, cocky little guy. He reached up, grabbed my lapel and said, "Hell, you would do it even if you *knew* you were going to get killed."

Not that he would have been any different.

I know it sounds strange but one comes to like the excitement, the challenge, the danger, and the prestige of being a test pilot and flying something as exciting and demanding as the SR-71. As Chuck Yeager wrote of test pilots, "We're all adrenaline junkies."

Kelly and I agreed that for the first few flights of the SR-71, I would be the only one on board. Normally, the aircraft seats two people in tandem, the pilot in front and the RSO (Reconnaissance Systems Officer) in back. We jury-rigged a small panel on the left side of the front cockpit so I could operate certain things that are normally wired only in the rear cockpit.

The first flight was relatively uneventful. Just one emergency, and another minor problem. A canopy-unsafe light illuminated at Mach 1.2 on the way to 1.5 at 50,000 feet, and later, during a fly-by requested by Johnson, fuel siphoning occurred. Not bad, as initial test flights go.

The SR-71 was, in many ways, a flying experiment. It was not just an incremental change from previous airplanes. It was a revolution. For example, the high heat developed at sustained Mach

3+ cruise mandated use of titanium for the skin and structure, but at the time titanium was a new metal in aircraft use. There were a lot of aluminum benders in Southern California, but nobody knew anything about titanium.

I feel very fortunate that I had Kelly Johnson and his boys, led by Ray McHenry and Henry Combs, and others designing the structure in this new substance. All design is a compromise between weight and strength, and sometimes the compromise goes a bit too far. This is usually unpleasant, or worse, for the test pilot.

The SR-71 has extremely high pressure recoveries in the inlets, which are situated far out from the center line of the aircraft because of shock waves generated by the long fuselage forebody. In the development days, it was common to experience unstarts, as they were called. These were very violent. When one inlet blew, or unstarted, it would go instantly from high thrust to high drag. With the other inlet thrusting, this would make the aircraft tend to fly sideways and it would bang around violently, becoming barely controllable. In this situation, it was imperative that the pilot's reaction be instantaneous and correct. You have only one shot to fix it, and you must shoot quickly to prevent overtemping the experimental engines, as well as regain controllability.

After more than 30 years, the SR-71 is still the world's fastest airplane. Kelly himself, way back in the sixties, used to say, "Nobody is going to come along and produce an aircraft with greater performance than this one by the end of the century." He was quite right.

Back then, I used to think it would be nice if I could remain alive until the next millennium to find out if that assertion—always made with a bit of belligerence—would turn out to be accurate. I did live that long, and the assertion has proved 100% correct.

Kelly knew better than anyone the extraordinary technological and financial difficulties and obstacles to creating such an aircraft. For him the obstacles were simply challenges to be faced, met, and overcome. Kelly Johnson creations, the F-104 and the SR-71, currently hold, respectively, the low altitude speed and high altitude speed records. The planes and the records are a remarkable monument to the man's engineering genius.

Biography

ROBERT J. GILLILAND

Bob Gilliland has logged more experimental supersonic flight test time above Mach 2 and Mach 3 than any other pilot. He is a former Naval Academy graduate and was a combat jet fighter pilot in Korea and he helped introduce the first American jets in Europe.

As project test pilot for the Lockheed SR-71, he was the first to fly the aircraft. It roared skyward amid the purple-orange blast of maximum afterburner on its maiden flight on December 22, 1964. Working with Kelly Johnson, the Skunk Works founder, and his small group of engineers, Bob was the first to achieve full-envelope expansion of speed and altitude in both the SR-71A and SR-71B. Prior to involvement with the A-11/A-12, YF-12A and SR-71, Bob was a Lockheed company test pilot in the F-104 Starfighter at Palmdale, Edwards AFB and in Europe. He holds the Kincheloe award as top test pilot by the Society of Experimental Test Pilots and is currently a trustee of ANA (Association of Naval Aviation). Anyone who has heard Bob's presentation of *The Supersonic Age, The Lockheed Skunk Works* or *Test Piloting* has come away awed, amazed, entertained and educated.

COLONEL RICH GRAHAM (RET.)

AN EARLY FLYING LESSON

My father was a former Navy F-4U Corsair pilot and also had his civilian instructor ratings. When my brother, David, and I were teenagers we got the urge to fly and my father said he would teach us both. To pay for my flying time I worked at the local airport in New Castle, Pennsylvania, cutting grass, washing and waxing planes, pumping gas and answering the unicom for local traffic... an all-around handy man.

My dad soloed both of us out in the Piper Colt... a tricycle gear, two-place, fabric covered plane (I have since often wondered how he had the nerve to trust us.). One day while I was working at the airport David took off on a solo flight to practice some of the flying maneuvers we were taught. He stayed up for about an hour and upon return to the traffic pattern he called in on the unicom, "New Castle unicom this in Piper N5545Z." I was near the radio and replied back, "Go ahead N5545Z." David said he was about to enter downwind for landing, but added in a calm voice, that he had heard loud "banging" sounds at the start of the flight, that had eventually gone away. I replied with the winds and runway and told him to taxi the plane to the refueling pits so I could fuel it up.

I hunted for Colin, our only mechanic, to explain my brother's strange banging noises. Colin and I met David at the pumps hoping to solve this weird noise puzzle. Colin approached the plane and knew the answer immediately. Dave had forgotten one of our dad's basic instructions, "Always buckle up the right seat belt when flying solo." When David shut the right cockpit door, the seat belt buckle was dangling outside. As the plane flew faster and faster, the wind hit the buckle and continually pounded it against the side of the fuselage, just behind the door. Eventually it punched a hole in the fabric and remained in there for the rest of the flight, thus no more banging noise. We both learned an expensive lesson early in our flying careers.

MY WORST EMERGENCY

In June of 1970 I received orders to fly the F-4 in Vietnam. After upgrade training at Davis-Monthan AFB, Arizona, I was assigned to the 555th Tactical Fighter Squadron ("Triple Nickel") at Udorn Royal Thailand Air Force Base in March of 1971. I had about 70 combat missions under my belt and I was leading a flight of four F-4s up into Laos for a bombing mission in an area we called the PDJ. It's an area in Northern Laos, called the Plain De Jars, where the ground actually looks like ancient jars coming up from the earth... if you can imagine that.

For this particular mission our F-4s were loaded up with six 500-pound bombs on the center station rack, called a MER (Multiple Ejector Rack), three 500-pound bombs under each wing station on TERs (Triple Ejector Rack), three AIM-7 radar guided missiles, and an electronic jamming pod.

Udorn was not that far from the Laotian border. As we crossed over the vicinity of Vientiane (the capital of Laos) I felt the aircraft shudder slightly. Immediately my wingman yelled out over the radio, "Lead, you just dropped your MER!" I couldn't believe it had departed the plane. I knew in case of emergency, the MER and TERs had small explosive cartridges that could be fired off to release them from the plane, but the pilot had to set up his bombing and arming switches specifically to release anything from the plane, and then, only at his command.

The first thought that ran through my mind was, "Oh hell, what have I done wrong now!" I knew I hadn't touched any switches at the time I felt the shudder... we were just cruising along in nice calm air to the target area. In the F-4C model, having the correct switches set for what you were trying to accomplish was not all that easy, especially in the heat of the battle. I know of many pilots who didn't get their MIG or correct ordnance release because of incorrect switchology. I glanced at my switches and found them all in the "SAFE" position. Then a bright red flashing "WHEELS" light illuminated in the cockpit and grabbed my attention.

On the F-4C/D models, the wing utilized Boundary Layer Control (BLC) to allow the plane to fly at a lower airspeed on landing. Very hot, high pressure air from each engine compressor section was routed forward by tubes and exhausted over the leading edge of each wing. This created additional lift for each wing, allowing us to fly at a lower landing speed. The plumbing of this additional air was such that if it came undone or cracked anywhere you would end up with very hot, high pressure air somewhere in your plane!

Our operating manual said that a flashing "WHEELS" light should be treated the same as a BLC malfunction light. The manual stated that a BLC malfunction light meant that you could expect everything and anything to happen, depending on where the hot air was being directed. Well, the book was right!

I began a slow 180 degree turn back to Udorn with my wingman while the other two planes continued on their bombing mission. While turning around numerous warning and caution lights began to flash in the cockpit. The only thing I was interested in was getting back on the ground ASAP. There were far too many lights going off in the cockpit to try and determine which systems were being affected by the hot air. On the way back, my wingman called out again, "You just lost your right TER... there goes your left TER." We had declared an emergency and at about 15 miles out the AIM-7 missiles began to fall off the plane.

The actual landing was uneventful, snagging the mid-field arresting barrier to stop the plane. We shut down the engines on the runway, and jumped out of the cockpit to inspect the plane. The flying safety officer met us, and as we walked around the plane it began to sink in just how much damage had been done by the hot air. With the trailing edge flaps down, molten metal was running profusely down both flaps and from every seam at the bottom of the fuselage. Large wire bundles were literally melted and fused together inside the plane from the hot air. If we had stayed airborne much longer, ejection would probably have been our only option. This incident proved to me just how much abuse the F-4 could take before falling completely apart.

DODGING SURFACE TO AIR MISSILES (SAMs)

After a one-year combat tour in Vietnam with the F-4, I trained further in the plane to be a Wild Weasel pilot. Wild Weasel crews were specifically trained to exterminate all electronic threats to other planes. Our F-4Cs were equipped with specialized electronic gear in the rear cockpit for the "Bear" (nickname for the GIB—Guy In Back) to find the electronic signals, analyze them, and help take them off the air. Each plane was equipped with four radar-seeking missiles, called the "Shrike," that would hopefully home in on the electronic signal and follow it to the enemy radar van or antenna.

Practically all of our Wild Weasel missions were into North Vietnam, going after enemy radar guided SAMs, which were lethal to our planes. We had encountered many SAMs during our tour and learned how to deal with them. Success in evading a SAM was directly related to being able to see it visually. Once you had a SAM in sight and could follow it, the rule-of-thumb was to wait until it looked about the size of a telephone pole, and then break (turn) sharply into the missile. The theory was that if you waited long enough, the SAM could not maneuver abruptly at the last second to track and kill you. Sometimes this worked. Unfortunately it was not foolproof.

Eight crews, including me, were sent to Korat Royal Thai Air Force Base to fly the Wild Weasel mission between September of 1972 and February of 1973. About halfway through our tour there we noticed a large increase in the number of SAM sightings at night. If you picked up a SAM visually at night, the best you could hope for was to see its exhaust and evade it accordingly. The more SAMs you encountered at night, the more you realized the difficulty in telling if it was actually coming towards you or going away from you.

The extensive cloud cover in North Vietnam made dodging them even more tricky at night. You could watch a SAM's eerie glow beneath a cloud deck get brighter and brighter as it got closer and closer to the cloud deck below you. Once it popped through the cloud deck it became easier to track. Even bombs going off beneath the cloud deck got your immediate attention. Initially it was difficult to distinguish between them and a SAM coming off its launching pad.

After several nights of evading more than the normal number of SAMs, we began discussing among ourselves and debriefing with intelligence this unusually high number. It continued like that for several more weeks until we finally learned what was going on. It turned out that the Navy had just acquired a new capability to improve the range and accuracy of its offshore shelling. The Navy was firing from its ships huge shells that had a rocket boost once the shell reached a certain distance. What we were seeing at night was the booster rocket igniting as the shell reached a certain altitude. To us it appeared like a SAM flying across the sky headed for someone. All this time we were jinking around the sky, making SAM breaks, on our own Navy's firepower. We felt like fools, but relieved to find out the answer to all the "SAMs" we had seen.

LONGEST SR-71 MISSION [Excerpt from *SR71 Revealed*]

The following is one of my favorite stories, as told by a former SR-71 pilot, Lieutenant Colonel Terry Pappas. He and his RSO, (Reconnaissance Systems Officer in the back seat), John Manzi, happened to be flying the SR-71 out of our detachment on Okinawa, Japan, when the requirement for a high priority reconnaissance mission came up. This turned out to be the longest operational sortie ever flown by an SR-71 crew. Here is Terry's story.

Every SR-71 pilot has a particular mission that he flew which ranks at the top of his list of memorable Blackbird experiences. For me it was easily our 11-plus hour mission flown out of Okinawa, during the Iran-Iraq war. We had 25 tankers, mostly KC-10s, plus several of our own KC-135Qs, supporting our five air refuelings. Four of our five refuelings had to be accomplished in the worst instrument weather conditions I ever had to deal with in air refuelings. Of the five hours we flew in air refueling tracks, I spent three and a half hours flying on the boom.

That grueling mission, which had us in our pressure suits for nearly 13 hours and on 100 percent oxygen for 12 hours, required every trick I had ever learned, plus a few new ones. The relatively small confines of the mission's target area required that we fly slower, permitting tighter turns. Our speed of 2.67 Mach in the target area meant a correspondingly lower altitude was necessary to make the Blackbird's inlet system run smoothly and allow for enough aircraft turn performance to stay on the black line. Lower and slower is not what we prefer, especially in close proximity to enemy fighters and surface-to-air missiles.

I remember one critical turn point in the take area vividly. We had just rolled out of a high banked turn and were racing straight at a hostile country's coastline. With 20 seconds to go before turn initiation, John quickly informed me that we had tailwinds 60 knots above forecast. This meant that a higher ground speed could sling us wide on the turn, causing us to miss some vital intelligence. We had planned the turn within two degrees of the maximum allowable bank angle for control of the aircraft. I selected minimum afterburner on both engines, but she didn't want to slow down. I knew that coming out of burner would mean a descent—wrong time, wrong place for that. I remembered a technique that I'd heard recently from one of the old heads. I quickly down-trimmed each engine's exhaust gas temperature (EGT) about 50 degrees. Painfully, the Blackbird relinquished some of her excess thrust and slowed just enough for us to make the turn.

John did a masterful job navigating us through those winding turns, out of the sensitive area, and into our third refueling. He had no idea what was going on when I said, "Man, what a beautiful sight." I described to him the three KC-10s waiting to give

us our gas, with Navy F-14 Tomcats flying escort. We were still dangerously close to the bad guys to be "low and slow" on the boom of a tanker. That day I became a genuine supporter of the U.S. Navy.

Hours later, after the fifth and last air refueling, we were cruising the last hot leg of that unbelievable mission. John and I were exhausted. Our bodies must have been on a metabolic roller coaster that matched the climbs and descents of our aircraft. We had focused so hard for so long. Just an hour-and-a-half to go until I could pull it out of burner for the final descent into Okinawa and a night landing.

Suddenly, I couldn't read cockpit instruments. Everything was blurred. I could see the round dials and gauges but couldn't *read* them. My mind was racing, and I'm sure my pulse was too. I didn't say a word to John. I was in near panic, trying to think of some way to recover my vision. I considered opening up the helmet faceplate but remembered that could prove fatal if we lost cabin pressure while it was open. Finally, I tried squinting hard. I kept trying, for what seemed like minutes, but must have been only seconds, until finally I was able to squeeze out a tear into each eye. Miraculously, the moisture brought back my vision. Apparently, the long exposure to 100 percent oxygen and helmet faceplate heat had dried my eyes completely.

With over two hours to go still, I knew my body was in bad shape at that moment. I could feel it. I had been unable to urinate for hours. I could feel my body trying to come down from the adrenaline high that I had hit several times already on the flight. I fought hard to keep my level of concentration up and the shakes to a minimum. The detachment on Okinawa called us to say that we could cut the arrival short and land on the opposite runway if we wanted, I told them, "No thanks." I didn't want to make any changes to our planned and briefed recovery unless they were absolutely necessary. I knew my body was running on fumes, and I had to get this machine on the ground safely, and soon!

When we taxied into the hangar that night, there must have been 150 members of the detachment waiting for us, cheering and clapping. Many of them had been up over 24 hours to make the mission work. You should have seen the pride on their faces as they celebrated that moment. It wasn't just the aircraft, or the aircrew, or any one member of the team. They were celebrating the magic and spirit of the Blackbird program. I don't think there has ever been anything quite like it in the Air Force, and I doubt there ever will be again.

THE SR-71 PRESSURE SUIT

A special altitude chamber located at Beale AFB, California allowed us to test our pressure suits at 85,000 feet. It was a small chamber, incorporating heating elements and the SR-71's ejection seat. The purpose of the chamber was to expose new crew members to the mating of the pressure suit to the ejection seat, build his confidence in the suit, learn how to operate and control the suit's temperature and pressure, and finally to experience a loss of all cabin pressure (called a rapid decompression, or RD for short) at 85,000 feet.

Every time we flew, we put our lives in the hands of the Physiological Support Division (PSD) technicians. Wearing the pressure suit made it next to impossible to strap yourself into the ejection seat and make all the necessary connections satisfactorily. Consequently, we were taught to extend our arms out each side of the cockpit and sit there patiently while several PSD technicians did all of the mating to the aircraft and our ejection seat. Trying to help them out merely hindered the process. They were extremely professional and safety conscious at their jobs, alert at all times to the dangers of becoming lax.

In the small altitude chamber, surrounding mirrors gave you an unrestricted view of how the technicians accomplished strapping you into the seat. You had time to stop and ask questions and discuss each item on their checklist. Once strapped in, they sealed the chamber and started the climb to altitude. The altitude chamber ride consisted of first climbing to a low altitude to check for any sinus problems you might have developed, and then it was on up to 85,000 feet.

On the way up, the first thing to grab your attention was a flask of water sitting on the inside windowsill. As you passed through 63,000 feet the water slowly began to bubble. At 70,000 feet it was boiling rapidly and at 85,000 feet it had all evaporated. It was placed there to give you an appreciation of what would happen quickly to your blood and other body fluids without a pressure suit on. The explanation goes like this. At sea level, water boils at 212 degrees F and our normal body temperature is 98.6 degrees F. A law of physics (Armstrong's Law) states that as you go higher in altitude (less pressure), the boiling point of water decreases. It turns out that the boiling point of water at 63,000 feet is around 98 degrees F, our body temperature.

Once the altitude chamber reached 85,000 feet, heaters could be turned on to get the chamber up to around 435 degrees F. The idea was to simulate the temperature that the cockpits could reach if your air conditioning systems quit at Mach 3 speed. We gained confidence in the pressure suit's ability to maintain a comfortable temperature inside the suit, regardless of the outside temperature. It was an eerie feeling in the chamber when your body was very comfortable, and yet you could see loose threads on the exterior of your pressure suit giving off wisps of smoke from extreme heating. It was hard to believe your suit can give you so much protection from such a harsh environment.

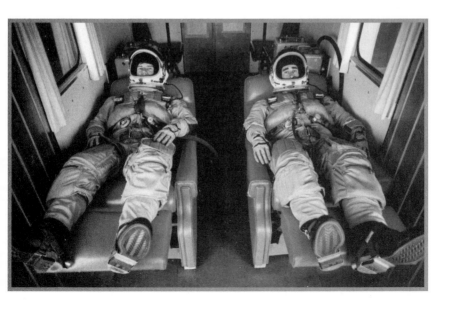

To prepare for the rapid decompression, the supervisor briefs you over the intercom on what to expect before throwing the decompression switch. I was told there would be a loud, explosive "BANG" accompanied by immediate fogging, and then rapid clearing inside the chamber. Simultaneously, the pressure suit would inflate. He recommended that the pressure suit tie-down strap be pulled tighter in preparation for suit inflation. After the briefing, the supervisor asked if I was ready. "Ready as ever," I replied. Peering through the thick glass window that separates you from them on the outside, I watched the PSD technician slowly lift the red covered safety guard and place his thumb on the switch. When he moves the switch, instantly your 26,000 foot cabin altitude will be at 85,000 feet.

It went exactly as he described... a loud "BANG"... immediate fogging... suit inflation... all simultaneous, followed by rapid clearing of the fog. I stayed at 85,000 feet for a while to experience the full suit inflation and to practice several cockpit chores in the rigid pressure suit. I was surprised that trying to pull on your tie-down strap or even turning your head in the helmet was more difficult than I imagined in a fully pressurized suit. The most important task to practice at this point was to reach for the ejection seat handle, located directly between your legs, grasp it firmly and give it a sharp upward pull. Hopefully I would never have to experience an RD for real, but for now, I had a chance to practice one in a controlled environment.

Biography

COLONEL RICH GRAHAM (RET.)

In Rich Graham's 25 years of Air Force service, he flew the world's fastest and highest flying aircraft, the SR-71 Blackbird. He flew 210 combat missions in Vietnam with the F-4 Phantom while assigned to the "Triple Nickel" Squadron. He has also flown the T-33, T-37, T-38, F-4 Wild Weasel, U-2 and the KC-135Q aircraft. Rich worked four years in the Pentagon and ended his military career as the 9th Strategic Reconnaissance Wing commander at Beale AFB. He currently flies the MD-80 aircraft for a major airline. Col. Graham speaks with authority on the SR-71, having spent over 15 years with this "TOP SECRET" program and has over 765 hours in the Blackbird. His book, *SR-71 Revealed, The*

Inside Story, describes flying operational reconnaissance missions over and around hostile countries, cruising faster than a speeding bullet (2,100 mph) at over 80,000 feet. With his pleasant demeanor, Rich has a wonderful ability to relate his Mach 3 experiences, enthralling both aviators and non-aviator audiences. Using his incredible depth of knowledge, he entertainingly answers all questions concerning the SR-71 program. You'll find this once highly classified information about the SR-71 Blackbird truly amazing. And you'll marvel at how an aircraft, built by Kelly Johnson's famed Lockheed Skunk Works, could be so far ahead of its time.

BARRY SCHIFF

[Reprinted by permission from *Flying Wisdom, The Proficient Pilot, Volume 3* by Barry Schiff. *Flying Wisdom* is published by Aviation Supplies and Academics, Inc. and is available from ASA dealers worldwide.]

DESTINATIONITIS

I am fascinated by how a comment made in casual conversation can have a profound and lifelong effect on how we regard and value the events in our lives. At least that is how Jim Taylor's remark affected me.

Jim and I were on a flying safari in East Africa using a rented Piper Arrow. On the day in question, we were heading from Arusha, Tanzania, to Nanyuki, Kenya. We were to spend a couple of days there lounging at William Holden's Mount Kenya Safari Club and raising "sundowners" in honor of whatever suited the moment.

While enroute, we were confronted by a line of thunderstorms that challenged our right of passage. There appeared to be some clear spots in the line, so I advised our wives in back to tighten their seatbelts in anticipation of a rough ride.

Jim was riding shotgun and knew how excited we were about getting to Nanyuki. We had been planning this vacation for months, and our expensive accommodations had been paid in advance (without possibility of a refund).

But Jim looked ahead at the ominous cells and put a father-like hand on my shoulder. "Barry," he said, "in a few years, it won't make any difference whether we get there or not."

That was in 1969. And Jim was right. It eventually didn't matter at all. But it might have made a great difference had we continued.

Jim's profound observation has served me well since then and probably has saved my life more than once.

A year later, my closest friend, Hal Fishman, and I were ferrying a turbocharged Piper Aztec C to Europe. Hal was and still is a news anchor for KTLA-TV in Los Angeles. The primary purpose of our flight was to produce a documentary film about the safety and reliability of general aviation airplanes. We had even made extensive arrangements with AT&T for Hal to transmit a live broadcast via high-frequency relay from the aircraft to his Southern California audience.

And because the flight was to originate in Los Angeles and terminate in its sister city of West Berlin, Mayor Sam Yorty had given us an official proclamation to be presented to West Berlin Mayor Klaus Schutz at a banquet to be held in our honor. Much depended on the timely completion of this mission.

The flight to Gander, Newfoundland, in N6649Y had been routine except for the automatic direction finder, which failed over the Gulf of St. Lawrence. Fortunately, Eastern Provincial Airlines had a first-class radio shop at Gander, where the faulty ADF could be repaired.

But the ADF could not be repaired and was declared a lemon. We called Piper and were promised a new unit would be shipped to us "as soon as possible."

In the meantime, a forecaster at the Gander Weather Bureau gave us the bad news about the meandering isobars on the constant-pressure charts. An intense low-pressure system was moving northeastward along the coast of Nova Scotia. We were advised that unless we intended to log some serious sightseeing time in Gander (not recommended), we should leave soon.

This was before the advent of the global positioning system and satellite navigation. The only checkpoints between Gander and Shannon were a pair of low-frequency radiobeacons aboard two enroute weather ships: Ocean Stations Charlie and Juliett. But an ADF was needed to find these waypoints. The approaching low also would create a net headwind along the direct route to Ireland and require using some of our fuel reserves.

The only other options were to take one of two longer routes to Europe. The first involved heading southeast to the Azores. But the first half of such a flight would be plagued by that deepening low-pressure system. It would produce the kind of strong crosswinds that hinder pilots from finding little islands in the middle of big oceans.

The other alternative was to head northeast and use Greenland and Iceland as stepping stones across the Atlantic. But the approaching low was pumping warm, moist air across southern Greenland. Widespread icing conditions were in the forecast.

Our plans, however, could not tolerate lengthy delays. Consequently, we decided to leave without the ADF and before the arrival of the low-pressure system.

By then I began to remember Jim Taylor's avuncular admonishment from our flight over the Serengeti Plain: "In a few years, it won't matter whether we get there or not."

It has been more than 20 years since Hal and I congratulated ourselves for postponing the ferry flight and allowing our plans to fall by the wayside. And as traumatic as that decision might have been at the time, it never did make any difference.

Thanks again, Jim.

When a pilot focuses so intently on reaching a destination that he loses his safety perspective, he is suffering from a syndrome known as "destinationitis." Although seldom cited in accident reports as a probable cause, it undoubtedly is an underlying reason for a great number of general aviation tragedies.

This is one reason why airline flights are typically safer than private operations. Airline pilots seldom are personally involved with the destination and do not become emotional or irrational when confronted by conditions that could delay or cancel a flight.

But general aviation pilots can develop an equally safe philosophy about any flight simply by recognizing that "in a few years, it won't matter whether you get there or not."

What does matter is whether or not you survive to think about it.

MY FAVORITE FLIGHT

I don't know what time it was, but I will never forget the date: August 27, 1991. We were flying on the back side of the clock over the middle of the North Atlantic at Flight Level 370 enroute from New York to Berlin, Germany.

The radios of our Lockheed 1011 were silent. It was one of those peaceful moments when the mind begins to drift. I recall staring out the left cockpit window, gazing at those friendly pinpoints of light dotting the celestial dome. They are my compatriots of the night sky that accompany me wherever in the world I wander.

It was one of those times when a pilot's eyelids tend to become heavy.

My head might have begun to bob a bit, but only for a few seconds. I was stunned back to reality by the sting of a rolled-up newspaper used by the flight engineer to swat me on the back of the head.

The young man blurted, "Sleeping is not allowed on the flight deck!"

The first officer, Bob McLoskey, was not surprised by such disrespectful and mutinous behavior. This is because the engineer was my son, Brian. This was our first flight as crewmembers on the same TWA flight.

Brian had come a long way since I had taught him to fly in the family Citabria. And no father could have been prouder. It brought a tear to the eye, a tear that I was careful to hide.

Brian's addiction to flying apparently was born before he was. This is because his mother, Sandy, was not content to sit at home knitting booties while pregnant with Brian. Instead, she busied herself learning to fly. I was her instructor.

But Sandy encountered a roadblock. The doctor was uncertain about approving a woman in her ninth month of pregnancy for a medical certificate. The FAA, however, unexpectedly came to the rescue by declaring that "being pregnant is a normal, healthy condition and not a basis for denial."

She soloed the next day. Or did she? Local "hangar lawyers" asserted that she did not solo because she had carried a passenger. That may be true. After all, Brian did make her flight safer. His "presence" made it impossible for his mother to bring the control wheel far enough aft to stall the Cessna 150 (intentionally or otherwise).

Brian was born a few weeks later, on September 8, 1967, and almost immediately embarked on an aeronautical career. It began with crayon drawings of TWA airplanes. (Thankfully, I still have one.) He couldn't wait for me to come home from my flights so that he could grab my captain's hat and run around the house pretending to be a TWA pilot. He cut out and saved TWA advertisements from newspapers and magazines. He made models of TWA airlines.

But we knew that this passion wouldn't last. We knew that he would grow out of it (or so we believed).

On the flight to Berlin, I occasionally found myself looking back at Brian. He would be hunched over his small engineer's table making fuel calculations or entering engine data in the aircraft log or reading a company bulletin.

Barry with sons. Brian (right) is now a Captain for TWA. Paul (center) works for Jeppesen-Sanderson, Inc. and is a certified flight instructor.

He turned around once and caught me looking his way. I pretended to be checking something on his panel, but he knew better. And I knew that he knew. We smiled at each other. Without saying a word, I was telling him, son, I am proud of who you are, what you have accomplished, and where you are going. Brian's smile said thanks for helping me get here. These were thumbs-up smiles filled with love.

This was the passing of the baton, a highlight of my career, of my life.

I turned away, misty-eyed. It was a time to reflect on my own beginnings.

My first exposure to aviation occurred 13 years after I was born. My parents shipped me from Los Angeles to spend the summer with my grandparents in New Jersey. And so it was that a North American Airlines DC-6 whisked me in the dead of night from Burbank, California, to Wichita, Kansas, to Chicago's Midway Airport to New York's LaGuardia. It was my first flight ever.

During the journey, I kept staring at the left wing. There it was, this huge iron thing that seemed like the outstretched arm of some giant predator. Noisy, too. And blue fire streaked from the engines bolted onto its leading edge. And those iron wings didn't move. They didn't seem to do anything. No flapping, no nothing. I couldn't understand how they managed to keep the beast in the air.

Curiosity drew me to the library in that little New Jersey town (partly because there was little else to do except throw eggs at the chickens running around my grandmother's back yard). There, I encountered those words now so familiar: Bernoulli. Venturi. Airfoil. Camber. It was so beautiful, so elegant. The wing did so much work—without really doing anything.

After returning home, I headed straight for the local airport, a place called Clover Field, now known as Santa Monica Municipal Airport. I desperately wanted a ride in one of those little airplanes. Any one would do. I wanted to look at the wing in flight with the smug awareness of what it was doing. I wanted to visualize the air caressing the curvaceous upper surface.

Not knowing better, I stood at the edge of a taxiway and tried to hitch a ride. Really. Thumb out. A pleading look on my face. A begging look.

I got kicked off the airport three times before I learned how to hitch a ride without getting caught. My first was in a Bonanza, an original one with a small engine. There was a painting of a glass of beer and a shot of whiskey on the side of the fuselage. That was because the owner of the Bonanza, Ed Grant, was in the business of making boilers. The whiskey and the beer together made what bartenders call a boilermaker.

The flight was infectious, addictive. I knew immediately that I would become a pilot. Flying was to become the most passionate and compelling aspiration of my life. It was Ed Grant's passion, too, but it killed him. Boilermaker's engine caught fire one day, and couldn't get down in time.

My first aviation job came within months of my Bonanza flight. it involved painting the men's room at Bell Air Service, a local flight school. The toilet there faced a wall that was uncomfortably close to your knees when you sat down. It was almost claustrophobic. But it was the perfect reading distance. So I glued a poster containing airport regulations to that wall so that everyone who sat there—having nothing better to do—would learn the local rules. This was my first attempt at instructing and it apparently went over pretty well. Somebody did the same thing in the ladies' room.

My TWA career began in 1964 as a first officer flying Lockheed Constellations. Those were exciting times. It was when people went to an airport hoping to witness a Connie or a DC-7 crank up, belch smoke, and come to life. It was when people dressed up for an airline flight. Flying was an adventure, not a bus ride.

TWA hired Brian in 1989, a quarter century later, as a flight engineer on a Boeing 727. His career will not be the same as mine. Times have changed. But it still will be rewarding and gratifying, as mine has been. His first flight as captain of a jetliner will be as memorable as when he first soloed our Citabria on his 16th birthday. His first command flight to the other side of the world will be as cherished a memory as his first solo cross-country up the coast to Santa Barbara.

He will continue to be awed by a world of experiences and sensations about which ordinary people only dream and which forms the bond that unites all airmen, especially when they are father and son.

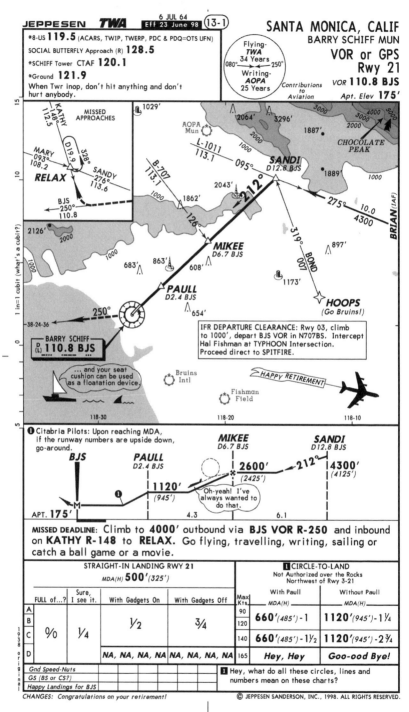

Designed by Paul Schiff to honor his father's retirement

Biography

BARRY SCHIFF

Barry Schiff retired as a Lockheed 1011 captain for TWA holding eight type ratings and all available flight instructor ratings. His 26,000+ hours include having flown 258 different types of aircraft. He has served as an FAA designated check airman on the Boeing 767, a general aviation designated examiner and has been appointed as an FAA designated accident prevention counselor at large. Barry's contribution to aviation is legendary. In addition to holding five world speed records, he's the recipient of a Congressional Commendation, the Louis Bleriot Air Medal (France), Switzerland's gold Proficiency Medal, an honorary doctorate in aeronautical science, and AOPA's L.P. Sharples Perpetual Award, to name just a few. Barry has authored more than a thousand magazine articles on flight safety, operation procedures, techniques and aeronautical theory. Many of these articles involve the development of original concepts, procedures and techniques that received considerable international and industry attention. Over the years Barry's prolific and skillful writings have earned him nine journalism awards. Barry is no ordinary educator. He presents outstanding programs on aviation safety, airspace and flight proficiency.

SHANDA LEAR

My dad was Bill Lear. Yes, *that* Lear.

"Call her Shanda," my grandfather, former comedian Ole Olsen, told my mom and dad when I was born. "People will always smile when they say 'Shanda Lear'."

My parents agreed. They loved going against the status quo and giving me a stage name was just another example of their unusual way of thinking.

AT HOME

At the dinner table, my parents taught us the fun of solving problems using *mental engineering.*™ They proved, time and time again that, in order to be successful, it is important to trust and *get excited about* the ideas that come to you to improve the quality of life. What you see (in your mind's eye) is what you get.

Many famous people jumped into the pool at our home in Geneva, Switzerland. During the Cold War, Commanding General Smoky Caldera, head of the Strategic Air Command, and many other generals came from all corners of the globe to a secret 150 proof "Bulsh" party. Mom and dad would turn in early, so I usually ended up hosting parties, even though I was only 15. My folks didn't want the guests to feel the party was over just because they didn't stay up late. The highest-ranking Conga line in military history danced through our house that night.

From left to right: Gordon Cooper Jr., Eddie Rickenbacher, Shanda, General Curtis Lemay, General Chuck Yeager.

This meeting was such a well-kept secret that the KGB never found out about it. Thank goodness. The only fallout occurred when the Conga line erupted into the room of Colonel and Mrs. Alex Rankin, who had already retired for the evening. So many people were pushing from behind that there was no way we could just say "Excuse us" and quietly close the door. I'll never forget their saucer eyes and bare shoulders as they clutched the sheets, watching us fall over ourselves trying to back out of their room. I'm sure they'll never forget *us,* either.

In 1960, General Igor Sikorsky (inventor of the helicopter) came to visit dad in Switzerland. He spent hours helping my father capture 28 of the relentlessly multiplying finches, which had accidentally escaped from my softhearted brother's room-cum-aviary. The two great inventors had to scrap their first plan for capturing the birds when my brother protested vigorously about the use of a vacuum cleaner. Those two massive minds thought about it some more and finally decided to try darkening the two-story, glass-walled living room so the birds would settle down. Then dad, manning the flashlight, would shine a spotlight on a finch while Sikorsky threw a multicolored beach towel over it and gently retrieved it.

MY PARENTS AND MY LIFE

My parents' teachings and their lives influenced mine enormously.

At 14, I convinced my mom she'd be lonely traveling around the world by herself. Within a week I had all my shots, left school, and saw Saigon when it was still a French colony.

At the age of 17, in Switzerland, I soloed. This was after only 8 hours and 44 minutes of dual time. I received my pilot's license with 30 hours and 50 minutes total time.

By the time I was 20, I was recording for Decca Records, in Italy. After Saigon, mom and I moved to Switzerland where dad later joined us. It was here that he started building the Learjet. I didn't return to the U.S. until much later, as an adult.

I'll always remember a night in Switzerland when dad, sitting in his lawn chair, pointed to a corner of the garden and said, "If aliens landed over there, I'd go with them. I know I'd probably never see you or mommy again, but I'd learn so much."

Learning something was always important to my dad. He embarrassed his mathematics teacher by solving an equation in a revolutionary way. The teacher's constant harassment forced him to quit 8th grade. He received the rest of his education from the public library. There, he discovered books by Robert Collier and began a lifelong quantum leap into the infinite ways of demonstrating there is only one mind and man is an inseparable spiritual idea of that mind.

Dad's parents divorced when he was a baby. His gentle stepdad, Otto, defended him against the onslaughts of his violently abusive mother. Later, his mother had a fit when she found out dad owned an airplane. No matter what dad said to justify having an airplane, in his mother's mind only bootleggers owned airplanes. Imagine if she had known that one day dad would own a Learjet! Dad learned parenting from these two.

My daughter, Mara, was born a few days after dad admitted he'd lost $17 million trying to develop an ecologically clean, steam-powered engine for automobiles. He was determined to clean up pollution, but his engine needed gas—lots of it—to burn clean and this was 1976, in the midst of the Arab oil embargo. Dad sat quietly in the twilight as I breastfed my newborn daughter. Almost inaudibly, he said "I wonder if anyone ever did that for me?" Suddenly, my father, the great icon, seemed so human, so fragile. My heart went out to him.

Dad's persistent question was "What does the world need?" His goal was to use all of his talents to bring good to the world. Making money was never his sole or even his major purpose in life. He had no doubts his needs would always be met. After WW II ended, government cancellations threatened to shut down Lear Incorporated. Dad told mom "Don't every worry about bankruptcy. They can never bankrupt my mind."

Dad wouldn't hear of retirement. He was 60 when he hocked everything to build a general aviation jet. He certainly wasn't going to stop when he was 75. My mother, and a roomful of engineers, claim he continued working to build his all-graphite twin turbine pusher prop airplane even after he died. During a heated discussion about whether or not to put some metal in the all-graphite aircraft, a bolt of lightning struck the building just outside their window.

"All right, Bill," they gasped in unison. "You win!"

Bill Lear: "They can never bankrupt my mind!"

THINGS DAD *DIDN'T* UNDERSTAND

Although my father was smart about almost everything, there *were* certain things he just could not understand. Me, for instance. He thought the world revolved around *him,* and that I should choose a guy who was right for him. He wanted me to marry one of his favorite engineers. That way he could continue to control me and, as a bonus, he would have an engineer son-in-law to talk shop with at Thanksgiving and Christmas dinners.

It didn't work out that way. He never could figure out why I protested. At the 30th anniversary of the first flight of the Learjet, Don Gromish, Learjet's chief engineer, told me he remembered dad slamming the phone down when I fought for what I thought was right. Dad was frustrated to find out that he could fire his employees but not his children.

My sister Tina and I both rebelled. I married an Italian writer and television producer. Tina married a world-famous sculptor when she was only 19. We both married glamorous, successful, self-made, older men—men just like dad.

A FEW I KNEW

When I was 18, I had a date with Jim Muntz. Some girls discover romance in the back seat of a limo. I discovered the four-track car stereo. I talked Jim into skipping the view from L.A.'s famed Mulholland Drive so we could pick dad up at the airport.

Dad was so excited about the stereo that we went directly to meet the inventor, Jim's father, Earl "Madman" Muntz.

RCA's president, General Sarnoff told dad, "Find a way to put an album's worth of songs on a cartridge." And thus the Learjet eight-track stereo was born. The rest, as they say, is history.

Then there was Frank Sinatra. Sinatra wanted the West Coast Lear distributorship (so did a lot of other people), so the Lear family was invited to Mia Farrow's birthday party in Las Vegas.

Each guest received, as a party favor, a golden bag with 100 silver dollars. I was delighted, thinking I could use the money to buy songbooks I wanted which cost $50 each. Not sure if that was OK, I asked dad what to do, and he told me the proper etiquette was to bet the money at Frank's casino and not cash the gift in.

Seeing my glum response, dad told me to play red or black at roulette. "You have a 50-50 chance of winning," he said, making it clear that money I *won* was mine to do with as I pleased. I *did* win, and set aside $100 worth of winnings then played the rest until it was all gone. I still use those songbooks today.

MOM'S ROLE

Since dad's purpose in life was to make the world a better place, he attracted what many considered his secret weapon—my mother, Moya Olsen. My dad's success can't be fully understood without first understanding my mother.

From her religious beliefs, mom learned to see the womanizing, mercurial, selfish, bullying side of dad as a mask. She could see past the mask and understand the original loving child that was dad's real nature. Her ability to recognize the

Moya and Bill in 1964

Shanda riding an EMX Racer in front of Dad's
personal Learjet now owned by Clay Lacy.

goodness in my father helped him feel safe, and allowed him the freedom to succeed. Her deep sense of security came from her understanding of Divine Love's caring presence and power.

She brought that understanding to the boardroom. She'd come to meetings armed with a piece of needlepoint, which she worked on during the proceedings. Quietly, metaphysically, she would handle the thoughts and fears of dad and his employees. Her presence brought comfort to friend and foe alike, and paved the way for Bill Lear's success and accomplishments.

IN HIS FOOTSTEPS

"What can I design that the world needs?" was always my dad's question. When I saw the fold-a-way electric scooter for which my husband had made the pattern, I thought, "Dad would have loved this," and founded Lear Ground Transportation to sell the scooters at airshows.

I continue walking in my parents' footsteps. Every day I act on what mom and dad taught me—see a need and fill it, and have fun. Life's a ball.

Biography

SHANDA LEAR

Shanda gives a very heartwarming presentation about Bill Lear. "Dad was always scribbling ideas and designs on restaurant napkins and tablecloths, all the while telling jokes and discussing the infinite possibilities of the mind. His charismatic presence would always turn heads when he entered a room." From her father she learned that impossible dreams come true—with determination. Shanda earned her Swiss pilot's license at 17 and is now an accomplished singer and entertainer. Her tribute to flight, *Out of the Blue* is an audiotape of aviation songs. Audiences enjoy her touching and inspiring presentation ending with singing. Her inspiring story of *The Secret to the Success of Bill and Moya Lear* is complemented with slides and spiced with interesting and little known facts about her father. Shanda will customize her program to wrap up with one to six songs, ensuring she ends on a "high note." Shanda has a medley of aviation songs, WWII songs and aviation military sing a long tunes. Among her most requested are *God Bless the USA* and *The Star Spangled Banner*.

BURT RUTAN

Pioneer. Engineer. Inventor. Aviator. Entrepreneur.
Educator. Designer. Visionary. Nice guy.

Major Projects Developed

VariViggen	Predator	SU25 ¼ scale ROAR
VariEze	ATTT	Ultralight show car
AD-1	Triumph	Eagle Eye
Defiant	CM-44 UAV	DC-X
Quickie	Scarab	Raptor D1
Long-EZ	Wing Sail	Vantage
Biplane Racer	Searcher	Z-40 Bladerunner
Grizzly	ARES	Comet
Next Generation Trainer	Pond Racer	Raptor D-2 ERAST
Voyager	TFV	Freewing Full Scale
Solitaire	PLADS/Rockbox	Kistler Zero
PARLC	Gondola for Earthwinds	Boomerang
Catbird	Pegasus flying surfaces	VisionAire Vantage
Microlight	Model 191	Williams V-Jet II
NGBA Starship POC	B-2 RCS model	Proteus
		Adam M-309

When Irene "Mom" Rutan asked three-year-old Dick what game he was playing he answered that he wasn't playing at all. He was making a runway (left) so the airplanes he saw flying overhead would have a place to land.

Later, as a teenager Dick pressured his dentist father, who was also a pilot, into buying an airplane with a partner.

The George Rutan Jr. family in 1944. Left to right: George, Dick, Irene, and being held are Nellie Ann and Burt. Dick Rutan was destined to become the pilot of the Voyager and Burt Rutan a prolific aeronautical engineer. It was their sister Nellie Ann who managed to accumulate more flight time than her brothers and father combined. How? As a flight attendant for American Airlines.

Burt flies one of his models in 1952. You can almost hear the engine noise coming from young Burt's lips, "Bbbbbbbbbbb."

George "Pop" Rutan was concerned about Burt. The boy had a habit of sitting alone and staring into space for long minutes at a time. One day he asked Burt what he was doing. "Thinking," answered the youngster.

A happy Burt at the age of 16 with a trophy for his Bonanza RC scale model. Year 1959.

Beech Aircraft Corporation
Wichita, Kansas

L. WINTERS
ASSISTANT SECRETARY

February 27, 1958

Mrs. G. A. Rutan
481 Lincoln
Dinuba, California

Dear Mrs. Rutan:

We have your February 20 letter, and were pleased
Elbert could use the material we sent.

Since you mention he is planning to build other BEECH-
CRAFT models now (in addition to his Bonanza), we're
enclosing photographs and blueprints of our other commercial models; also, the T-34 (Army and Navy
trainer), and hope this material will assist him in his
future model building.

I hope, too, since Elbert is so air-minded, he can use
this talent - perhaps he will be an aeronautical engineer some day!

Sincerely yours,

L. Winters

L. Winters

LW:tg
Enclosures
  Bonanza - brochure
  Travel Air - blueprint #95-001012, brochure,
          photos #13539 & 13456F
  Super 18 - blueprint #414-180005, brochure,
          photos #13541 & 13529D
  Model 50 - blueprint #50-001015, brochure
          photos #13540 & PL 21477o
  Model 45 - blueprint #45-001012, photos #10869H & 11717

- *Founded in 1932 by Walter H. Beech* -

In 1966, Burt, pictured on the lower right, with the C130 Test Crew, El Centro, California—low altitude sled delivery. Burt was employed as a civilian engineer by Edwards Air Force Base after he graduated from California Polytechnic University, San Luis Obispo. As a Flight Test Project Engineer, he conducted 15 USAF flight test programs in his seven-year tenure.

Burt Rutan's Defiant Model 40, First Flight 1978

Burt Rutan's Long-EZ Model 61, First Flight 1979

Burt Rutan's Boomerang, August 1996 (Photo by Tonya Rutan)

Artwork by Stokes

BURT RUTAN
**Pioneer. Engineer. Inventor. Aviator. Entrepreneur.
Educator. Designer. Visionary. Nice guy.**

Burt began flying in 1959. His flight time has been in over 70 types of aircraft, including 10 military aircraft, which he flew in hazardous tests. His FAA ratings include multi-engine, single-engine sea, instrument airplane, and single-engine helicopter. However, Burt is more widely known for his aircraft designs, rather than his flying. His designs include the VariViggen, VariEze, NASA AD-1, Quickie, Defiant, Long-EZ, Grizzly, scaled NGT trainer, Solitaire, Boomerang and Catbird. His record-breaking design, the Voyager, was the first airplane to circle the world non-stop without being refueled. All of Rutan's airplanes employ some of the most advanced design in use today. Hollywood featured the avant-garde beauty of his designs in three films, *Death Race 2000*, *Octopussy* and *Iron Eagle III*.

Rutan's company has developed projects as diverse as a sail for an America's Cup challenger and the gondola for Virgin-Atlantic's Richard Bransen's attempt to balloon non-stop around the world. His company also developed an all-composite car body for General Motors that averages 100 miles per gallon. People are inspired by Rutan's enthusiasm for what individuals with vision can achieve. "An engineer in a normal company structure," says Rutan, "gets to work on two or three airplanes in his whole career. We've done twenty-three airplanes in twenty years." Burt founded Scaled Composites, Inc. in 1982 to develop research aircraft. The prodigious output of Scaled includes innovative configurations for a myriad of applications from agricultural to space launching, from reconnaissance drones to close air support, from air racing to ocean racing. Burt has received a multitude of prestigious awards for his many designs.

Artwork by Stokes

Burt Rutan's Designs

BILL COX

THE FERRY PILOT

Ferrying little airplanes over big water isn't for everyone. Few pilots can appreciate the solitude or tolerate being out of sight of land for hours at a time. I don't get many calls from passengers wanting to ride right seat, which is just as well, so I usually travel the world alone.

The proof that international delivery flying is intolerable to many pilots was never more clearly demonstrated than on one late December Atlantic crossing when an owner asked to ride shotgun from Florida to South Africa in his new single-engine aircraft.

On our first overwater leg, 1,400 nm from St. Johns, Newfoundland to Santa Maria, Azores, only an hour into the trip, my likable passenger looked down at the cold Atlantic whitecaps atop 20 foot swells, being driven by 40 knot winds, and asked, "Be honest with me. Would we really stand any chance of surviving if we had to ditch in that ocean?"

I glanced down at the angry, windswept sea 11,000 feet below, no worse than typical for that time of year, reflected on his question for a minute, then smiled and answered as honestly as I could, "Not much."

An unusual, but not unfamiliar, expression came over his face. Thirty seconds later, he threw up all over his jacket. When he finished, he cleaned himself as best he could. I didn't say a word. Just first flight over water jitters, I thought. We flew on in silence.

Four hours out, with the St. Johns beacon now faded from range and nothing but water everywhere, my companion asked, "How long until we see land?" A little wiser, I paused, studying his face. We had barely started the longest overwater leg. Would he or wouldn't he?

Finally, I said, as calmly and nonchalantly as I could, "Five hours." The same look came over his face. Sure enough. At least, he found the sick sack the second time.

The old saying about long distance flying, "Hours and hours of sheer boredom punctuated by brief moments of stark terror," certainly applies to ferrying small airplanes across large bodies of water. Some folks think pilots who have ferry tanks installed in single-engine airplanes and head out across 1,500-2,500 nm of water are simply deranged. Others think we're brave. Still others believe we're a little of both. Most delivery pilots prefer to think of themselves as adventurers, but I know my wife, Martha, probably believes the deranged explanation to be more accurate. Read the next two stories about adventures in single-engine airplanes, and judge for yourself.

AFRICA

[Originally appeared in *Plane & Pilot* Magazine, April 1983]

Though it is late December 1982, the equator knows no season but summer. The sun rises fat and wet above the jungle, and we are sweltering in our airplanes with engines running at 0630 as it breaks the humid horizon. Today, we fly south out of Libreville, Gabon enroute to Windhoek, Namibia. Heat hangs heavy in the still, morning air, with occasional rain marching through in brief squalls. I am happy to get off the ground, but the airplane doesn't share my enthusiasm. It struggles to climb away from the city, prolonging my 11,000 foot ascent to almost 20 minutes.

As I look down on solid jungle an hour after takeoff, approaching the last VOR we will use for 10 hours and 1,600 nm until we reach Windhoek, I'm amazed at the intensity of the color. A green so vivid and indelible in the early morning sun, it seems almost psychedelically imprinted on my brain when I close my eyes. And I thought Ireland was green.

We left Lakeland, Florida six days ago on our 10,000 nm trip to South Africa, three new airplanes, a Mooney 231, Piper Seneca III and "my" Cessna Crusader, the first of its type ever to leave the U.S. We flew north to Bangor, Maine to clear Customs, then to frigid St. Johns, Newfoundland, Canada, the jumping-off spot for transatlantic flights to Africa and southern Europe. Funchal, Madeira Islands was our third stop, 1,700 miles out in the Atlantic.

At Funchal, 400 miles off the Portuguese coast, I was forced to refuel from a gas trailer. The trailer ran dry with the aft fuselage ferry tank only half full. Pumping the bottom contents of a Portuguese fuel trailer into my airplane was scary, but there was nothing I could do about it. Customers don't take kindly to ferry companies cutting holes in an airplane's belly to install sump drains in auxiliary fuel tanks, so there was effectively no way to check ferry fuel for contamination. About the best I could do was peer down through the filler hole with a flashlight and get high on the fumes in the process.

The problem waited three days to bite me. After Funchal, we continued across the southwest corner of Africa's vast Sahara Desert, above bleak Mauritania and desolate Mali to Abidjan, Ivory Coast. On the fifth morning of our trip, we hopped the short 900 nm across the Gulf of Guinea to Libreville, happy that our trip was only two days from over... or so we thought.

Flying Africa is definitely a different experience for a Western pilot. Though I've made two dozen other ferry trips to points international, they've all been to Europe where the major cultural difference is the menus for McDonalds aren't always in English. This is my first trip to a place where fast food is a gazelle. Much of Africa is still primitive and undeveloped, a throwback to a time when life had absolutely no resemblance to a lite beer commercial. I shudder to think of the consequences of an engine failure above such a totally primeval and unforgiving environment.

The Cessna twin is on autopilot, cruising in uncharacteristic smooth air and sunshine above the perpetual heat haze of the equatorial jungle. In weather circles, this area is known as the infamous ITCZ, the Inter Tropical Convergence Zone (slanderized simply as the "itch"), where the weather gods throw their parties. Weather systems from the northern and southern hemispheres merge at the equator, spawning huge thunderstorms that live in the itch almost year-round. Today, the sky is insidiously clear.

The Crusader's left seat is full back, the right full forward and my legs are across the cabin, my feet resting on the right seat cushion. I see the VOR pass below me, make my turn to head offshore, and once again look up the VOR on the Jepp chart, Tchibanga, a name straight out of a Tarzan movie. In these parts, the locals are infamous for shooting at airplanes with everything from .22s to TOW missiles, so I'll track offshore and parallel the coast of Angola 20 miles out to sea to avoid any unnecessary encounters.

I'M LOSING THE LEFT ENGINE. Abruptly, the props unsync, and the left fuel flow and manifold pressure begin to fluctuate wildly. I sit stunned and frozen in disbelief for a moment, a Pepperidge Farm chocolate chip cookie halfway to my mouth. I am painfully aware that there is nothing below but double canopy rain forest rolling in all directions to the horizon. The left manifold pressure stabilizes for a moment, continues to fall, stabilizes, then drops again. As I watch in amazement, waiting for training and experience to overcome momentary panic, the RIGHT fuel flow also surges once and begins to slide backward down the scale.

It's not possible, I think. This can't be happening. I'm losing both engines. Abruptly, my brain re-engages, and reflexes and training overcome shock. I delete a few expletives, disengage the autopilot, punch the pumps on high, switch the fuel system from the ferry tanks back to the Cessna Crusader's wing tanks, double check the mags and promise to be a better person. Mixtures go forward, and I ease the throttles toward the panel. The engines respond only slightly with ragged, sporadic power, causing the Crusader to wallow from side to side. Within 30 seconds, it's apparent I'm going down.

"Tom, you're not gonna believe this," I tell lead-dog Tom Willett on the radio, trying to sound as matter-of-fact as possible with a voice at least an octave above Mickey Mouse, "but I just lost both engines." Without a word, Willet, the consummate professional, flying point in our loose, three-plane formation, wracks his new Mooney into a steep bank and turns back toward me from his position a half mile ahead.

10,000 feet. I search frantically for a place to land, knowing that a descent into the dense rain forest below probably would not be survivable. At first glance, the only possible landing site appears to be a narrow jungle river, winding lazily toward the South Atlantic. Lacking a better choice, a river ditching seems my only choice. Better to lose the airplane in a ditching and live to fight off the crocodiles than to buy it on impact in the jungle.

8,000 feet. In desperation, I start a series of S-turns and suddenly spy a short, dirt strip almost directly below me, its brown earth partially overgrown with jungle moss. I later learn it is a missionary medical emergency strip intended for picking up natives bitten by bad snakes, but right now, it looks like LAX to me. Still a half-ton over gross with ferry fuel, the Crusader glides like a set of car keys toward the dark ribbon of salvation two miles below. The engines cough and stagger, developing only about 17 inches per side under full throttles.

6,000 feet. Damn, that looks short, probably less than 2,500 feet long. Willett follows me down in my steep spiral toward the jungle, smart enough to stay off the radio and let me do my job. Meanwhile, Ernie Kuney loiters above in his Seneca III at 11,000 feet to maximize radio range, and I hear him transmitting a Mayday for me on 121.5. An Air Angola 727 answers his call and circles overhead at 35,000 feet, relaying a running account of my situation back to Libreville.

4,000 feet. I have all the help I can use. Now, if I just had one good engine. As I descend toward the jungle, I have little time to speculate on the cause of the problem, but I'm certain it has to be fuel contamination.

I line up for a high downwind entry at 3,000 feet, holding 120 knots for lack of a better number and watching the VSI steady on 1,200 fpm down. Meanwhile, I try to remember everything I ever learned about dead-sticking a twin-engine, flying rock onto a short dirt strip in the African jungle at 1,000 pounds over gross. I also try to forget that I'm flying a very live bomb, carrying almost 350 gallons of fuel, 220 of it in the temporary fuselage tanks directly behind me. My main concern is that I'll have a hell of a job explaining this to the owner of the ferry company if I blow the landing. On the other hand, I probably won't have to worry about it, as "blow" is definitely the operative term.

Though I've flown two dozen ferry trips, many at even higher gross weights, I've never landed an airplane at this weight. And for my first time, I have to do it without power. Why am I here?

2,000 feet. Wonder if this puppy will have any flare left under these conditions? Wonder how the gear will handle a power-off landing on a rough, dirt strip at this weight? Wonder if I have a snowball's chance in Tchibanga of stopping this thing before I slide off into the trees? Wonder who'll take care of my dog?

1,000 feet. Judging the approach toward the indistinct threshold is akin to guessing the glidepath of a fully-loaded Peterbilt. I misjudge the key position and am forced to hurry the turns to base and final. At 200 feet and still looking short, I extend the rubber to meet the mud, go to full flaps, then reach across the cabin and pop the copilot's emergency hatch.

The runway rushes up at me as I slow through 100 knots without the foggiest notion of the flare characteristics or stall speed at such a heavy weight. The threshold is indistinct, merging with the jungle as I take my best guess on where the runway begins. If I'm more than a few yards short, I will clip the trees on the edge of the clearing. If I land long, I'll run off the end into a solid wall of jungle. Either way, I probably won't have to worry about explaining my mistake.

As I turns out, I'm short. My questions about flare and gear strength are answered as I drag the gear through the trees, and the Crusader begins to sink right through any semblance of ground cushion. I begin a flare off the end of the runway and come full back on the yoke, but the airplane still slams down ungracefully in a full stall 10 yards short of the threshold in light brush and mud. The Cessna bounces once, lands the second time on the runway, and I stab my Reeboks hard into the brakes, grateful for mud or anything else that will slow my headlong rush toward oblivion.

The Crusader loses speed reluctantly, sliding on the moist dirt, but I'm able to slow the airplane to a crawl well before reaching the opposite threshold. There's a small parking ramp near the end of the runway, and I steer onto it with the little momentum I have left. I retard the throttles and both engines die almost simultaneously before I can even reach for the mixtures.

Willett taxis his Mooney in beside me and shuts down, as I sit in the Crusader listening to the tick of the engines, oblivious to the heat, grateful just to be alive. Finally, after a full minute to contemplate the wet spot on the seat, I climb back over the ferry tanks to the double clamshell door and step out onto the ramp.

Fifteen minutes later, after I've calmed down and had time to reconsider all those promises I made in exchange for my life, a French innkeeper from the village of Tchibanga shows up in an appropriately rickety Citroen to ask if we need assistance. He drives us back to his tiny hotel and alerts Libreville to our situation on his HF radio.

Within two hours, a Cessna 310 from Libreville Air Service, the Cessna distributor for Gabon, lands with a mechanic and a full tool chest on board. Following my description of the problem to the 310's British pilot, who translates it into French for the mechanic, the Frenchman pulls the wing sump screens and discovers massive fuel contamination by some kind of fabric material.

Though the mechanic speaks no English, the cause of the double engine failure is obvious. The fabric has almost completely clogged every injector and filter in both engines. The ferry system fed both engines from the same source, and I was burning fuel from the aft ferry tank when the engines quit, negating the redundancy of independent fuel sources.

Ironically, the worse the contamination, the better the fuel sample. The fabric contaminant, later analyzed by Shell Oil and determined to be an outdated cloth filter from a fuel trailer (remember Funchal?), was effectively filtering the fuel before it came through the strainers, making my fuel samples look as clear as Chablis.

While the mechanic cleans the injectors and filters on both engines, Willett and I try to drain fuel from the ferry tanks to lighten the load for the coming late afternoon takeoff. I know the fuel contamination will still be there, but it's only an hour back to Libreville, and I'll have to take my chances that the airplane will run for another hour.

It does. I stagger off the ground at almost 100 degrees F, struggling to clear the trees, and Willett and I sneak back into Libreville just before dark. The following morning, Air Service inspects Willett's airplane and finds more contamination. His Mooney was filled immediately before mine at Funchal.

The mechanics drain nearly 300 gallons from my Crusader plus another 150 gallons from the Mooney into 55-gallon drums. By noon, there's a line of 20 cars next to the maintenance hangar, all waiting to fill their tanks with contaminated avgas, apparently reasoning that no matter how bad it is, it can't be much worse than local car gas, and anyway, it's free.

The next day, Willett and I refuel totally empty tanks and try one more time. We depart Libreville at daybreak, pass over Tchibanga, uneventfully this time, angle 20 miles offshore to be well outside missile range and parallel the Atlantic coast for 800 miles. Then, we turn back toward land abeam the stark, white Tiger Peninsula, cross the short Namib Desert and touch down at Windhoek, Namibia only 13 hours after departure.

The final abbreviated leg to Johannesburg across the Kalahari Desert the following day is similarly anticlimactic. I land in Johannesburg on New Year's Day, 1983. For me, it has been an eventful 10,000 mile enduro, an eight-day flight test halfway around the world, my 26th international ferry trip.

ANATOMY OF A CATASTROPHIC ENGINE FAILURE

[Originally appeared in *Plane & Pilot* Magazine, November 1989]

July 3, 1989, had already started off as one of the worst days of my life. Then, it got worse.

I'd just returned from delivering a new Mooney 252 TSE across the Atlantic from Hayward, California to Glasgow, Scotland and was flying my own Turbo Mooney back to Long Beach from Northern California. Enroute weather was excellent with virtually unlimited visibility and not a cloud in sight. The entire Los Angeles Basin was luxuriating in a modest heat wave, with temperatures in the high 90s, but uncharacteristically for summer in Los Angeles, the air was clean and clear.

I'd been watching the oil temperature on the Mooney's Lycoming as I drifted southeast at 11,500 feet, pushed by light tailwinds. The IO-360's cylinder heads had remained relatively cool, and the EGT on cylinder number one (the first to peak) was still reasonable, but the oil temperature had been running well above normal, though below redline. I'd been careful not to use any turbo boost that might have raised temperatures even higher and instead settled for normally-aspirated power.

The engine continued to hum happily in all other respects, and I wanted to keep it that way. In 23 years of flying, I'd had seven previous dead-stick emergency landings, and I didn't want to make it eight. I resolved to have my resident engine expert, Scott Jackson, check the powerplant at Long Beach the following day before my next trip.

Scott never got the chance. I let down around the west side of the Burbank ARSA (now Class C airspace), then threaded the needle through the narrow Los Angeles TCA (now Class B airspace) corridor along with four other airplanes, all on the same radial and at the same relatively low, 3,500 foot altitude. Given my druthers, I would have flown much higher over one of the largest cities on the planet, but the Feds, in their infinite wisdom, had taken the decision out of my hands and decided 3,500 feet was the only acceptable altitude. Thanks a lot, FAA.

Just south of the TCA, I turned slightly left toward Long Beach, began a slow descent and watched Hawthorne Airport slip by to my left. A year earlier, I'd visited Hawthorne unexpectedly when a fuel line ruptured and I was forced to find a parking spot. Today, the little Mooney was running smoothly, though oil temp was still high, just below redline. I passed south of Compton, descended below 2,000 feet, made my initial call to Long Beach for the downwind entry to runway 25L and began my prelanding check.

Without warning, everything went to hell. The prop suddenly ran away, shrieking up to 3,300 rpm, 600 above the normal redline. Even through the padded David Clark headset, I could hear the wail as the tips screamed up near Mach 1.0. I chopped the prop control to the back stop and saw no change, so I pulled power and finally managed to bring rpm back down to the redline 2,700 at 18 inches of manifold pressure. Things were smooth, but the oil temp was now going bananas, climbing practically as I watched.

A few seconds later, nearly within gliding distance of Long Beach Airport, there was a violent vibration out front, almost as if part of the prop had separated. Practically before I could bring the throttle back, there was a loud bang, and the prop seized, coming to an abrupt stop horizontally. Instantly, it got very quiet in the cockpit.

There was a moment of shocked disbelief before my brain grasped the seriousness of my situation. Nothing below but houses and freeways clogged with rush hour traffic. There was the L.A. River off to my left, easily within reach but crisscrossed by power lines. No good. Long Beach Airport was still too far away. No chance. Oil fields below, Torrance Airport too far away to the right. Compton was my only hope. I punched the push-to-talk button: "Long Beach, Mooney 65 Victor just blew the engine. Gonna try to make it back to Compton."

Compton Airport was behind me now. Altitude 1,500 feet, airspeed 110 knots. I racked the Mooney into a quick 45 degree bank, trying to recall the optimum power-off bank angle for minimum altitude loss (by sheer coincidence, 45 degrees is about right). Not much reason to try a restart, I thought, as I held the nose up to avoid bleeding off too much altitude. Just to be sure there was no power left, I switched tanks, blipped the fuel pump switch and touched the starter. The prop wouldn't even budge. Probably a broken crankshaft, I speculated. I turned off the fuel and mags but left the master on for electrical power for the gear, noting again how quiet it was. Only 1,400 feet left.

It would be convenient to report that I was calm and collected through all this, but in reality, I was beginning to hyperventilate as I rolled out with Compton Airport straight ahead. I knew I'd better do this right the first time. I wouldn't get a second chance. I was already down to 1,200 feet.

Compton looked barely within gliding distance. No, wait, perhaps I was even a little high, I guessed, setting up for a wide left base entry to the seldom-used right runway. I couldn't remember the best glide speed, so I settled instead on 80 knots (close—the proper speed was 71 knots). It was so quiet in the cockpit.

I watched the airport settle into my sight picture, attempting to keep the threshold at roughly the same spot on the windshield. 1,000 feet remaining. I'm still high, I thought, bouncing through the hot thermals of choppy air. Gotta lose some altitude. Save the gear and flaps for later, I told myself. I rolled out on a long final and began a series of gentle S-turns, never turning away from the airport and losing altitude as slowly as possible. Quiet.

Looks about right, I thought, as I rolled out of my final S-turn and lined up with the centerline again. Incredibly, as I watched the airport creeping closer, I saw the threshold ever-so-slowly *rising* on the windshield. I WAS TOO LOW.

I shouted in anger at myself, "You idiot." I'd given away precious altitude too early. The trees off the end of the runway were coming up, and it looked as if I wasn't going to make the airport. Years of ingrained habit had made me aim for the threshold rather than well down the runway, as I should have. Now, it appeared I was going to be short. No time to pick an alternate landing site now. Nothing ahead but the inevitable series of apartment buildings that seem to surround every airport. I was amazed how quiet it was in the airplane.

Fighting the temptation to put in more back pressure, I continued down toward the buildings, hoping I was wrong about the approach angle. 400 feet. Gradually, I realized I just might make it after all. The Mooney drifted down, descending through a bubble of superheated air, temporarily halting its inexorable descent. 200 feet. It would be close.

The trees and apartment buildings were rising to meet me. I held my breath and lifted up in the seat as I approached the obstacles. Resisting the urge to haul back on the yoke, I watched the buildings loom larger through the side window. I still had three hours fuel remaining, enough to make my airplane into a huge Molotov cocktail if I didn't make the airport. Please don't let me screw this up, I thought as I ran out of sky.

I watched in near amazement as the obstacles drifted by what seemed only inches below. I cleared the fence by a few feet, toggled the gear handle to down and was grateful for the Mooney's quick electric gear. I felt the reassuring thunk of the wheels locking in place a few seconds before the airplane touched the runway 200 feet short of the displaced threshold.

I rolled out halfway down the runway, turned off onto the south ramp and pulled to a stop in front of the T-hangars. Now, it was truly quiet except for the soft whir of the gyros spinning down and my own rapid breathing. I sat in the cockpit for several minutes, glad to be alive, waiting for the rush of adrenaline to leave my system. I barely noticed when two helicopters, one from L.A. County Sheriff and the second from L.A.P.D., both alerted to my emergency by Long Beach tower, landed near me and shut down. After a few question to determine that I was OK, the officers climbed back into their choppers and departed.

Somehow, despite several dumb mistakes, I'd made it down without breaking anything. I'd had what I'd always feared most over the Los Angeles metropolitan area, a total, catastrophic engine failure. Hindsight is always 20/20, but I still can't help wondering if I could have avoided the problem altogether. Should I have terminated the flight early, say at Van Nuys, because of the high oil temperature? Had the unusually warm outside air temperature seduced me into believing the high oil temp was "normal"? I should have known my airplane's best glide speed by heart, and I certainly shouldn't have set up my dead stick approach to Compton's runway threshold.

A few days after the engine failure, my mechanic and I returned to Compton to check the damage. There was a jagged, quarter-sized hole in the top of the number three cylinder, with a half-dozen cracks emanating out in all directions. Apparently, the engine had thrown a connecting rod in the most violent manner possible. We were amazed that no pieces had blown through the top of the cowling. We checked the oil before pulling the engine, and there were six quarts left, no big surprise since I knew there'd been seven quarts out front when I left Hayward.

In retrospect, the emergency hadn't turned out as badly as it might have. The airplane was still intact, though the engine was obviously history. Most important of all, at least to me, my tender pink body was still intact and no worse for wear.

Biography

BILL COX

Aviation writer Bill Cox began flying as a CAP cadet in Anchorage, Alaska more than 30 years ago. Since then, he has gone on to earn commercial, multi, instrument, seaplane, glider and helicopter ratings and own half a dozen aircraft. Bill has logged over 11,000 hours in some 265 types of flying machines, ranging from Champs, Chiefs, Luscombes and Cubs to the Goodyear blimp, Swearingen SJ-30 biz jet and the F-15 and F-16 fighters.

Bill is the author of some 2,000 articles for magazines such as *Flight International, Flying, AOPA Pilot, Air Progress, Private Pilot*, and more recently, *Plane & Pilot*,

where he's listed as a senior editor. Bill was also a writer and on-camera host of the ABC-TV program *Wide World of Flying* in the '80s and early '90s. When not on deadline for the magazines or television, Bill delivers a variety of airplanes overseas to Europe, Africa, Australia and the Middle East and recently logged his 100th international delivery.

PATRICK O'DOOLEY

A LESSON THAT COST ME MY BOOTS
[Excerpt from *Flight Plan for Living*]

I have always taken a professional attitude toward my flight duties in the private planes I have flown. I've always sought instruction in new planes and kept up my flying skills. Nonetheless, there are still times when routine assumptions about our currency are not enough.

I was engaged to speak in Hot Springs, Arkansas, and decided I was going to fly there. When I got to the airport, the plane I usually flew was in pieces all over the hangar.

When I asked what was going on, the shop owner told me that my plane was down for its 100-hour check. "But don't worry," he said. "I've made arrangements for you to fly another plane over to Hot Springs. It's just like yours except that it's five years newer."

"Okay," I said, and went out to start my normal preflight checks.

The replacement was brand new, with only six flight hours on it. I completed my checks and departed for Hot Springs, which was about a two hour flight. I landed safely, and went back to the airport at about 11 o'clock that night.

The weather for my return trip wasn't bad, but it was starting to mist fairly heavily. Because of the mist and the fact that the airplane was parked in a dark area of the airport, I did something I don't usually do. I didn't have a flashlight so that I could see to complete my preflight check, so I said to myself, "It flew in, it'll fly out."

In pilot talk, this is known as "kicking the tires and lighting the fires." When I started out, I had taken on plenty of fuel for six hours of flying. Since it took two hours to get to Hot Springs, I decided it should take two hours going back, and I thought I would be in good shape.

After I took off I suddenly encountered some fairly heavy rain. I got on the instruments and rechecked everything thoroughly. That was when I noticed that my gas gauges read almost empty. Let me tell, you, flying at midnight, in a rainstorm over southeastern Oklahoma and nearly out of fuel, is not a good situation.

Feverishly, I dug out my charts to find the nearest airport so I could land pronto. I soon discovered Broken Bow International in Oklahoma. It wasn't much, but when I broke through the clouds and saw the lights of Broken Bow, it looked like the world's greatest airport to me.

I landed, parked near the fuel shack, and got out to see if I could find anyone to fuel my plane. It was raining so hard that I was soaked by the time I sprinted into the shack. Inside, I found a sign that read, "After ten o'clock, if you need fuel, call this number..."

There was a pay phone in the corner. I went over to use it, stuck my hand in my pocket and came up with a total of eight cents in change. I had more than $100 in my wallet, and back then it only took a dime to make a call, but none of that paper money was going to do me any good.

At that point I had two choices: I could hang out in the shack until the airport opened at seven in the morning, or I could hike down to the airport operator's house, which, according to a map in the shack, was about a quarter mile down the road. There wasn't anyplace in the shack to lie down, not even an old couch, so I decided to wake up the airport operator.

When I stepped out of the shack and onto the road behind it, my boot sank into nothing but mud. The only way to get to the operator's house was to take a dirt road in the pouring rain. I was wearing a brand new pair of expensive boots, a recent gift from my wife, but I wanted to leave Broken Bow that night, so I pressed on.

I sloshed through mud up to my ankles, disgusted with myself because it was all my fault. If I had done what I was supposed to do in Hot Springs, I would have been starting my descent into Dallas instead of ruining my new boots.

The airport director was a model of Southern hospitality and was happy to come out and fuel my plane. He drove me to the shack, brought the fuel truck around, and within minutes was yelling in to me, "What do you want me to do about these auxiliary tanks?"

My mind flashed and I asked, "What auxiliary tanks? My plane doesn't have auxiliary tanks."

About that time, he yelled again, "Oh, never mind, they're already full."

That was when I remembered that, though it appeared the same as the one I usually fly, this airplane was newer and had a different fuel system. Because I was not current in that particular plane, I didn't know it had auxiliary tanks and didn't know how to put them to use. I could have crashed with all that fuel on board.

I learned a lesson from this experience. I was reminded of the importance of staying current with the equipment you use so that you can tap the hidden reserves when you need them. In this situation, I could have crashed due to what I thought was fuel exhaustion, and burned up because of the fuel in the auxiliary tanks that I didn't know were there.

Biography

PATRICK O'DOOLEY

Patrick O'Dooley has inspired audiences in all 50 states and seven foreign nations. His goal is to make his meeting planners look good by giving his audience more than they expected. He offers the same commitment to his readers with his book *Flight Plan for Living*. Patrick draws upon his background as a college athlete, military officer and pilot, as well as his very successful years in business with IBM and Steelcase to bring stories and techniques to help you "fly" through life. He has chosen the flying analogy because, as a for-

mer professional pilot and now a private pilot, he sees many parallels between living a successful, happy and healthy life and techniques pilots use on today's high-speed jets. Patrick O'Dooley's research has given him a treasure trove of popular and effective anecdotes that illustrate simple principles of everyday living. He is a Certified Speaking Professional (CSP), the highest designation given by the National Speakers Association, on whose board of directors he has served. Patrick's programs are: *One Down and the B.E.S.T to Go!!* (Motivation*), How to Take the Cuss out of Customer Service, 8-1/2 Ways to Increase Sales* and *Team Building*.

COLONEL ROBERT K. (BOB) MORGAN (RET.)
Pilot, B-17 Memphis Belle (5th from left)

IT'S A LONG WAY TO WALLA WALLA

During my B-24 and B-17 transition training at MacDill Field, Tampa in 1942, I made a cross-country flight to my hometown in Asheville, North Carolina in a B-17. I had already earned the name of "Floorboard Freddy" because I constantly landed hot and burned out brakes.

Upon arriving in Asheville, I kept my reputation intact. I landed hot and burned out the brakes. The only solution was to call my commanding officer in Tampa. He had to send a crew to Asheville to fix my brakes, but he allowed me to fly the B-17 back to MacDill Field.

Since nothing was said upon my return, I thought I had eased right through this incident with my C.O., that everything had been forgiven and forgotten. But a couple weeks later I learned that he had neither forgiven nor forgotten the brake job.

My class was ordered to Walla Walla for advanced training, over 2,000 miles away. Much to my chagrin, my C.O. dealt me a shameful punishment. I was the *only* pilot grounded to surface transportation. While my pilot buddies sped through the skies, I slowly snaked across the United States riding the troop train from Tampa to Walla Walla, Washington.

We shot craps all the way.

I'D NEVER WALK A MILE FOR ONE

If you watch the 1943 William Wyler combat documentary, *Memphis Belle,* you will see me wildly waving a cigarette prior to boarding the Belle for her 25th mission. My wife, Linda, has seen the video numerous times and never commented on the cigarette. One evening, when it was shown prior to my being introduced at a banquet, she finally focused on the cigarette. She leaned over and whispered, "You never smoked! What were you doing with that cigarette?"

By the time this part of the documentary was filmed, the crew knew the film was going to be shown nationwide. In the 40's, cigarettes weren't considered a health concern. I figured I, the pilot of this historic flight, could make a killing doing Camel ads, but only if I made it quite evi-dent in the film I was a smoker, which I wasn't. You know... war hero, macho man, Camel man. I was already spending the money I would earn from becoming the new Camel spokesman. Flicking the ash, I was thinking, this is my big chance for Camel cigarettes to *find me.*

Much to my chagrin I never heard from Camel or any other tobacco company.

Colonel Robert K. (Bob) Morgan (3rd from left)
and crew of B-17 Memphis Belle

LIGHTS—CAMERAS—ACTION!

During one of my personal appearances in 1993, a bright
young man in the audience posed an interesting question. Why
was the Memphis Belle the first plane to take off on the 25th mission run, but the last to return? The 25th mission took us to Saint
Lorient, France to bomb German submarine pens and was actually quite uneventful. The suspense builds in the Wyler documentary as all eyes are focused on the horizon for the Belle. Was
she going to make her 25th mission or had she been mortally
wounded? William Wyler, being a hot Hollywood producer, did
some staging for our grand return to Bassingbourn. Just to keep
the ground crews tensely waiting, he had us circle north until all
the planes returned to base. Then, as the cameras rolled furiously to capture that golden moment, the Belle made her grand and
final entrance to Bassingbourn. Until that question arose 50
years later at the Seattle Museum of Flight, no one had ever
asked me about it. That's Hollywood!

Biography

COLONEL ROBERT K. MORGAN (RET.)

Col. Morgan was captain of the first B-17 to fly 25 successful missions in WWII. Actor Matthew Modine portrayed him in the movie, *Memphis Belle*. "In the 1990 movie it shows how the B-17s were entrusted to kids just out of high school or college," says Morgan. "A lot of war movies are fought by people John Wayne's age. But we were so young. We fussed and argued with each other, but on a mission, everybody fell into the puzzle and did their job." Eighty percent of the 91st Heavy Bombardment Group were lost

Bob, his wife Linda & pooches

after three months. "You wised up fast. The thing was to have the attitude that 'we were going out and we were coming back.' None of us knew the others had good luck charms, until the subject came up in the movie. We all had one, but kept them to ourselves. I kept my girl's picture on the instrument panel. We didn't *depend* on these things, but we had to have something to hang onto." After the Belle's 25th mission, the crew flew the war-torn bomber on a three-month goodwill tour to 20 U.S. cities. Bob banked the mighty flying fortress 60 degrees and flew right between his hometown courthouse and city hall, a distance considerably less than the width of the wings. Following the war bond tour, Morgan trained in B-29's and flew 25 more combat missions in the Pacific. On November 24, 1944 he led the first B-29 bombing raid on Tokyo.

MICHAEL MAYA CHARLES

PIREP: "SLICKER 'N OWL SNOT"

It was the worst winter storm in years. Sleet, freezing rain, ice pellets, snow and plunging temperatures had turned the Memphis International Airport into a skating rink. Only one runway, 9-27, was open. Traffic was backed up for hours. When ground control gave the OK to taxi, we began a slow plod toward Runway 9, behind another 727.

As we felt our way south to Runway 9, I noticed our lead 727's main gear was oddly misaligned with the nosewheel. A moment later, the mains were even more to the right of where they should have been. It took a moment for my brain to interpret the picture I was seeing. The 190,000 pound 727 in front of us was slowly weathervaning into the 12-knot east wind.

"Look at that!" I said to the crew, pointing to the Boeing as it spun slowly 50 degrees to the taxiway. The picture was unreal, but I automatically moved the tiller to maneuver our 727 into an area of rough snow and ice at the edge of the taxiway—just in case.

Curiously, the crew of the skating Boeing remained silent through the taxiway tour and made no comments on ground frequency. Perhaps, I thought, the crew was so surprised by the event, they didn't know what to say. I was sure they were careful not to call the braking action "nil." Our airline's ops manual prohibits us from taking off in "nil" runway conditions and therefore, the "n-word" is rarely spoken for fear of shutting down the operation.

When a lull in the ground chatter presented itself a few minutes later, I piped up, "Hey guys, the taxiway at the intersection of Quebec and Victor is slicker 'n owl snot."

A pregnant pause followed on ground frequency while the 60 tired pilots listening and an overtaxed ground controller digested my pilot report. Finally one pilot, with tongue planted firmly in cheek, asked, "Uh... ground, what was that about a slick taxiway?" You could hear the snickering in the cockpit when he depressed his mic button.

The ground controller, playing along with admirable professionalism and a straight face offered, "Uh, I think 'slicker 'n owl snot' is the same as 'poor'."

A PANTYHOSE PERFECT LANDING

Landings. Everybody makes such a big deal about landings. They're the only real measure of a pilot. Or are they?

We were flying a load of foul-mouthed, foul-smelling, forestry smoke jumpers around the hot, dry West in an attempt to save it from rampant summer fires. The girls in the back, though they smelled better, were about equal to the smoke jumpers in language and experience. These were no new sky waitresses. They had seen it all, done it all, and heard about the rest.

The Boeing 727 has a rather well-deserved reputation for occasional landings that make the one holding the little wheel up front look like a perfect beginner. I've seen pilots with thousands of hours in type make spine-shortening crunches, regardless of their best efforts. I'm certainly not without blood on my hands.

It had been a hard week of flying and we were heading back to our home base in Idaho, already tasting the cold beer waiting for us. We had one more landing to make, and then we would be off for a few days. The pilot flying was a kind, but scattered gentlemen who had lost his medical for a while then regained it some years later. His heart condition had cost him his major airline job. Now he flew for the non-scheds because they were the only ones that would hire him.

The last landing of the day looked like a piece of cake from where I sat, but my hands were not on the controls. The wind was from 300 degrees at seven knots. The air was smooth. Runway 29 was clear and dry. The jumpers in back were as quiet as falling ash. On final, the old man had the Boeing configured and slowed just like The Book instructed us. But The Book has a way of leaving you at about 50 feet. From there to the runway, it's all up to you.

Touchdown was a teeth-chattering cruncher and the old Boeing bounded into the air for more. But wheel spin-up on the brief touchdown had popped the spoilers from the upper wing surface, so the second landing was not pretty.

We taxied to the ramp without a word among us and shut down the 727, running our checklists and gathering our things, waiting patiently until the last passenger was gone before opening the cockpit door. When the door swung open, three flight attendants stood in a tight diamond formation in the entryway with their pantyhose rolled down around their ankles, smiling. "Who made *that* fine landing, boys?"

FOOTPRINTS IN THE SAND

[Originally appeared in *FLYING Magazine*, January 1992]

Perfect evening. Winds are light and variable. High, thin cirrus draw across the sky as the day begins to lie down. From just behind the row of trees off the end of the runway, I hear the unmistakable growl of a radial engine. Eyes darting for the first sign, I catch a glimpse of a worn yellow ag plane, heading straight for the airport at treetop level. The big single is aimed purposefully for the first third of the 3,300-foot concrete runway. Over the numbers, the power is slowly reduced to idle and the radial backs off with a fart and a pop. Without a bump or a bobble, the big tires of the ag plane smooth on the runway, tail high. Speed bleeds off and the tail comes down gently without a swerve or a dart. At midfield, the tired looking yellow biplane turns off the runway and taxies to the waiting tank truck parked beside the T-hangars. The plane rolls into position for the fill up, spins perfectly around without scrubbing the tires, and the mixture is cut. Impressive.

I went back to reading my *Trade A Plane* from the bench in front of the small FBO, wishing I was flying on such a perfect evening. Every airport that wishes to survive the onslaught of future rulemakers ought to install such a bench—preferably under a big oak tree—to view the runway, so that arrivals can be properly judged.

After a few minutes, the ag plane chugged back to life, and began a deliberate taxi for takeoff. The power was constant from startup to the end of the runway. No cowboy in that cockpit. His old, round engine would last forever with that kind of care.

At the runup area, the radial's symphony increased, mags and prop were checked. "Good for him," I mused. Even though he had been herding that old yellow bird around the tops of the trees all day, the pilot took the time to check his engine carefully before every flight.

The sound rose again to a fury, as the power smoothly came up for takeoff, late evening sun gleamed off the big, broad prop. The biplane's yellow slab sides drank deeply of the late sun, glowing richer and more beautiful than they probably were close-up.

Tail up, again, the unwavering precision and smoothness I'd witnessed on the landing. The airplane just rose from the runway without a change in pitch. I felt that I had seen something quite extraordinary in this simple bit of flying. There was a real artist at the controls of that airplane.

This pilot, whom I later saw from a distance, looked more like someone's doting grandfather than our usual concept of skill and professionalism. His thick, powerful legs told of many hours herding the biplane around the turns and between power poles. Blue jeans and gray work shirt, tail out, paunchy middle looking desperately for an escape, his flying told more of the story than his appearance.

Often, the pro in this aviation business is thought to be the one with the shiny shoes and tie, burning obscene amounts of kerosene at high altitudes. But the truth is, the pro is found many places in aviation. I've witnessed the pro flying banners along the beach above Daytona, flying night mail in a tired Twin Beech, sneaking along in a Jet Ranger between a 700 foot overcast and the Gulf of Mexico, or shoehorning a Twin Otter in among the boats of Vancouver Harbor. I've also ridden in the back of airliners on flights that began with a deliberate smoothness during taxi and no perception of turns or stops, and continued until level off at altitude without a noticeable pitch change or G-load. I'm tempted to genuflect as I pass the cockpit on the way off the airplane after such a flight.

A few weeks after witnessing the flight of the biplane, I rode with another professional pilot, only this one was not the type most would want to emulate. He flew the 727 as if to punish it—and all aboard. Just taxiing with this pilot was to brace for all turns and stops. The landing was without flare, too much reverse thrust was used on rollout. It was painful to ride with this fella, yet he called himself a professional. Like a few others in this business, he might even consider himself "God's gift to aviation."

Though most airplanes, including the Boeing, are built to take a real pounding, the care and consideration given a piece of equipment is an easy measure of a pilot's professionalism. My father's advice to me as a 10-year-old lad on the family farm tractor—my first piece of real machinery—was simple, "Treat the equipment right and it will treat you right."

Smoothness is one sure mark of a professional. Being smooth takes more effort and indicates a higher degree of intent, a willingness to work harder to polish the stone. It requires attention to the many subtle details of flying, and a willingness to make fine corrections before large ones are needed.

It takes very little study to perceive the difference between an airplane driver and a real professional pilot. Professionalism is simply an attitude, one's approach to the task, the desire on the individual's part to "do it right." Being professional requires a higher degree of personal discipline and self-mastery, a unique combination of raw talent and practiced skill that few are willing to work for.

We are judged more by the many subtle things we do than the grand overtures that are more easily observed. As pros we must remember that all the rhetoric in the world, including our former lives as an ace with Uncle Sam's Air Force or as a freight pilot for some fly-by-night operation, will not speak so loudly as our thoughtful attention to every moment of our flying.

I was grateful for the example shown by the grandfather in the yellow biplane. The aviator's attitude, not the cockpit's altitude, determines professionalism. Whether we fly a Grumman Yankee, a Grumman Gulfstream V, a 747-400 or an old, tired, yellow Snow ag plane, our approach to flying should be the same. We should fly as if someone is watching us, evaluating our every move. Because they are. No matter where we step, we leave footprints in the sand.

SAY... DIDN'T YOU USED TO FLY FOR THE NAVY?

It's often helpful to learn the backgrounds of the pilots with whom we share our cockpits. I usually ask my crew about their previous flying experience and often learn things that help me understand why they make some of the choices they do. On one night's descent into a major airport, this information proved handy.

A winter cold front had passed the area and the wind had shifted to the north behind the front. When we arrived from the northeast, the controller first offered Runway 36 Left. Winds were 010 degrees at 18 gusting to 22 knots. But traffic was heavy and a few moments later, the controller said, "You can have Runway 27 if you'd like. Wind is now 350 at 18 knots. I looked at my first officer and offered him the choice since it was his landing. A bit of a crosswind, but nothing that couldn't be handled.

"Sure," he said, "...if you'll back me up."

I thought he was kidding about backing him up, but grinned and told the controller we'd take the east-west runway.

As we descended through 8,000, it occurred to me that perhaps he wasn't kidding about "backing him up." "Say, John... didn't you tell me you used to fly for the Navy?"

"Sure did," he replied, a little puzzled about the timing of the question.

"And don't they always turn the ship into the wind when you land?" I asked.

His sheepish grin and nervous laugh spread throughout the cockpit. I watched him closely on landing. He smoothed it on, upwind wheel first, just like he had been taught in T-34C's during primary flight training.

Some guys do well in spite of their training.

FAMOUS COMEDIAN HELD PRISONER IN A BIZJET!

There's more to corporate flying than gentle landings, leveling off smoothly at altitude and being available when the boss needs to go somewhere at 3 a.m. That's the easy part. A corporate pilot is judged more by the way little details are handled, such as hotel reservations, limos, taxis, rental cars, and of course, catering.

Our flight was from home base in Little Rock, Arkansas to Burbank, California to pick up comedian Bob Hope. Old "Ski Nose" was to speak in our little Southern town at a gala to raise funds for a worthy cause. As often happens in the world of money, favors, influence and appearances, the ride was provided free by my boss, one of the town's wealthiest magnates.

Our brand new Canadair Challenger was an impressive airplane, one of the first to have the new "glass cockpit." The wide-body cabin had passenger-pampering capacious seats, a full bar, a bathroom with gold fixtures, a TV monitor continuously showing our exact position (updated by VLF-Omega), a fantastic 10 speaker stereo system and even a foldout king-sized bed. Opulence fit for the king of comedy.

The forward galley was normally stocked with all the little nibbles and libations one could ever want. But this trip was a last-minute addition to the schedule and we were very low on those "stores." Unable to restock before the flight, we called a trusted caterer in Burbank who agreed to have food and drinks waiting for the trip back to Little Rock.

During descent into the murky Los Angeles basin airspace, I called the FBO to request a quick-turn refueling and asked about our catering order. "Not here," they said. "We'll call them." After landing, we taxied up to the FBO and shut down, 10 minutes early.

While I was explaining the required fuel load to the line supervisor, a new Cadillac rolled up and parked next to the shiny white jet. An older woman drove. In the front passenger seat sat the famous comedian looking a little aged, but his smile and eyes still had that magic sparkle. We introduced ourselves, then Cory, our flight attendant, took Mr. Hope into the cabin to make him comfortable while we loaded his baggage.

The refueling went smoothly, but the customer service representative told us the caterer still had not arrived. Our frantic call to the company was met with assurances that "the food should be on the way." A driver had called in sick and the caterer was running late with deliveries. We told Mr. Hope and his manager of our problem. Should we wait for the food or cast off for Little Rock? The decision was to go.

Normally our creative flight attendant would have been able to take the missing catering in stride by substituting something from the galley. But with our low supplies, even Cory was hard pressed. As I strapped into the cockpit seat, I suggested Cory try card tricks, or perhaps a tap dance routine.

Somewhere over New Mexico, I left the flight deck to relieve my aching bladder. The short turnaround in California had left no time for personal needs. In the tradition of oceangoing vessel captains, I stopped to chat with the passengers as I headed aft through the cabin. When I reached Mr. Hope, I asked him how we were treating him. With typical dry wit and comedic timing, he said, "The flight is fine, but I feel like I'm in a concentration camp. All they'll feed me back here is water and dry crackers!"

Biography

MICHAEL MAYA CHARLES

Michael Maya Charles began flying at age 11 and started his aviation career as a line boy for a small FBO. By the time he was 21, he had earned an ATP and CFII and chalked up over 4,000 hours. Through the years, he managed a Part 141 flight school, owned two Part 135 charter companies, sold new corporate turboprops, and worked as chief pilot for several corporations.

Michael's interest in journalism began in high school, when he was editor of his school newspaper, and continued through his college years at Ohio State. He began contributing photography and writing to *FLYING* magazine in the mid 70s, though he is perhaps best known as author of the popular monthly column *Pro's Nest.*

Now with over 18,000 hours, Michael is a captain for a major airline as well as a licensed A&P. His current writing can be found in the pages of *AOPA Pilot* magazine and a monthly column in *AVweb,* the *Internet Aviation magazine.*

In addition, Michael offers his expertise as a consultant and expert witness.

For more of Captain Charles' stories and flying philosophy, read his new book, *Artful Flying.*

ROD MACHADO

CAPTAIN GWINN'S LAST TWA FLIGHT

Captain Dave Gwinn is a well-known radar expert whom I've used as a resource many times. He is a dear friend who has an awesome sense of humor. We're always kidding each other. An opportunity to fly in the cockpit on an airline captain's last flight is rare. It is especially rare when the captain is a dear friend. I was fortunate enough to have that experience with Dave.

On November 12th, 1998, I flew from Orange County, arriving at the TWA gate in St. Louis as Captain Dave was punching in the door combination to board his DC-9.

From 20 feet I yelled, "Hey, let's see your boarding pass, mister."

I must have startled him because he patted his left shirt pocket, in search of either a boarding pass, chewing gum or heart palpitations.

He had no idea I was going to be there. Since Dave enjoys playing pranks and practical jokes on others, I took great satisfaction at seeing the look of surprise on his face. We hugged like lost buddies. Then I showed him my cockpit authorization. Of course, I showed it to him from a distance, then pretended to read from it.

"Dave," I quipped, "it says here that I'm not only allowed to ride in the cockpit on both flights, but that I can fly the airplane if I really want to."

Suddenly he began patting his left shirt pocket again.

"Hey, I was just kidding about that boarding pass," I said.

"I'm not looking for a boarding pass," he responded "I'm checking for heart palpitations."

And that's the way the flight began.

For years I've been telling people that Dave calls me from the cockpit just so I can talk him down. Well, let me quash any rumors. I didn't go along on his last flight just to save long distance telephone charges.

We departed St. Louis flying to Chicago on a round trip that Thursday morning. On board were several of Dave's friends. The copilot, Tom Hernon, had specifically bid to fly with Dave on this flight. Several other TWA admirers also bid for this copilot slot but Tom beat them to it and wasn't about to give it up.

As we taxied for takeoff, Dave, true to form, commenced giving me the business. "Hmmm, what does that switch do?" he mused out loud. Nice try. Then I mentioned that I probably wouldn't see much of his takeoff since it's difficult to see things with my hands over my eyes. Well, it was obvious that I wasn't about to nonplus the master with my shenanigans.

The takeoff was spectacular. The mechanical action of lifting tens of thousands of pounds of metal into the air with a simple curl of the yoke is an impressive sight. Dave rolled the airplane into a 30-degree left bank, flipped a few switches and we were on our way to Chicago. As my friend guided his airplane through a departure, I was filled with an enormous sense of pride. "I know this man to be a gifted teacher, skillful communicator and masterful writer," I thought. "Now I'm finally getting to see him do what he's done most of his life, and done so well—fly airplanes."

It's in the nature of an instrument instructor to watch the needles. I did. And they weren't moving. Not that I'm surprised by an airline pilot's ability to hold altitude, heading and airspeed, but there was such an economy of motion in Dave's actions. Every movement seemed purposeful and calculated, not wasted.

Dave made it look easy.

So easy, in fact, that I thought, "Hey, I could fly this thing just like Dave." But I know better. Experience taught me a long time ago that a master makes a complex task look effortless. The illusion of effortless action is the ultimate manifestation of skill. When I leaned over and said, "Captain, you make this look so easy," I realized that I had just given the highest compliment one pilot can give another.

Dave was the essence of professionalism. I even mentioned this to him and commented on how surprised I was that his use of the phrase "Center, who-dah-man?" would be so well received by ATC on every call. OK, he didn't really say that.

Out of 12,000 feet, we approached a vertical wall of clouds. Dave quipped, "These are the times that make me wish I had an instrument rating." He was at it again. In response, I desperately wanted to say, "Ah, Captain, I think the PA system was active when you said that." But I didn't. I couldn't stop laughing long enough.

Enroute, Tom informed the Captain that he could expect a right crosswind at Chicago. Dave slapped his left leg, patted his right hand, then joked, "OK, that means we gotta push this leg and twist that arm."

Dave Gwinn and Tom Hernon

Hey, I did my homework. I was prepared for my pal's mischievousness. You see, I've heard the stories about Captain Dave pointing out the Euphrates and Nile rivers to unsuspecting passengers on the St. Louis to Chicago route. I wasn't about to fall for that ruse. Besides, I was too busy looking for the pyramids. On the return flight Dave announced the presence of the large arches in St. Louis, which, he explained, commemorated Missouri's annual croquet tournament.

The return trip was too quick. "I could get to like it up here," I thought, "this is fun." Yes, it is fun, especially when Dave's the captain. ATC gave us permission to level off at cloud-top level where we skipped along puffs of stratus. "Isn't this beautiful?" Dave asked, "isn't it simply beautiful?" A pilot who can still say that after decades of flying is someone who has never lost sight of what flying is all about.

Pulling the DC-9 into a smooth steep climb, he pointed skyward toward the wispy contrails of an invisible airplane. "Look up there," Dave said. "That's the Hale-Bopp comet. Can you see it, Rod?"

"Oh, I'm sorry, Captain," I replied, "I was busy looking outside trying to find the Euphrates River, and I'm really upset that I didn't get to see the Sphinx, either." And that's the way it went on the trip home.

There were quiet moments, too. These were moments of existential reverie, which stayed cockpit banter, moments when I mulled over the thought that Dave would never fly as a TWA pilot again. "This was the last time," I thought, "the last time he'll land this airplane, the last time he'll move those throttles, the last time he'll pull into this gate." It was sad in that way, but then I remembered that the general aviation community now gets Dave full time. TWA's loss is our gain!

As we approached the terminal, I peeked out the window at the jetway. Lining the walls were Dave's friends, a gathering of fellow pilots, admirers and well-wishers. Among them were several young pilots who credit Dave for helping them with their airline careers. "How sad, how sad, how sad," I thought. "All those people out there and not one of them is wearing a Groucho Marx nose and glasses. How could I ever forgive myself for letting that happen?"

As we walked through the terminal a confused elderly lady asked for help. Though we were on our way to a celebratory lunch, Dave, the consummate compassionate instructor, stopped and patiently gave her directions.

It's obvious that Dave is like many of us. He's a pilot who has never lost his passion for aviation and never lost sight of what flying is all about.

This was one of the very best times I've had in aviation. I was proud to share it with my friend and the friends of my friend. It's an experience I'll never forget.

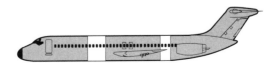

GOTCHA

Aviation flourished in the early 70's. Its technology seemed to change every nanosecond. The delivery of each new airplane brought an air of excitement as pilots rushed to glimpse the latest gadgets and gismos on the instrument panel. As two fledgling flight instructors, Tim Peterson and I were no exception. Tim was my instructor for my multi-engine flight instructor rating. I was Tim's instructor for his certified flight instructor instrument rating. Tim and I each relished acquiring and sharing knowledge. We were both equally fascinated with aviation's latest gadgets.

One day, Tim casually mentioned to me that he had just purchased a mechanism akin to an HSI, only better. Tim claimed it had numerous navigational capabilities and also displayed DME information. Remember this was years before GPS and Loran were even a glimmer in the eye of some clever engineer. Tim excitedly described the new avionics as combining four separate instruments into one. I voiced my skepticism. Tim insisted. His new purchase had multiple capabilities in a single black box. In fact, he had the $7,000 exotic piece of equipment in his car, if I would like to look at it.

Unbeknown to me, the impressive looking black box was a gift to Tim from a military buddy. The unit was no longer in production, nor was it of any use, unless you happen to be a master prankster.

Tim had doctored the black box. He had removed the retaining screws and packed the case with extra screws, wires and electrical gadgetry, then carefully slipped the instrument back into its casing without the screws. Straightfaced, Tim opened his car trunk, took out the black box and proudly displayed it for me. To distract his victim's attention, Tim kept up a continuous monologue as he handed me the box upside down. I couldn't examine the instrument face with its many dials and cards, so I turned this marvel of technology to the vertical position.

SWOOSH! CLANG! CLATTER!

The innards of this instrument dropped from the back of its casing, crashing to the ground. A million screws, pieces of wires and extraneous electronic parts scattered everywhere.

To have seen my face! A number roughly the size of the national debt, the number of students times the number of years it would take to pay for the damage, flashed before my eyes. I saw myself in perpetual bondage to flight students in Cessna 150s.

Tim interrupted my higher math and started hollering like a banshee. "Rod," he shouted in mock outrage. "How could you be so careless? That's an expensive piece of precision equipment!" The commotion drew a large crowd of onlookers. After a few minutes Tim could no longer contain himself and started laughing. When I realized I had been duped, boy, was I mad.

Twenty some years later, we are still best of friends. However, Tim is still a bit nervous. Because some day, some time, some place, when he least expects it... it's payback time!

Biography

ROD MACHADO

Rod Machado "MACH 2 WITH MACHADO" is the byline Rod Machado has earned for his rapid fire delivery at his lively safety seminars and keynote speeches. Rod has three distinctively different types of programs: information-packed, psychological and purely humorous. He has spoken in all 50 of the United States and in Europe. As a writer for *AOPA Pilot* and *Flight Training* magazines, Rod reflects his fresh approach to education. He says, "People learn best when they are having fun." This is

why humor is omni-present in *Rod Machado's Private Pilot Handbook*, a complete general aviation resource filled with over 1,100 of Rod's original illustrations and photos. *Rod Machado's Instrument Pilot's Survival Manual* is an example of how Rod simplifies the difficult and uses humor to help the lessons stick. He is the instructor voice and wrote the lesson plans for Microsoft's Flight Simulator 2000. With degrees in psychology and aviation science he is ATP rated with all fixed wing flight instructor ratings. His 8,000 hours were earned the hard way, one CFI hour at a time.

DEAN S. ENGELHARDT

DUANE COLE'S EYE EXAM

I started flying airshows in a Ryan PT-22, but my favorite air-show airplane was the Aeronca 7AC Champ with a C-85 engine. My Champ was specially rigged and licensed to fall apart in midair. I could drop up to three of the control surfaces: the rudder, left elevator and the right aileron. If I was doing a full aerobatic routine, I would only drop the left aileron, since it was most difficult to control the airplane in unusual attitudes with the rudder, left elevator and right aileron missing.

With the three control surfaces missing, I could turn left by applying either left or right aileron—adverse yaw swung the plane left. To turn right I had to reach behind me to open the door as far as possible for adverse yaw in that direction. I enjoyed pulling people's legs at strange airports with the Champ and would sometimes lose pieces on takeoff or landing.

One weekend on my return flight from an aerobatics show, I stopped off in Reno at Duane Cole's Flight School. Duane taught aerobatics in a Citabria. I stayed overnight with Duane and his family.

In the morning, as we drove to the airport, Duane asked me if he could borrow my Champ. I was puzzled by the request but said, "Sure!" As we entered the flight school, his first student was already there, waiting for him.

Duane told the student, "My plane is not flyable today, so I'm using another Citabria that's painted up for an airshow. So ignore appearances and just preflight it."

What was Duane doing? My airplane was restricted from flying passengers and from instruction. In addition, the left aileron was stowed in the cockpit, leaving a gapping hole in the left wing. As the door closed behind the student, Duane turned to me and said, "This is the same student who preflighted my Citabria and didn't see that the propeller was missing!" At that, everyone in the flight school turned to watch the preflight.

Presently, the student returned and announced the plane was ready. "You've checked everything?" Duane asked.

The student responded, "All set to go."

Duane said, "Well, I don't see a left aileron on that airplane!" Turning, the student had the most incredulous look on his face when he saw that the plane was indeed missing a major piece.

"Ohmygosh!" was all he could say.

THE PROFESSIONAL STUDENT

Seems everyone in Alaska flies. It's the only way to get around most places. When I worked in Alaska as a bush pilot, I picked up some extra money by flight instructing out of Anchorage International. One day, a student came to me wanting to get his private license. He showed me his logbook with 260 hours of dual. He had never soloed. As I flipped through the pages, I saw a number of instructors, none staying with him for more than a few hours. I asked why no one had soloed him.

"They tried to cheat me out of my money," was all he said.

I figured, after 260 hours, he should be able to fly the plane, so I had him fly the pattern to see how he flew. We flew the pattern several times. I didn't need to grab the controls, but I had this nagging feeling that something wasn't right. I finally realized that I was telling him every time when to turn.

I told him to make a full stop and taxi back to the runup area. I reviewed the turn points for the pattern and asked him to repeat them back to me. He did. It was clear he had a full understanding of the appropriate turning points to fly a standard landing pattern. We took off to try again. Each time we flew the pattern he would continue every leg straight ahead. Again, I would have to tell him when to turn.

After touchdown I had him stop and told him, "This time, you fly the pattern without me saying anything." We took off. As I expected, we flew past the point where he should have turned crosswind. Ten minutes later, we passed over the shoreline on the Kenai Peninsula. 45 minutes later, Kenai could be seen in the distance off our starboard wing. 90 minutes after takeoff, Seward passed beneath our nose. Ahead was Seattle—more than 1,500 miles away. Since I doubted that the Cessna 150 could fly that far, I asked, "What are we doing?"

"Touch and goes" was the answer as he continued to fly straight-ahead.

"When are you going to turn crosswind?"

"Oh!" he said and turned crosswind.

He logged another hour-and-a-half of dual that day.

A LASTING IMPRESSION

As I sit at my desk, I can see a photo of my father, my inspiration, standing with the entire Curtiss design team in front of a Condor biplane airliner. This wasn't Lloyd Frederick Engelhardt's first design effort. That honor belongs to the Curtiss Robin, the same plane that Douglas "Wrong Way" Corrigan flew to Europe shortly after Lindbergh's famous flight. I asked him why he made it so heavy. Dad replied that he was unsure of his first practical stress analysis attempts, so he just added wall thickness to the entire structure. Certainly none of the Robin aircraft ever suffered structural failure.

One of dad's first military efforts was the Curtiss F9C Sparrowhawk. This Navy fighter hooked on to the trapeze on the underside of a giant dirigible. The F9C had a gull-shaped upper

Lloyd Engelhardt, designer of the Condor, is second from right.

wing to allow good visibility toward the airship's trapeze and the airplane had a hook on a framework attached to that wing. The pilot could reach outside the cockpit to a handle that would open the hook mechanism to fly away from the mother airship. Historians have said that the Sparrowhawk was a failed carrier fighter that was later modified for airship hook-on duties.

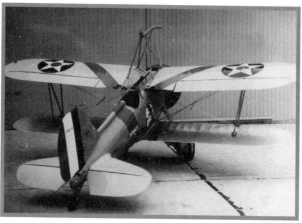

Curtiss F9C Sparrowhawk with hook.

Dad said that this was a ruse to preserve security during its development and that it was always intended to land on airships, not sea ships. (Historians persist in thinking that dusty archives always tell the truth! They think that governments never lie.)

After a lifetime of work, dad's final efforts were on Mercury and Gemini spacecraft. Following the launchpad fire with the Apollo One astronauts, McDonnell received the contract to redesign the escape system. Dad came up with a concept that included reducing the time requirements to open the door from 90 seconds to three seconds. Because of this important contribution, NASA honored dad by naming a crater on the backside of the moon after him. Engelhardt Crater is just above the Korolev Crater on the equator.

Lloyd Frederick Engelhardt

On clear nights with a full moon, my family wishes the moon would turn 180 degrees so we could see "our" crater.

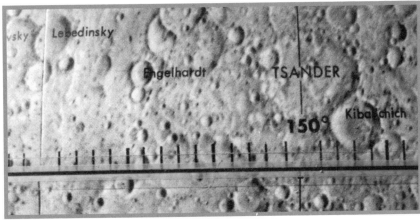

Dad's highest honor. His own crater.

IDENTITY CRISIS

My introduction to movie stunt flying came while I was an aerobatics instructor. One of my students was a director and stunt pilot wanting advanced instruction. He decided that the flight that he was training for was too dangerous, so he offered the job to me. With one flight for a television episode of *Mannix*, my career was on its way.

While flying for movies and television, I doubled for the actors.

For another television show, I was made up as a 20-year-old buxom blonde helicopter pilot. To double for the actress, they gave me the works: latex face remolding, long hair, large breasts, tight blouse and slacks. It took two hours of work. With my new look, I walked over to the crewmember who was guarding my helicopter. He immediately started flirting with me. I gave him about 40 seconds then I said, "John, I flew you here in this helicopter!" He reacted as if I'd stuck his fingers in a light socket.

On the set of *Birds of Prey* David Janssen was very friendly to all cast and crew. His motorhome that he kept on the set was half playboy bedroom.

With padding under my blouse I doubled for a pretty young Ann Lockhart in a balloon crash. (I'm the one on the left.) Working as Second Unit Director on the movie *Ole Ole Oxen Free*, I snapped this candid shot of screen legend, Kate Hepburn. She was genuine and nice to everyone.

To look like Buddy Epson my hair was sprayed white.

FIRST FLIGHT

When I first started dating my wife Jeanene, she knew I was a pilot although she had yet to fly with me. Since she had flown in a Cessna 172 with another boyfriend, I wanted to take her up in something more impressive. I borrowed a C-18 Twin Beech from a friend at Flabob Airport, put her in the copilot seat, and climbed out to the north to show her the snow on Mt. Baldy.

As we circled the summit, the prop governor failed on the left engine. No problem. I shut the left engine down, turned for home, and reset the manifold pressure on the right engine at 34 inches. Within two minutes of shutting down the left engine, a fire started in the right engine. No problem (Right!). I immediately executed the emergency procedures and had the right engine shut down in moments.

With both engines out, the C-18 glides like a brick, so I wasted no time in restarting the left, not caring if I damaged the engine during the return to Flabob.

After the plane was safely on the ground, I took Jeanene out to Elsinore to go glider flying. I wanted to show her you don't really *need* engines to fly. While preparing to leave, I found out what she thought of losing two engines over the mountains when I heard her describing our morning adventure to someone nearby. "I knew something was wrong," said Jeanene, "because I had never seen him that serious or quiet before."

WHAT AIRLINE DO YOU FLY FOR?

In the movie, *The Island*, starring Michael Caine, I was hired to fly the DC-3 in the Bahamas and crash it. The crash sequence was pretty spectacular. The DC-3 would bellyland and slide into the rocks on the side of the runway, burst into flames and explode. The director wanted to shoot the crash sequence separate from the explosion, so my copilot and I would crash the airplane and the explosion would be a separate shot. Even though the explosion was to be a separate shot, they needed footage of the crew in the explosion. So, our airline uniforms were made up to look like we'd been in the explosion.

After the crash, I asked my mechanic to tear out the control wheel, which I kept for a souvenir. I took the control wheel, picked up the flight manual and quickly headed for the company charter plane to Nassau. I didn't bother to change because I was in a hurry to meet my wife, who was flying in to join me for a few days' vacation.

As we taxied in, the DC-10 carrying my wife was also taxiing in. I asked to be dropped off at the terminal. As I walked through a gate door into the terminal, I was confronted with a long line of people waiting to board their flight. They all stared at me—wearing an airline uniform that looked like it had been through an explosion and carrying a control wheel with broken cables hanging off of it in one arm and a flight manual in the other. The fifth passenger in line asked me, "What airline do you fly for?"

I read the name of the airline on his ticket holder, which I'll call "X" to protect the innocent. "Airline X", I replied, whereupon he spun on his heels and left the terminal.

Shot on scene of the movie *The Island* in which
Dean crashes a DC-3 surrounded by pyrotechnics.

Biography

DEAN ENGELHARDT

Dean Engelhardt is the wacky and witty stunt pilot who has successfully crashed 14 aircraft on purpose! He has been featured on television shows such as *Banachek, The Rockford Files, The Six Million Dollar Man, Chase, Little House on the Prairie* and *Cannon.* Dean's film work includes *Airport 79', Charlie* and *The Great Balloon Chase* and *Breakout.* Among aircraft he has flown (and crashed) are a DC-3 and several hot air balloons. His 14,000 hours in the air includes every class and category of aircraft and his pilot experience ranges from experimental-test, movie stunts, Alaskan bush, seaplane instructor and aerobatic airshow to competition flying. Dean's two programs are crowd pleasers. Recommended for all groups, *Crashing Aircraft for Fun and Profit* is a very humorous, illustrated talk about the little-known career of a motion picture stunt pilot. *How to Survive an Aircraft Crash* draws on Dean's experiences as an engineer and test pilot. This presentation shows pilots what to do when the chips are down and they're going in.

WALLY FUNK

WALLY'S WING WALKING

In 1961, I taught aerobatics in a T-6, a Waco and a Stearman out of Wright Flying Service in Hawthorne, California. Communications were pretty basic in the Stearman, there were no fancy headsets or voice-actuated microphones or intercoms. We communicated with the tower by wiggling our wings in response to the light gun. I had my own special means of communicating with the student pilot flying in the back seat of the Stearman. Whenever I wanted to talk to him, I would slow up the Stearman, crawl out of the front seat, place one leg on the wing running area, keep the other leg in the cockpit seat and face the student. I was half in and half out.

The guys in the tower used to get a real big kick when they saw me on downwind half in and half out of the cockpit. I was usually giving the student the dickens for making a lousy landing and not keeping the stick back to keep the tail down. If the student didn't keep the stick back, the Stearman tail wheel would bob up and down, up and down, right into a ground loop. In those days airplanes parked close to the edge of the runway. If the pilot did not make a pretty deadeye straight landing, the Stearman would ground loop right into those planes. I didn't allow any student to solo until he was making perfect landings.

VERONICA LAKE

In the 60's and 70's, when I could arrange a three-day weekend, I instructed students out of Palm Springs. I scheduled students in the early hours of the morning, around 5 a.m., when it was cool and there was no traffic. It was great. I got to fly, get away from the FAA and the NTSB and have fun with my friends.

One of my more memorable students was a celebrity hair stylist named Erma, who had a Veronica Lake hairdo. Erma entertained us in the flight office with her stories of Pierre Salinger and the Kennedys and $100 tips for a haircut.

She was a very skilled young lady. She did everything well, except land an airplane. She'd botch up the last bit of the flare-out. She performed all the other maneuvers just perfectly.

Her husband was getting on my case, "When are you going to solo her? When are you going to solo her?"

"Don't bug me," I told him. "She'll solo when she feels right, I feel right, the plane feels right, the day feels right, the tower feels right, the sun feels right, and she's ready."

Next time she came in for a landing and started her flare, everything looked great. Then everything fell apart in the last 15

Wally at Hawthorne Airport, 1962

seconds. She just plopped it in. I thought, "I have to do something to fix this. The poor nose gear can't take too much more of this abuse." So, on her next landing, I leaned around and looked at her square in the face. By golly, I saw the problem. She couldn't see through her Veronica Lake hairdo. The Veronica Lake hairdo is long hair down the back and over the left eye down on the left shoulder. Without her left eye, she had to use her right eye to see over the cowling and down the runway, and of course, she never really saw where the runway was. Her depth perception was absolutely obliterated.

I said, "Erma, I'll fly the airplane. Get that hair out of your eyes. Tie it back." I grabbed an old rubber band wrapped around my clipboard. She used it to make a pony tail out of her hair. I gave her back the airplane and she started another landing. Every time she turned her head to look around for traffic, her ponytail swished into my face. She came in for her first landing, and greased it on. It was beautiful. I said, "Okay, make two more of those and we'll see if it's not a fluke."

She took off, flew around the pattern, called, came in, and flared right past the numbers every time. She did a beautiful job.

Kissed that little main gear on the runway and held the nose gear up just like she was supposed to. We taxied down to the south end of the runway. The wind was out of the north. I said, "Okay, kid, I'm sick of flying with you. Let me watch you from down here. You go make three takeoffs and landings. Make your first two touch and goes, and don't forget to come back to pick me up."

Her husband and all their friends watched from behind some bushes up at the north end by the terminal, while I stood on the south end watching. She made three beautiful landings. After the third landing, instead of taxiing down to pick me up, she just turned around and back taxied on the runway to the terminal. I stood at the edge of the runway watching the airplane get smaller and smaller. Oh my gosh, here I am a mile and a half away from everything, and she forgot me. Those were the days before hand-held radios, so I had no way to call the tower. I didn't have much choice, so I ran up the side of the runway. It took me a good 10 to 12 minutes to run it.

When I reached the airplane, the champagne was already flowing and the caviar was out. Erma and her husband and friends were whooping and hollering it up and hugging each other. When I made the last few feet to the airplane, I asked, "What in the world do you think you were doing not coming back to pick me up?"

"After my last landing," said Erma, "I was so excited I did it, I completely forgot about you."

When she was part way in, the tower called her and said, "Well, hey, go back and get Wally."

Erma said, "Oh, the heck with her. I'm mad at her because she soloed me. Let her walk." That brought down the house.

MERCURY SPACE CANDIDATE POST PROGRAM ADVENTURES

When Valentina Tereshkova made her historic flight in 1963, Russia beat the United States in the race to put the first female astronaut in space. I had just completed three phases of the Mercury Space Candidate-training Program, including being measured for a space suit. Then the U.S. scrapped the Mercury Space Program and we were left up in the air.

I decided to travel to Europe, see the Paris Air Show, and then on to Russia. I didn't meet Valentina then because the Russians didn't want anyone from the West talking to their cosmonauts. They didn't want the West to discover the type of launch or reentry procedures they used.

(Years later, I met Valentina. We talked about her training and missions. She confided, "Oh, well, we can tell you now. As soon as we hit the troposphere I exited out backside of space capsule. It was like being shot out a cannon." She floated down in her parachute, next to the capsule with its parachute. Of course, the capsule floated a little faster than she did. The Russians had claimed their cosmonauts reentered in their capsules. Valentina was picked, in part, because she was a parachutist. She had no technical knowledge whatsoever.)

After Europe, I traveled in North Africa and Egypt. I couldn't visit Sudan because many main roads were mined in 1965. So I drove my Volkswagen camper across the northern part of Egypt and Libya. I ran into a 29-man Marine station in the middle of Libya. To see the American flag out in the middle of the desert was really incredible. I wheeled right in. They welcomed me with great gusto. I ate American peanut butter and drank coffee and spoke with Americans. It was great fun. I even got to wash my clothes in a real washing machine instead of using the Mediterranean Sea.

One evening while sharing stories from the good old USA, one chap said he worked on the Mercury Space Program in Pensacola where the last phase of training was to take place. He said if the program hadn't been canceled, he would have suited me in my space suit. He told me a name like "Wally Funk" was hard to forget.

I missed the Gemini program, which started in 1965. I was overseas from 1965 to 1968 on a goodwill ambassador trip, lecturing on space, and learning about flying in different parts of the world. I traveled Africa and found it quite interesting. After driv-

In 1961, Wally Funk was one of 13 women aviators selected as astronaut candidates for the Mercury 13 program and sworn to secrecy. These women took the same rigorous tests as the male candidates, many times outperforming the men. In spite of each woman's outstanding test results, these talented women would never get a chance to fly into space with the NASA program. Undaunted, Wally has trained with cosmonauts and astronauts in preparation to go into space with the civilian sector.

In 1960 Wally was the first female flight instructor at Fort Sills. She soloed 400 U.S. Army military officers.

ing across Northern Africa, I took a ship down the west side on into Angola for a couple of safaris, then into South Africa and Mozambique where I spent six months studying their ways of flying.

Obtaining a pilot's license in Africa, or even getting a medical, was very difficult. It took months because everything had to go to Victoria for approval. Their standards were very high. I couldn't get into Tanzania, so I turned back and took a ship to Madagascar and the Spice Islands. I spent some time in Kenya learning their flying techniques. Eventually I made it to Israel and back into Europe. It was quite a trip and quite an adventure.

13 DAY ORIGAMI PILOT

When I lived in Taos, New Mexico, I got a phone call from a young lady named Susan from Topanga, California. "Wally, I understand you can teach people to fly in two weeks."

I told her it was possible. I could set up an intensive flight training program where a student could get her license in two weeks. She told me that's what she wanted to do. "Okay, Susan, get your medical, a second class medical (I wanted to make sure she was real healthy), and after you pass the private pilot written, call me." She agreed. I thought I'd never hear from her again.

Two months later I got a another call from Susan. She had her medical, made a 98 on the written, saved some money and wanted to come out to Taos. I said, "That's great, Susan! When do you want to come to Taos?"

She said, "How about in two weeks?"

I told her that was pretty soon, but I thought I could manage it. I found her a place to stay on the mesa and made sure the Cessna 150 was available for two weeks. Since I hadn't met her, I thought I had better ask her some personal information. I said, "Susan, how old are you?"

She said, "21."

I said, "Well, that's good. Do you drink?" She said, "No." I said, "That's good too because alcohol and flying don't mix. Do you smoke?" She said, "No." I said, "That's terrific, because smoking cuts down on your night vision."

I went on, "Now we start out at 7,000 feet MSL, we do our maneuvers at 10 and 12,000 feet. I need to know how much you weigh." She said 150 pounds. My experience in the Cessna 150 at Taos altitudes suggests a student limit of 150 pounds. I prefer the student to be around 130 pounds. I weighed around 115 pounds. "Susan," I said, "I think we may have a problem with the altitude in Taos. Is there any way that you could lose some weight? I could probably drop one or two pounds and we could wear some real light clothes. What do you think?"

She said, "Well, gosh, I don't know... I might be able to lose a couple of pounds."

I said, "Well, how come you can't lose any more than that?"

"Because I'm 6-3," she replied.

I didn't know how I was even going to fit her into a Cessna 150.

Wally and Susan

So I told her to come on out and we'd see what we could do. She arrived at midnight and we started flying at "O-dark-thirty" the next day. I had to fold her into the cockpit, legs underneath her chin, in front of the yoke.

We flew. And we flew. Because of the density altitude, we never really got to pattern altitude too many times even though we began flying at 5 a.m. Nevertheless, we'd fly until the winds picked up at 9 a.m. Then we started in again around 6 p.m. and flew until 10 at night. I soloed her on the third day. She did an excellent job.

I found out she had two engineering degrees and designed satellites for Hughes Aircraft. She just did such a wonderful job. She got her private license, starting from scratch, in 13 days!

Susan had never been in a little airplane before. We became good friends. Now I babysit her 1957 Cessna 172 when she's in France on business.

Biography

WALLY FUNK

At age 16, Wally entered Stephens College in Columbia, Missouri and graduated first in her flight training class of 24. By the time she had turned 20, she had a B.S. in secondary education plus enough ratings to become a flight and ground instructor at Oklahoma State University. At OSU she captured top honors as The Outstanding Female Pilot, The Flying Aggie Top Pilot and took home the Alfred Alder Memorial Trophy two years in a row. After graduation, Wally was selected as the first female flight instructor at Fort Sill, Oklahoma. She taught U.S. Army officers, soloing

more than 400 servicemen and sending a total of 500 on to private, commercial and instrument ratings. She has flown everything from balloons to gliders to DC-3s. Wally has competed in many air races, including the Pacific Air Race where she won first place in 1975. As the 58th woman to earn an ATP, she applied for and was granted an interview by one major carrier. Her accomplishments put her head and shoulders above the male applicants, but the company's lack of a women's restroom in the flight department prevented them from hiring her. She has served as chief pilot for three schools, was the first female FAA Inspector in 1971, the first female in the FAA's System Airworthiness Analysis Program in 1973 and the first female Air Safety Investigator for the NTSB in 1974. With 13,600 hours of flight time, Wally now dedicates herself to educating pilots on how to put safety and common sense into flying.

JOHN NANCE

ONE SMALL LEAP

God protects fools and little children, goes the old adage, but the pundit who coined that phrase left one out: God also provides an inordinate amount of protection for what we used to call (in Air Force pilot training) "a hundred and seventy pounds of dumb" —student pilots.

All "highly experienced pilots" lug around at least a few stories of that finite point in time when the sum total of our aviation knowledge was exceeded only by blind confidence. For those who first entered the cockpit in the military, the rigorous demands of the pilot training syllabus kept the period of student narcissism blessedly short. But for those of us who—despite later military service—entered through the civilian route, that student pilot certificate was an invitation to fly (probably upside down) through the valley of the shadow of death, laughing maniacally at the Grim Reaper riding unseen in the back seat.

In short, we didn't know that we didn't know!

Every now and then, either from the cockpit of my King Air E-90 or the left seat of a B737-400, I'll flash back to the first of those close encounters of the student kind, wondering how I survived.

It was December 29th of 1964, a mild-mannered day of blue skies and fluffy clouds. My instructor pilot had just told me to taxi the tiny Cessna 150 I was wearing back to the flightline at Dallas' then-remote Addison Airport. (Cessna 150's are extremely small, and the seats are so close that one female instructor I flew with turned as she strapped in and said she'd respect me in the morning).

So here I was home from college over Christmas, eager to begin pilot training, and trying to fly every day. Why were we going back?

"Keep it running," the IP (instructor pilot) commanded as he undid his seatbelt and opened the door.

He needs a quick trip to the can, I decided. Why else? We'd only been up fifteen minutes and at the time I'd had a total of only three hours of flight instruction. Count them. Three! I could barely start the thing.

"Okay," the IP said, standing in the doorway, his feet safely attached to the concrete. "Take it around."

"Take what around?" I asked.

"The airplane."

"To the hangar?"

"No, in the air. Three touch and go's and a full stop."

"You mean, when you get back from the bathroom, right?" I said, my eyes undoubtedly as big as fried eggs.

"Wrong. I mean now. While I watch from the ground."

"But...that would be a solo."

"Very good! This is why I instruct college boys, your instant grasp of obscure concepts."

"But...I haven't soloed yet..." I stammered.

He stroked his chin, looking thoughtful. "I'm not sure, Nance, but I think that's the whole point."

"By *myself*?"

"You know a better way?"

"But, I'm not ready...am I?"

"Would I get out of the airplane if you weren't?"

"Yes. Maybe. I don't know. Why are you doing this to me? Did my check bounce from last week?"

I'm sure the entire flight school, such as it was, heard the sound of my swallowing. The confident self-image of a big college freshman was welling up to quell the fears, but my Michael J. Fox confidence was facing a Schwarzenegger of virtual panic, and Arnold was winning.

"I can't do this!" I said to the empty right seat.

It was too late. He'd closed the door and walked away, waving me off.

I swallowed another lump the approximate size of Cleveland and called ground for taxi clearance in a voice two octaves higher than normal. That, I figured, was the first step. Everything else would probably follow. If he'd asked me my name at that point I would have had to research it.

"Roger Nine Seven Tango. Taxi runway one-five."

Dang! I remember thinking. *He cleared me*! I guess I'd been hoping for a reprieve. I'd been hoping he'd refuse the request, press his microphone button and say: "Negative, Nine Seven Tango. You're too green and far too scared. We're not sure you can even drive, and you're too young to drink. Park that thing and live a while longer!"

Instead, he'd cleared me to the end. Obviously part of the conspiracy.

Bobby Evans, my sadistic IP, was standing by the doorway of the flight school office now, shooing me away as if getting rid of a reluctant dog. I'd always thought he liked me.

And what about the plane? Why would he want to hurt a perfectly good airplane?

Insurance. That's the ticket! If I crack this one up, they can get a new Cessna 150!

Somehow I had arrived in the runup area at the end of the runway with no memory of the trip.

What if I just shut down right here, put on the parking brake, and leave. I could be in Oklahoma by midnight. Evans would never catch me!

But my car was in the flight school parking lot, and I loved my car.

Resigned to my fate, I ran the engine up and checked the magnetos, praying they'd fail the check.

They were perfect.

I checked the fuel.

There was more than enough.

I tried the flight controls, the flaps, the radios, the vacuum readings, the ash tray, *anything* to find a maintenance problem that would ground the plane.

Nothing! The darn plane hadn't worked better the day it came off the Cessna line in Wichita.

I picked up the microphone for a few last words. "Tower, ah, Cessna Nine Seven Tango, re...ready to go, one-seven, I mean one-five."

The clearance came swiftly in a different voice. "Cleared for takeoff," it said.

So they were *all* in on it!

"Ah, Nine, ah, Seven Tango, rolling," I stammered.

But the airplane didn't move.

Actually, I realized, *it'll probably roll a lot easier if I remove the parking brake.*

Moving onto the runway was simple. Pushing the throttle up was simple too. So was gently lifting the aircraft off the ground, and even banking left to what they called a crosswind leg and throttling back at a thousand feet.

It was just like I remembered. You pulled the yoke, the houses got smaller. You pushed, they got larger. Right now they were steady, and that was a good sign.

Say, I thought, *maybe he was right. Maybe I am ready.*

The alternative was a bit too problematic to think about.

I sailed along the downwind leg then with growing confidence, turned base with supreme enthusiasm, and turned to final approach with a manly flourish of confident words on the radio.

"Roger, Nine Seven Tango, cleared to land!"

Simple! I thought, tempting Murphy, the little green devil with whom I'd share the rest of my aviation career.

The runway was holding nicely in the middle of my cowling, my Before Landing checklist was completed, and the wind was steady at five knots straight in my face.

Piece of cake!

Actually that wasn't the phrase that ran around my head. That one I learned later in the Air Force. It was more of an instantaneous feeling of well-being, immediately punctuated by a growing reality: The cowling of my engine and the runway ahead weren't matching up.

First the runway was in the middle of my windscreen. Then the Cessna yawed a bit, and the runway moved off to the right about a mile, and then to the left about the same distance.

I tried to steady the aircraft, wondering why panic was rising once again from the black hole where my stomach used to be. My carbon-based analog brain was rapidly convincing itself that this meant that if I encountered the slightest gust of crosswind over the runway, I'd be shoved a mile sideways in either direction, and,

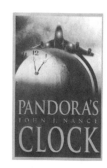

John J. Nance has been authoring fiction and nonfiction books since 1984. Foreign language editions and English versions of his six novels have been printed and sold all over the world in French, Spanish, Dutch, Finnish, German, Swedish, Norwegian, Russian, Polish, Italian, Chinese, and Japanese. *Both Pandora's Clock* and *Medusa's Child* were filmed and aired as major, two-part, successful mini-series for television.

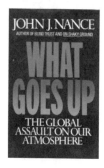

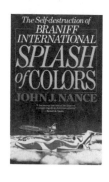

after all, that so-called runway had already shrunk to the size of a bike path.

Hence an unavoidable conclusion: There is no way I can ever land this airplane!

Understand, that wasn't a conscious conclusion. My brain, having decided that my conscious self was the suicidal idiot who had wanted to go hurtling through the air in the first place, had also decided that the conscious me couldn't be trusted. So I got the conclusion, not the calculation: "I'm doomed!"

I tried hard. I flew it to about 50 feet, where the back and forth gyrations were only a few hundred yards. But Bobby, the homicidal IP, had taught me the loyal and trustworthy institution of the go-around, and I decided that this was a pretty good time to practice.

Back on the downwind I took stock of the situation and decided to try again. This wasn't bravery, of course. It was gravity versus fuel. Better to try while the fan in front was still rotating, and guess what? My second go-around was even better than my first!

Back on the downwind for the third time, I remember thinking that Bobby-the-Ripper Evans had probably left the field, his murderous plan realized. I must have done something to him in another life. Or maybe I'd dated his daughter. There had to be a motive.

"He'll never get down!" I imagined Bobby cackling. "He'll be up there all week!"

There's another old adage about third tries being charms. In aviation, it simply goes to show you how fast unjustified confidence can build, sort of like a cumulonimbus on a summer day.

This time I'm going plant it!

The runway was getting closer, but this time my side-to-side gyrations were under control because I was riding the rudder pedals back and forth with the concentration of a brain surgeon at work. This time I'd keep that runway right in the middle of the windscreen.

And I did, the touchdown coming as a bit of a surprise, scoring somewhere below three on the Richter scale.

Good grief, I'm alive!

That recognition came slowly, and right on its heels was the thought that maybe I'd better shut it down for the day. The taxiway seemed to be bouncing, until I realized my feet were chattering on the rudder pedals as my bloodstream dealt with about a gallon of adrenaline. I turned the 150 toward the ramp, startled to see Evans standing there with his right thumb in the air, a dumb gesture at best for a grown man. So he'd stayed to see the carnage, and I'd cheated him. Ha! I remember being furious at him, and proud at the same time that I'd actually done it. And, in fact, after I shut down the airplane and set the brake and climbed out on a pair of wobbly legs, I had every intention of walking right over and decking him. If it hadn't been for that sudden case of rubber legs, I would have, too!

Instead, the following spring, as I continued flight training while attending the University of Hawaii in Honolulu, I'd think about how far I'd come as a pilot—every time I made a few residual mistakes, such as trying to take off with the wrong flap setting, nearly running out of gas on a cross-water cross-country, trying to stall on short final, and coming close to bouncing the main gear off a building on an ill-advised downwind takeoff. Ah, the confidence of youth!

The Air Force had it right.

Charlie Gibson and John Nance on location during the filming of *Good Morning America*.

Biography

JOHN NANCE

John Nance is best known to television audiences worldwide as an aviation analyst for the ABC Radio and Television Network, and as the Aviation Editor for *Good Morning America*. He has appeared on Larry King Live, PBS News Hour with Jim Lehrer, Oprah, NPR, NOVA, ABC's 20/20, the Today Show, and many others. He is internationally recognized as an air safety analyst and advocate. John is also the internationally known author of eleven major best-selling books such as *Splash of Colors, Blind Trust, On Shaky Ground, What Goes Up, Final Approach, Pandora's Clock, Phoenix Rising, Medusa's Child, The Last Hostage and* his latest, *Blackout*. John presents programs both here and abroad as keynote addresses on such diverse topics as team creation and leadership, crew management methods, resource management, communications and motivation, and is well known for his involvement in human factors flight safety education. John is a native Texan who grew up in Dallas, holds a Bachelors degree from SMU and a Juris Doctorate from SMU Law School. He is a licensed attorney. With over 12,000 hours of flight time, he is a decorated Air Force pilot; a veteran of Vietnam, Operations Desert Shield/Desert Storm; a lieutenant colonel in the USAF Reserve; and a Boeing 737 captain for a major airline. He is also one of the founding board members of the National Patient Safety Foundation of the American Medical Association.

JAMES "DOC" BLAKELY

TWO BIT LAW

It was one of those beautiful spring days. I began a routine private flight to Sherman, Texas. Sherman is so close to Oklahoma that a high school dance on the nearby Indian reservation can cause a six-inch downpour in north Texas.

Weather was forecast to be "partly sunny." As I neared my destination, I saw darker skies between my position and Sherman. "Partly sunny" turned into what appeared to be "partly inside a car wash." I called Flight Watch. "Unexpected line of thunderstorms," they said. I retreated and landed at Commerce, Texas. Absolutely nobody was around. Tried to call into town to rent a car, or see about getting fuel in case the storm passes. No quarter. Operator informs me I can't use my credit card.

There is a strange Federal law and if it weren't for dealing with lawyers and politicians, I'd work to have it changed. The law is you can't charge a 25 cent call on a local pay phone to your calling card—for any amount of money. I tried to make it worth their while. Even told them I was a personal friend of the governor. No soap.

I practically live off plastic. Money burns a hole in my pocket. Bums are always asking for a small handout, so I never have any change. But, enough about my relatives. I love plastic because it's not like spending the hard stuff. I've got a plastic personality, plastic friends. Plastic surgery for me would be to cut off my credit cards.

So it irritates me when people say irrational things like, "We don't take American Express." It's also unnerving if the guy saying it is the arresting officer.

Leaning against the phone booth, I got creative. I called a friend in Oklahoma on my credit card. I asked him to call City Hall and ask them to call me on the pay phone because I don't have a quarter. He laughed, said, "Sure, right away," and hung up. Nobody called. Made me regret being a known prankster.

The storm passed and I saw a clearing to the west. I'm 30 minutes away by air. I take off again. Free at last, free at last! I talked on the radio to pilots from Beaumont to Bangladesh. Just to be on the safe side, I landed at a nearby city airport for fuel. They *did* take American Express and somebody was actually there. "How'd you get so wet?" asked the attendant.

"I used a pay phone installed in a shower," I replied.

"Why didn't you turn off the shower?"

"God was operating it at the time."

"Pay phone out in the open and no quarter?"

"You got it."

A trip to the restroom made the incident even more profound. The airport was built with funds from a federal grant. They had a pay toilet. Naturally it took quarters—which I didn't have.

JUST HOW BIG IS IT?

Australia is slightly larger than the U.S., but has only 16 million people. Most of them live in a ring around the country, sort of like a doughnut with a big hole. The hole is called "The Outback." The weather there is said to be uniform, but some places are hotter.

We wanted to experience the real Outback but were not sure just where it started. We also wanted to see the largest stone in the world, Ayers Rock (or Uluru Rock). For some unexplained reason, I got the impression it was at Alice Springs.

"Would Alice Springs be considered the true Outback?" I asked an Aussie friend.

He cocked his head, rolled his eyes upward as he answered, "Oh yeah, mate. That's the middle of the middle, that one."

We flew nearly all day from Brisbane to Alice Springs. I looked in every direction. No rock. "Where's Ayer's Rock?" I asked when we landed. Four-and-a-half hours west, I was told.

Brushing the flies from your face with both hands is called the "Aussie Salute." We saluted every few seconds. After a couple of hours, our ability to salute was thoroughly tested, so we landed on a gravel strip at an oasis called Carton Springs.

A sign over the doorway behind the bar confused me. It was written in a language I knew nothing about, all in one word. "WYBMABIITY." I turned to a stranger and asked, "What does the sign mean?"

"Will you buy me a beer if I tell you?" he asked.

"Sure," I replied, even though I knew I couldn't drink one myself.

"That's what it means, mate... <u>W</u>ill <u>Y</u>ou <u>B</u>uy <u>M</u>e <u>A</u> <u>B</u>eer <u>I</u>f <u>I</u> <u>T</u>ell <u>Y</u>ou."

"Of course," I laughed as I caught the meaning.

"That's two beers now, mate."

Clever marketing strategy. Poking fun with a purpose. Then he added the clincher to his strategy. "If you're willing to buy a couple of beers for a stranger perhaps you'd give 25 cents to the Guide Dog Association for the blind children in the Northern Territory. Let's forget the beers." A ceramic guide dog piggy bank with a slot in its back was produced and the bargain sealed. This little game has raised money for hundreds of dogs for needy kids. A noble purpose.

"Where you from, mate?" my newfound friend asked.

"Texas," I replied.

"Ah," he said, "I run a sheep station here that is larger than the state of Texas. That's the truth, mate. Waddya think of that?"

"Tell you what," I countered, "is it for sale?"

A roar of laughter rang out in the middle of the middle. Quarters came from everywhere and a new dog was ordered on the spot. They wouldn't even let me pay for my own drink. And buttermilk is expensive in the Outback.

HOME OF THE BRAVE

In the Atlanta airport, our designated plane was delayed two hours. It was stuck on the ground in Alabama because of thunderstorms. I glanced around at the crowd. Everyone was trying to be patient. A group of about 20 school kids, probably ages 13 to 14, on some sort of sponsored trip, were seated in a row of seats across from a lone soldier dressed in camouflage. He couldn't have been more than five years older than the kids on their spring fling. They were white. He was black. They wore the garb of kids on a spring fling. He wore an Army uniform with a shoulder patch that read, "Desert Storm."

Sadness in the young soldier's eyes and the weight of wartime experiences on his shoulders gave him a confidence and bearing far beyond his years. For an hour, the kids chattered while the soldier gazed afar, lost in the corridors of his mind. All of a sudden, the kids moved in unison, the way a school of fish moves in response to some unseen signal. My hunter's eye immediately picked up the sudden activity. I was curious, but too far away, to hear more than fragments of excited questions from the youths, their knees on the floor, sitting on their Reeboks.

Hands shot in the air as the soldier nodded in the direction of a questioner. He responded quietly. Bits of the conversation drifted my way through the static of competing noise as the entire waiting area grew progressively more silent.

"It was my job. I accepted the risk when I enlisted..."

"No, I was scared to death..."

"We all made out our wills..."

An announcement over the airport speaker interrupted the interview. Our plane was off the ground in Huntsville and would be available for boarding in another hour. The interview continued.

"Actually, I felt sorry for the Iraqis..."

"My crew had two kills. Soviet-built tanks..."

"I sold my car, gave away all my clothes. I didn't expect to come back..."

"Yes, I'd do it again... hope you don't have to... proud to be an American...."

Finally the plane arrived, unloaded, was cleaned, and the call was given for immediate boarding. A sea of blond-haired boys and girls stood up and circled the seated black soldier. As I passed by the huddled mass and peered inside the human circle, I saw a sight I'll not soon forget. Twenty hands thrusting 20 scraps of paper.

And a hero signing autographs.

LEAP FOG AT NIGHT

If you are one of those fainthearted who is afraid to fly, you may get white knuckles just reading this. From the Archives of the NAA (National Aeronautics Association) comes a handwritten account by Charles A. Lindbergh, dated September 16, 1926. Pilot Lindbergh, then an unknown mail carrier, recorded significant flying events that occurred when he flew the St. Louis-Chicago route that evening. He left St. Louis at 4:25 p.m., landed at Springfield and again at Peoria. About 25 miles east of Peoria, it got dark (don't you hate it when that happens?). So Lindy took up a compass heading (are you paying attention to this—he's flying by a compass!) checking on the towns below until a low fog, that extended from the ground to about 600 feet, rolled under him. The following are excerpts from Lindy's account:

"Unable to fly under it [the fog], I attempted to drop a flare and land." No mention of an airport, just gimme a shot at a turn row in a cornfield.

"The flare did not function and I again headed for Maywood [Chicago's airmail port], hoping to find a break in the fog." Oh, sure, we'll laugh about this later, but I'll bet he didn't say at the time, "Darn, that flare didn't function."

Eventually he writes, "I saw a dull glow on top of the fog indicating a town below." (Probably Maywood by his reckoning. However, he was not able to locate the exact position of the field.) "I understand the search lights were directed upward and two barrels of gasoline burned in an endeavor to attract my attention."

He circled for a while, then headed west until his fuel was almost gone. He tried another flare. This one worked but disappeared into the solid bank of fog below. It was still about 600 feet above ground level and probably thicker than a student pilot's skull. "I turned towards open country and nosed the plane up. At 5,000 feet, the engine sputtered and died. I stepped up on the cowling and out...." Try that on a 747. "The parachute functioned perfectly. I was playing my flashlight towards the top of the fog when I heard the plane's engine pick up. Apparently when the ship nosed down an additional supply of gasoline drained to the carburetor." Now the ship is flying in descending spirals "headed in the general direction of my parachute." Lindy slips his chute to avoid the plane, but drops his flashlight. It disappears into the fog (so he can't see anyway) and works all this out by sound. He still has the presence of mind to cross his legs "to keep from straddling a branch or wire, guarded my face with my hands, and waited." I don't know about you, but I don't have enough hands for guarding purposes in a case like this.

He landed in a cornfield. Not a scratch. Visibility was about 10 yards. The plane crashed two miles away but did not burn. The last entry in his report was "The sheriff from Ottawa arrived and we took the mail to be entrained at 3:30 a.m. for Chicago."

Ever wonder why they called him "Lucky Lindy?" Lindy caught a train back to St. Louis. The one to Chicago had an accident—a dead cow lying on the track derailed it. The investigators suspected foul play. The cow had been killed by a blow to the head... from a falling flashlight.

PRE-BOARDING ONLY

There is a retirement village in Florida where airline pilots go to file their final flight plans. Every house has a hangar for a small airplane. The streets all double as taxiways leading to the nearby private airstrip.

The names of the streets are in keeping with the aviation theme of the project. There you'll find Barrel Roll Lane, CAVU (Ceiling and Visibility Unlimited) Drive, Blue Angels Avenue and Scattered Showers Boulevard. The entrance is at 747 Boeing where you'll find a visitor's center named "Scud Runners Rendezvous."

The golf course and country club can be reached by going down Airway. Right turnoffs are at American, Delta, Continental on down to Western. The lone exception is a left turnoff at Southwest. It leads to a miniature theater where customers take turns providing floor shows for each other. Seating is in the round, so everybody will have a middle seat.

Meanwhile, back at the golf course, everyone signs up for their "flight" in "Funny Teams" of four: "Divot in Command," "Co-Divot," "Agitator" and "Some Clown from the FAA."

Periodically, flight attendants show up long enough to serve junk food and marry one of the pilots.

The game's aerial flights continue over water, sand and forest with many more landings than takeoffs... just like in the old days.

The holes are not numbered. They have initials like DFW, JFK, and ATL. However, it's easy to tell when you get to 18, because it's marked RIP.

Then the teams go to the AVJet bar until closing time. The seat belt light goes off and everybody takes turns standing at the door, putting on a cap, and trying to say, "Have a nice day."

I like this community. It's so much more imaginative than the mail carrier's retirement project. The only thing that differentiates the carrier's community from others is a large sign, "NO DOGS!"

On the national television show, *Nashville Now*, Doc gets his share of the laughs. "A hurricane came through my small hometown in Texas. It did $250,000 worth of improvements."

Biography

DOC BLAKELY

Doc Blakely is the winner of the National Speakers Association's highest honor, the Cavett Award, the speaking equivalent of an Oscar. Doc has spent 20 years presenting his own brand of humor to clients, including Fortune 500 corporations and national associations. He is exceptionally witty and has given talks in 49 states and several foreign countries, making about 100 appearances a year. Doc grew up in the ranch country of South Texas where he learned the skills and music of working cowboys. Long before he earned his Ph.D. in animal husbandry, his friends were calling him "Doc" for his knack of treating horses and cattle. A multi-talented musician, Doc plays the fiddle, mandolin, guitar and even the musical saw. He is the author of numerous books including *Shoot Luke, the Air Is Full of Pigeons* and *Doc Blakely's Handbook of Wit and Pungent Humor*. Doc is also a mentor to many professional speakers. As a pilot, he has collected funny stories for a special presentation to aviation groups, *To Soar With Eagles*. He can incorporate his music and funny songs into his solo program. Doc also teams up with his son, Mike Blakely, a musical storyteller, to form the Swing Riders. This duo performs a wonderful one-of-a-kind, humorous, foot stomping show. It's always a big hit.

RICH STOWELL

TWISTED PASTA

Spinning through 3,500 feet, the islands below us began to merge. Forest green and pacific blue smeared across the canopy of the Pitts S-2B as the rate of rotation increased. It was now time to start the recovery.

"Okay, talk me through the procedure as you do it," I commanded.

Teaching other instructors how to conduct spin training is one of my favorite assignments. The interaction usually proves educational for me, and it's a lot of fun besides. The dramatic sensory stimulation of a spin often makes it difficult to verbalize recovery actions while simultaneously performing the control inputs. Effective instructors, though, develop the ability to talk and fly at the same time.

Spin training certainly demands good communication skills. Recovering the airplane always seems to be the easy part. Untying the instructor's tongue, however, usually takes a bit of concentrated practice. Even though he was also a 727 captain, this case was no different. The instructor was progressing well, and I was sure this would be the spin where it all came together. He spoke deliberately as he manipulated the controls.

"Power, off; ailerons, neutral; rudder, opposite..."

"He's got it wired," I thought, nodding my head in approval. He sounded like a test pilot: cool, collected, assured. Just one more input. But then it happened. From where in the recesses of his cerebral cortex it came I don't know, but the volume rose in my headset as he loudly proudly proclaimed his final input:

"Elevator, NOODLES!!!"

Suppressing the urge to laugh, I shot back, "Elevator, NOODLES! Are all these spins making you hungry?" Laughter filled the cockpit during the climb back to altitude. We spun some more. We laughed some more. We had a great time during that flight high above the Pacific Northwest, and another spin instructor was born.

THOSE WHO HAVE, AND THOSE WHO WILL

Without warning, the Pitts biplane swerved hard left as if pulled by a tractor beam. "You got it," crackled over the intercom, but it was already too late. The airplane was beyond control. All I could do now was hang on until the ground loop stopped. The airplane skipped off the hard surface of the runway onto a mixture of sand and broken asphalt, crunching to a halt in a cloud of dust 150 degrees from our original heading.

We sat motionless, stunned by the brevity of the experience. The sound of the engine ticking lazily at idle faded in as our shock dissipated. There we sat, listing to the right. A layer of light brown sand covered the wing. The sky was bright blue, without clouds. The large bubble canopy soaked up the California sunshine and it was hot.

I never imagined I'd be instructing. I learned to fly to experience the thrill of aerobatics. Through serendipitous events, teaching evolved into a full time profession. The opportunity to take the school's S-2A to Edwards Air Force Base arose less than a year after I became a CFI. A team of pilots attending the USAF Test Pilot School designed a class project code-named, "Have Pitts." I was to be the safety pilot during a number of spin test sorties.

Admittedly, it was more than a little intimidating flying the Pitts onto the hallowed grounds where Yeager broke the sound barrier, where sonic booms from X-15's and the space shuttle echoed in the distant hills, where those with the right stuff pushed the envelope daily. Here I was, a relatively low-time civilian pilot, a new CFI, sharing the cockpit with the project leader, an F-16 test pilot, a graduate of the Air Force Academy. I was awed by it all. This was the first sortie, and we were practicing touch-and-go's at the North Base.

"Are you okay," I asked.

"Yeah. My God, what happened? I can't believe it! Oh no."

We shut the engine down, undid our belts, and climbed out of the airplane. Fortunately, damage was confined to the right side only—the landing gear had collapsed under the fuselage, the lower wingtip was broken, so were a couple of wing ribs. The aileron spade had punched a hole through the wing. The bottom aileron was damaged as well, and miscellaneous tears dotted the fabric.

The North Base seemed deserted. A half-mile away, the fire station's huge doors were drawn up in mock laughter. Yet the fire trucks stayed inside. They couldn't see us out here! We couldn't raise the off-site air traffic controller on the radio either. So we walked over to a guardhouse, materializing like apparitions before the surprised guard. After explaining ourselves, we were allowed to make a phone call to the test pilot school.

Our post-ground loop daze transformed into embarrassment as we waded through a sea of green flight suits enroute to the Commandant's office. Everyone we passed somehow already knew our dark secret. They looked at us differently now. I can't

recall the number of times we were asked to explain the details surrounding the event, or how many grins we feigned in response to the obligatory ribbing from other test-pilots-in-training. The serious part of our ordeal had yet to begin.

Following a debriefing with the Commandant and members of his staff, we drove to the infirmary for a preliminary checkup: pulse, blood pressure, and other routine poking and prodding. While there, another colonel and his aides pulled us aside for a debriefing. We then visited the base hospital where we left urine samples and about a half dozen vials of blood apiece. More debriefings ensued upon our return to the school. These closed-door sessions—all off the record—were low-key, professional, to the point.

Twilight was fast descending on the Mojave Desert when we returned to the crippled airplane. It had been a long day already. With the help of other pilots on the project team, we dismantled the Pitts and loaded it on a trailer brought in from Santa Paula. It was dark, windy, and cold when we left the North Base for the lonely drive home.

Time eventually healed our bruised egos. The airplane was repaired, and safety procedures were improved at the North Base. The pilots on the "Have Pitts" team were absorbed into other projects. The project team leader and I exchanged cloth patches as sort of a rite of passage. His depicts a duck landing on water, captioned "Taildragger and Bragger." Mine is an official "USAF Test Pilot School" patch. Last I heard, he was accepted into the Space Shuttle program. The Pitts went on to star in its own aerobatics video! Me? I'm still instructing, but I'm much less influenced by the flight experience of my students. The focus now is on the tasks ahead, guided by the adage, "You're only as good a pilot as your next landing."

Biography

RICH STOWELL

Rich Stowell holds a Bachelor's degree in mechanical engineering. After receiving his pilot's license he left his engineering career behind to become Chief Aerobatic Pilot at CP Aviation. He refined CP's existing emergency maneuvers course into the internationally recognized EMT® (Emergency Maneuver Training) program. It was Rich's unique style of instruction that helped popularize this life-saving course. The EMT® program and Stowell's teaching techniques have been featured in *FLY-*

ING, Private Pilot, Sport Pilot, Hot Kits & Homebuilts and *AOPA Pilot* magazines. A NAFI Master CFI, Rich was the Western-Pacific Region CFI of the Year in 1993 and the IAC President's Award winner in 1994. He has performed over 15,000 spins with students, which is the equivalent of 710 vertical miles traveled while spinning! Rich has written for *Flight Training* magazine and written, produced and hosted several educational videos on *Stall/Spin Awareness, Emergency Maneuver Training* and *Basic Aerobatics*. He is the author of two outstanding flight training books, *Emergency Maneuver Training* and *PARE®—The Emergency Spin Recovery Procedure*, based on the P-A-R-E acronym he developed as part of the EMT® Program. Rich lectures across the United States. Perhaps Amy Laboda said it best several years ago in *Sport Aviation* Magazine when she stated, "What Rich Stowell 're-taught' me was what I should have learned on those very first flights ten years ago."

KAREN M. KAHN

SIMPLE PILOT MATH

A favorite Second Officer's remark to the flight attendants is to tell them our part of the airplane preflight consists of multiplying the number of wings we count by the number of engines we count to get the number of tires. Or, to be different, tires divided by engines equals wings. I always wanted to walk back into the aircraft, while passengers were boarding, and mumble loudly to myself, "Let's see, was that two engines and three wings, or three engines and two wings?" I suspect some travelers—and flight attendants—may not have appreciated my sense of humor.

KABOOM at FL350

Most of our flights are routine and thankfully so. The old adage that flying is "hours of boredom punctuated by moments of sheer terror" certainly came true one afternoon. We were enroute from Houston to Los Angeles on the Fourth of July and not expecting any fireworks.

The flight was full. We had 144 passengers plus four flight attendants, two pilots, and one Air Traffic Controller occupying the jumpseat. After leveling off at 35,000 feet, we began to relax for the three-hour journey ahead. I was just about to begin my "Welcome Aboard" announcement with information about the route of flight, time enroute and weather in LA, when suddenly we heard a tremendous "KABOOM!"

We quickly scanned the instruments for a malfunction: cabin pressurization, door lights, and engine group. These would show if we'd had a rapid decompression due to a door suddenly departing the aircraft, or perhaps an engine explosion. The First Officer wisely reached up and turned off the power to the galleys. After checking all the instruments, we found nothing abnormal, but we *knew* there had to be something we were missing. That horrendous noise could not have meant anything but trouble.

Moments later we received a call on the cabin-to-cockpit interphone system from one of the flight attendants. The head flight attendant solved our mystery. The escape slide on the forward galley door had inflated in flight. The noise we'd heard was the slide filling the galley area, pinning two flight attendants to the wall.

We were relieved to hear no one was hurt. Then came the problem: how to deflate the slide so they could get on with their service. I suggested they use the blunt end of the knife on the valve stem, if they could find it. Barring that, I told them to stab it with the knife, but watch out for another explosion!

Unfortunately, we were unable to assist with the deflation process. We were trapped in the cockpit. Inside, our occupied jumpseat filled the cockpit doorway and outside, the head flight attendant was pinned to the cockpit door by the slide. He, too, was unable to help with the cleanup. Several minutes later, we received an "all deflated" call and I managed to get back to the galley to survey the damage.

There it lay, in a puddle of yellow rubber, the loudest sound I've ever heard in my 15 years of airline flying.

Later, we called our maintenance crew in Los Angeles to request a new slide. They humored us saying there would be someone out to reattach the slide to the door. That's the usual request. "No," I said, "that's not the problem. The slide inflated in flight and we'll need a whole new slide, package and all." Silence followed... I think it was a first for all of them... and hopefully a last for me.

Biography

KAREN M. KAHN

Captain Karen M. Kahn has been actively involved in aviation for the past 31 years. Holding all ratings through ATP, she was the first woman to be type-rated in a Lockheed JetStar. Her other ratings include flight engineer, seaplane, glider and helicopter. She is an active instrument and multi-engine flight instructor. Karen is presently captain on the MD-80 for a major air carrier. During the last 22 years she's also flown the DC-10 and Boeing 727 on both international and domestic routes. Karen is a frequent speaker at pilot seminars and career workshops as well as contributor to Pilot's Audio Update, a monthly aviation cassette series. She writes a monthly column for *Flying Careers* magazine and *International Women Pilots* magazine. Karen is at her best helping pilots improve their communications skills. She uses her in-depth knowledge of human resource management, both in and out of the cockpit, to assist pilots in achieving their career goals. Her engaging presentations are entertaining and filled with practical advice on how to survive and thrive both in and out of aviation. Karen's topics include *My Story, Surviving in Aviation, Women's Careers in Aviation* and *Succeed! or Just do It.*

Flight Guide *for* **Success**

Tips & Tactics for the Aspiring Airline Pilot

Captain Karen M. Kahn

CHAS HARRAL

A MEMORY THAT BRINGS A SMILE

As I remember, it was in the fall of 1967...

In warbird circles, I was considered one of the authorities, since I owned and flew a North American P-51D Mustang. I generally flew the Mustang when someone was willing to spring for the gas. Upon completion of the flight, my passenger received a very nice certificate, which I created just for the occasion. It included the speeds achieved during the flight, the acceleration in "G's" we recorded, and all the little details the passenger would want to know to brag about to his friends. Going for a ride in a sleek P-51 for something like $25 was a popular adventure in the Phoenix area at the time. By the way, 100 octane avgas was only 45 cents a gallon, and we got a rebate of eight to ten cents a gallon for non-highway use.

I was also the local person to call for dual instruction in the T-6 and SNJ series training aircraft. I always knew when someone had purchased a T-6 Harvard or SNJ. My phone would ring with requests to check out the new owner. What a thrill it was to train a doctor or an attorney or a state senator in his newly acquired playtoy. Each came fresh from his late model Bonanza or Cessna 182 with no tailwheel experience. Zip. Zero. Nada! I turned gray and lost hair at an early age.

The T-6 or SNJ would have no intercom or working radios and bucket seats with no cushions, so I usually got to sit on 6.00 x 6 airplane tires in the back seat and yell myself hoarse. I was young and enthusiastic, and no one told me I couldn't do it that way.

One day, a good friend, Big Jim, asked me to go to Canada and pick up the Harvard Mk-IV he had successfully bid upon in a Royal Canadian Air Force surplus sale. As I remember, Big Jim had negotiated his "very nearly no time since IRAN (Inspect and Repair As Needed)" Harvard for the sum of $1,300 American, including duties paid to U.S. Customs. (An interesting side note to this whole adventure was the name of the Procurement and Auction Officer: Mrs. Bidgood. Truly!)

I had never been to Canada before, so I elected to go to Calgary on Arizona's favorite airline at the time, Hughes Air West. I didn't need much for the trip: a very small overnight bag, an aviator's flying helmet, and a newly packed parachute, complete with my name stenciled in red on the ripcord panel on the back. The first leg of the trip was uneventful. I carried my helmet on board in a fish net bag and checked the suitcase and the parachute safely in the hold of the DC-9.

The plane arrived late in Calgary due to extremely strong headwinds. I didn't have much time to retrieve my suitcase and parachute and clear Canadian Customs prior to boarding my next flight. I thought I would breeze through Customs until the dour Canadian Customs officer became convinced I intended to sell the helmet and parachute to some Canadian pilot for megabucks. We argued as I attempted to explain to him that I intended to use them myself for the ferry mission. Ultimately, after signing all kinds of agreements and waivers and declarations, he reluctantly let me go. I rushed to catch my departing airliner, frantically trying to keep my possessions from getting away from me in the mad dash to the gate. I barely made it as the last call for boarding had been made. The ticket agents were in the process of closing the boarding gate door.

I handed my ticket to the attendant at the gate and rushed out on the ramp, then ran to the stairs to get into the plane before they closed the door. When I saw I was going to make it in time, I stopped at the bottom of the stairs, caught my breath, and readjusted my load for the steep climb up to the passenger entrance.

I climbed up the stairs with the parachute slung on my back, the crash helmet in my left hand, and the overnight bag in my right. Just before reaching the top of the stairs and the open door, I heard a tremendous booming voice shout, "STOP!" I froze in my tracks and turned around to see who had challenged me.

The captain of the airplane stood at the bottom of the steps. His resplendent uniform, magnificent beard and four gold stripes blazing in the bright lighting of the ramp commanded my full attention. He asked, "Surely you have more faith in Air Canada than this?"

I imagined myself walking down the aisle in front of the passengers and started laughing. After I regained my composure, I told him about my ferry mission. He arranged to have the baggage personnel open the hatch. They stowed my parachute with the rest of the passenger luggage. Thus, Air Canada Airlines narrowly averted an extremely embarrassing negative public relations scene.

I arrived at Saskatoon, Saskatchewan, and spent the rest of the night catching up on my sleep in a motel near the airport. I ran into George, a flying acquaintance, who was also in town to ferry another Harvard back to Arizona. We went to the airport together to pick up our airplanes and closely inspect them prior to our flight to Great Falls, Montana. The airplanes were as expected: rough yellow paint and Canadian insignia. From what we could tell, they were mechanically sound and ready for their new life in the States.

We both decided if all went well on the takeoff, we would skip the test flight and just continue on to Great Falls. We planned to fly in loose formation and navigate independently. After clearance to taxi, we rumbled out to the end of the runway together, canopies open, enjoying the great sounds of the radial engines and searching for any last glitches prior to our journey back to Arizona.

The runup and takeoff checklist went without a hitch, and I followed George down the runway. Just as the plane lifted off, a great cloud of oil sprayed off the engine and covered the windshield. I quickly realized this oil had been pooled somewhere on the engine. It was not a sign of trouble, but it effectively ruined my forward vision. The only way I could see forward was to yaw the airplane or look out the open sides of the canopy. I tried to communicate with George, but to no avail. My radio didn't seem to receive anything he said. No problem, I thought, we could fly into Great Falls as a flight of two.

I relaxed, sat back, loosened my seat belt and shoulder harness, and began to enjoy the Canadian scenery, occasionally looking over at George flying loosely off my right wing. I would wave every once in awhile. Was this a dream come true? Two young men, flying World War II airplanes on a beautiful day, without a care in the world. What could be finer? I relaxed even more, listened to the hearty roar of the 1340, reveled in the exotic smells of the classic warbird, and let my mind wander. I was a classic case of "Condition White" (a relaxed, passive mental state).

Then I noticed George pulling away from me about a mile or two. I wondered about this for a moment, then dismissed it. All of a sudden, my airplane lurched, staggered, yawed, and commenced to roll upside down. I almost fell out of the Harvard. My seat belt and shoulder harness were very loosely engaged and barely held me. I was terrified! I called upon all of my aviator's skill to figure what was happening to my airplane. It seemed as if it took hours to regain control, but just as suddenly as it started, it stopped and I managed to get the Harvard right side up, recover lost altitude and return to my heading. From the cockpit I could see no visible damage. All the big parts were still attached and the engine was still running. I scratched my head. I couldn't figure out if it had been structural failure or turbulence that caused the incredible ride. I guessed I was okay. I tightened every restraining strap to the point of pain. I was ready for whatever was next.

I looked around for George. He was nowhere to be seen. Since I couldn't communicate with him, I visually navigated to Great Falls, Montana, and landed uneventfully. I saw George's airplane parked on the ramp. I taxied up to it and shut down my engine, remembering to take time to run the propeller to the full decrease RPM position, even though I desperately wanted to get to the men's room (Too many cups of coffee prior to the flight!).

Just as I started to get out of the plane, the customs agent sauntered up and told me to stay in the airplane. He was fuming. I had not arrived with the other Harvard and had created extra work for him. Not being willing to be intimidated by this non-aviator, I gritted my teeth until he had vented all his frustration. Finally he allowed me to get out of the airplane, and I rushed toward the pilot facilities.

Once we settled with the unreasonable customs agent, we were able to breathe easily once more. We even had a few dollars left to rent a motel room and get a little dinner. When we got to the restaurant and settled in for a nice meal and some relaxation, George looked over at me quizzically and said, "Chas, I know you are a flight instructor, and respected as a pilot, but I need to ask you a question."

"Go right ahead," I said.

"I have been wondering all the way down here from Saskatoon. Why, for heaven's sake, did you fly directly into that great big nasty dust devil?"

The mystery was finally solved. How would you have explained it?

Biography

CHAS HARRAL

Chas Harral is renowned for his gripping presentation on awareness and personal vigilance entitled the Color Code System. This is no ordinary program. It's an experience. The audience gets so involved with his fascinating storytelling, they literally leap out of their seats at one point. He identifies various states of mind that have a direct effect on our ability to function safely both on the ground and in the air. *The Color Code System* enhances the mental state appropriate for whatever circumstances we encounter

and properly prepares us. His program, *The Paradox of Focus*, focuses on the concepts ingrained in us since childhood that may be inappropriate for our present situation or activity. Chas speaks to fire, police, military and aviation groups as well as industry, corporations and associations. His programs are broadcast on satellite television to subscribing cities and governments. This acclaimed safety program is appropriate for all. Companies score a big plus inviting guests to attend. In his 20 years as an FAA designated pilot examiner, Chas has collected a wealth of funny aviation stories. *As The Examiner Sees It* is his humorous and entertaining keynote for all pilots. Chas does double duty with a safety program and a keynote.

JIM JOHNSON

THINGS THAT GO BUMP IN THE NIGHT

Strange things can happen in good weather as well as in bad. However, as the witching hour approaches, the odds of such an encounter seem to increase.

Late night flights are always an interesting affair, especially when departing Las Vegas. Some people are tired. Everyone is either a winner or a loser. Some have had too much to drink. And some are reluctant to leave the casino atmosphere.

One night while flying the all-night flight from Las Vegas to Atlanta, we heard this "snapping sound" in the cockpit. It was not unlike the sounds made by circuit breakers popping. I looked at the First Officer and he looked at me. I turned up the lights in the cockpit. We both began looking around for one or more elongated circuit breakers that may have popped. We didn't see any. We looked over all the airplane systems. Nothing looked any different. There was nothing out of parameters.

So, I turned the lights back down.

Wouldn't you know it, not long after the lights were out we heard this "pop-pop; snap-snap." Once again, we looked at each other in puzzlement.

Before making another complete systems check, we stopped to consider all the possibilities. What could make that noise?

Our brows were furrowed as we each mentally sifted through the volumes of technical information we memorize for the aircraft. Then we heard it again. But this time we are ready for it with our ears on full alert. To our surprise, we discovered it wasn't coming from the instrumentation in front of us. This time it was obvious that it came from the cockpit door behind us. This is most intriguing, as there were no circuit breakers on the cockpit door.

To investigate further, I leaned over and opened the door. As the door folded open, two red dice bounced into the cockpit, stopping inches from us. I looked back into first class. There were two first class passengers down on their hands and knees staring at us with the same surprised expression we had. We had interrupted their game of craps. They had been rolling the dice down the carpet the length of first class using the cockpit door as the backstop to bounce the dice.

We stared at them for a few seconds. What should a captain say or do in such an instance? I did the only thing that seemed appropriate. As I tossed back the dice, I told them as tactfully as I could, "Just remember, the house gets 10%."

I closed the door as our first class passengers burst into laughter. We chuckled as we went back to flying our casino through the night.

CAT I APPROACH

I am privileged to be a member of the only six-ship civilian aerobatic team in the world. It's a joy to fly one of these beefed-up T-34s. Quite a change from my regular job of keeping the heavy iron level for passenger comfort.

After a morning practice flight in Wisconsin, our six T-34s joined up on a T-28. Our rendezvous was over Lake Winnebago, just outside of Oshkosh. While flying along in formation, one of our pilots noticed a dark strip of something flailing in the wind-stream underneath one of the T-28's landing gear doors. We presumed it to be a piece of rubber weather stripping and relayed our concern that it might begin beating against the underside of his wing.

One of the more common techniques used to get rid of this type of loose stripping is to simply lower the landing gear, allowing the weather stripping to fly away. Naturally, a good time to lower your landing gear is while on approach, so we radioed the Oshkosh tower for pattern entry instructions.

The controller had us fly toward Runway 18 for an overhead break. After the group came around on the downwind it was time for the T-28 to lower his gear and thus open the gear doors. To our surprise, as the gear door opened, we discovered it was not weather stripping after all. It was the tail of an animal that had crawled inside the well. As the gear door opened fully, the flying feline fell out of the wheel well and plummeted to its demise.

Copyright: Lou Drendel

Some days the sky can truly rain cats—poor kitty.

Biography

JIM JOHNSON

Jim Johnson talks about aviation weather without snowing you. Often referred to as a "pilot's meteorologist," he is just that—a pilot and a meteorologist. In addition to flying actively as a general aviation pilot, he is a captain and special projects manager of applied meteorology with Delta Air Lines. He is also a consulting meteorologist in Chicago. This gives him his unique perspective. He doesn't just know about weather, he flies in it and brings the audience into his cockpit every time he speaks. Listeners not only learn about weather, but judgment and decision-making as well. Jim is the author *of Pilot's Handbook of Hazardous Weather,* a contributing author for *World Book Encyclopedia,* an expert witness, and is a frequent guest on radio and TV talk shows. His civilian flying background makes him ideal to lead general aviation, corporate or airline weather training sessions. Jim has specialized in weather-related flight problems since 1980. As a trained Air Safety Investigator, Jim is a participant in many NTSB accident investigations. He holds an M.S. degree, is a member of the American Meteorological Society (AMS) and the National Weather Association (NWA). His presentations include some of the most beautiful weather photography you will ever see.

DANNY COX

The following two stories are excerpted from *Leadership When the Heat's On*, Published by McGraw-Hill, Inc. and available at book stores.

STAYING LEVELHEADED

Effective leaders are levelheaded people. They grasp the facts in a hurry. They have the ability to organize chaotic situations. They see things as they really are, as opposed to how they wish they were. Effective leaders don't react to problems, they respond to them. Reacting is like a reflex knee-jerk which will invariably produce the same type of behavior that helped generate the heat in the first place. Responding means invoking the type of common sense judgments that take the organization down a new and better road. When internal pressures combine with external pressures to produce a storm of uncertainty and disruption, the realistic leader can bring order and set corrective measures into motion. This is a leadership quality for tough, heated moments.

These people prefer to fix problems rather than talk about them. I'm sure you know the different types. Some people come to you constantly with worried expressions, reporting problems that seem unsolvable. These same people will discuss the problems at length with anyone who will listen. Interestingly, long after the problems are solved or no longer relevant, these people are still talking about them.

Not those who approach life realistically. They act without being told to because they understand that, in the real world, problems aren't stopping places. They are decision points. Problems are not to be feared. Problems are to be expected. The levelheaded leader doesn't go into a state of shock when he or she is on the hot seat, but calmly and confidently deals with the situation. To panic is to be unrealistic.

I learned about being realistic as a test pilot. I know what it's like to be flying a supersonic jet fighter, all alone, with 79,000 horsepower, at 60,000 feet, 1200 miles per hour, 20 miles per minute, upside down... on fire. There I was, with every red light on the control panel flashing in my face. At least I think they were flashing in my face. There was too much smoke in the cockpit to really tell.

Peter Drucker said, "A crisis must never be experienced—for the second time." Not having read Peter Drucker at that point in my life, I wound up in the precarious position just described more than once. At any rate, I did my best to be realistic in the face of disaster. It started with self talk, "Be realistic, Danny," I would think to myself. "You are a test pilot with the right stuff. You're used to living on the edge. This is America up here. The nation is depending on you. The whole world is listening in on the emergency frequency. Remember that before you touch that microphone button."

Sufficiently under control, I would reach over to shut down whatever I thought was causing the fire with one gloved hand and simultaneously press the microphone button on the control stick with the other. In the most macho voice I could muster, I hit the button and called control center. "Mayday, Mayday, Mayday. I'm at 60,000 feet, upside down, and on fire. Request landing instructions."

As I recall, each word of my transmission was clear, calm, and distinct. A Hollywood actor in a simulator couldn't have been more composed. As far as I could tell, I couldn't have been calmer ordering ham and eggs at the chow hall. Of course, after I managed to get down safely (don't tell me God doesn't answer prayers), the controllers would play back the tape of my emergency transmission for me to hear. For some reason, that calm, composed, macho voice ended up sounding like an amphetamine-crazed chipmunk to the controllers in the tower.

My mythical sense of realism in the heat of the moment gave way to the adrenaline coursing through my body at such intensity I didn't even recognize my own voice later. It never failed to

give controllers a chuckle or two. My high-pitched babbling was so fast that sometimes they recorded my prayer that was supposed to follow my transmission. I didn't get my thumb off the button quickly enough and I usually broadcast my negotiations with God. Test pilots' prayers are, by necessity, brief. Most of them sound something like, "God, get this thing back on the ground and I'll taxi it in for you." There has been a time or two in my civilian life when I've thrown up similar prayers. A good example was when my boss came in and told me he was looking for my replacement!

The people with the information we need to develop the leadership qualities are all around us. Remember, leaders are not born, they simply drink from Elbert Hubbard's "ocean of knowledge." Nothing promotes a levelheaded sense of realism as much as knowledge. Likewise, ignorance, prejudice, and narrow-thinking result from lack of knowledge.

NOW FILTERS AND MEMORY MOVIES

Influence can be negative as well as positive. I was flying with a guy once who knew how I thought. He flew in the back seat as a radar observer and really knew how to hit my buttons. Now that I no longer fly, I can confess that I used to spend quite a bit of time flying my supersonic jet inside the Grand Canyon. As it went, I was playing cowboy one day, darting in and out of the maze of caverns and canyons.

I leveled off just above the canyon rim and noticed a steel tower ahead and to my left at the edge of the canyon. I kept my eye on it and asked my radar observer if he had any idea what it was. In his coolly calculated voice, he said he didn't know but there was another one just like it on the opposite side of the canyon.

The wings nearly tore off that jet as I yanked the control stick back into my belly to change our course from straight and level to straight up. We were pulling about a million G's when I noticed the hysterical laughter coming from the back seat. A quick glance to the right revealed no twin tower as my now hysterical radar observer had reported.

He knew all too well how to switch on my memory movie and direct it. My memory check immediately recognized his input as high-power lines and my imagination kicked in to not only create the nonexistent second tower, but also to string the nonexistent cables between them and visualize the disaster as I flew straight into the wires.

What did I do with the input? I took evasive action, much to his delight. He exerted tremendous influence on my behavior through extremely simple, but effective, input. This guy wasn't through with me, though. On final approach to a base in New Mexico sometime later, he got me again. I tell you this story because it's fun and also to illustrate that we're always vulnerable to erroneous input.

I had never flown into this particular base before and wasn't familiar with the area, so naturally I was more cocky than usual. That 79,000 horsepower goes to your head pretty quickly. At any rate, as I turned onto final approach, I noticed some people standing beside the runway. I called the tower to confirm I was on the correct runway. The controller in the tower that day was as cocky as I was. He said the people were a surveying crew, but if I needed a wider runway, he would try to find one for me.

That's all it took to get my attention. Everyone has their weaknesses and their Achilles heels and this tower operator had just found mine. You can do many things to a pilot that he or she will ignore and let roll off his or her thick skin, because, after all, pilots are bred to coolly handle crises. Just don't cast aspersions on a pilot's ability to land his or her aircraft. That's crossing the line. The controller knew it. My ego was now on a mission.

I felt I had no choice at that moment but to execute the most perfect landing ever witnessed by that tower operator and the surveying crew next to the runway. I felt as though my entire career, as well as the reputation of the entire United States Air Force, depended on the precision of the landing I was about to make. However, I sealed my own fate by telling my radar observer my intentions. I told him my landing was going to be so perfect that we would have to ask the tower if our wheels had touched down yet.

There we were on short final and everything was perfect. My chest was swelling in anticipation as we approached the end of the runway at 220 miles per hour, which is about 10 miles per hour faster than the Space Shuttle lands. You had to fly those beasts down back then. I used to refer to my 20-plus-ton aircraft as a supersonic manhole cover. So we were moving right along as we crossed the numbers and a smile crept across my face. The air speed was bleeding off perfectly as we settled closer to the runway. Tears of joy were beginning to form in the corners of my eyes.

We were about 10 feet off the deck, only moments from the sweetest touchdown in history, when my radar observer made his move. "Danny, are you sure you put the landing gear down?" I panicked. Instead of gently kissing the runway with my tires, I struck the runway with my landing gear and bounced, not once but three times. Once again, my radar observer nearly wet his pants laughing. But he wasn't through.

As I taxied off the active runway, he said, "Danny, do you want me to log all three of those landings?" He could no doubt tell I wasn't amused because he tried to console me by saying, "If nothing else, you just impressed that surveying crew with how strong the landing gear is on an F-101."

Input—evaluation—response. In the two stories I just told you, I received input, I evaluated, and then I reacted. Kind of a knee-jerk reaction to be more exact. Please note that on both

The F-101

occasions, I set myself up to be victimized by his devious input. If I had used my "now" filter a little more judiciously, I would have placed myself in a better position to respond more appropriately.

The more familiar you become with your people, the better you are going to understand how they filter the "now," what is stored in their memory movie, and how they are likely to respond to the input you provide. The effective leader is one who is sensitive to each of his or her people on each person's level of evaluating and responding to data. A good leader also recognizes that pressure and heat often stem from inappropriate input. We can take a potentially enormous amount of heat off ourselves as leaders by paying more attention to the input we provide to those we report to and those who report to us.

Biography

DANNY COX

Danny Cox is known as an accelerationist—one who causes faster movement, higher efficiency and increased productivity. Danny spent ten years flying supersonic all-weather fighters for the U.S. Air Force. In addition to his duties as a test pilot and air show pilot, Danny was a speaker to civilian organizations in the surrounding cities that were hard hit by sonic booms. At the time, this experience earned him the international reputation and moniker, The Sonic Boom Salesman. If Danny can sell sonic booms to civilians, imagine what he can do for your company or program. Danny's real world experience, shattering national sales records as leader of a nationally known

sales company, makes him the perfect motivational speaker. Author of the best selling book *Leadership When the Heat's On, Seize the Day,* and his latest book, *There Are No Limits.* Danny's reputation makes him one of America's busiest speakers. Danny's presentations include leadership, motivation and achievement, team building, customer service and coaching and mentoring. Danny's unique, highly acclaimed high-flying humor and thought-provoking material make him an excellent keynoter, after-dinner speaker or seminar leader.

KEN DRAVIS

JESSE ON THE WING

It's been six or seven years now. I recall that memorable journey from a tiny Vermont town to the glittering lights of Las Vegas, Nevada. The event taking me west turned out to be more than just another aviation convention. It was my chance to meet a lady I'll never forget.

Though I am a pilot and a plane is always my preferred mode of travel, necessity sometimes requires use of my old Dodge van. On this occasion, the inside of the van was packed with cassettes and CDs, guitars, sound and lighting equipment, and my lone mind and body, all racing towards the Southwest desert.

Colorado and Arizona had been my life in the 80's. I felt in my heart that I was heading toward home. It would be difficult for me to explain these feelings to you in a thousand words. It has to do with the region's people, the color of the sky, the towering afternoon thunderstorms and the scent of the pine in the San Juans. I could go on about these feelings that resurface each time I'm in that part of the world or even heading in that direction. Memories of the Rockies, where I learned to fly, have always inspired my music writing.

This extended road trip went without incident. The days traveling through Colorado, Utah and Nevada filled my mind with ideas, melodies and lyrics for new songs. Over the past several years, I had been writing about airplanes and the people who love to fly them. In that short time, I had played for folks in many states. Faces and names were becoming familiar wherever I performed. We had a common bond... aviation.

It continues to surprise and comfort me to happen upon old friends when appearing at various aviation shows around the U.S. This trip to Vegas was no different. While setting up my Aviation Music booth, a number of friends dropped by to say hello. One of them was Steve Soper, an aerobatic pilot from Idaho. I met Steve and his wife while performing at the Grand Junction Air Show in Colorado. Steve asked if he could play some of my songs during his airshow flight routine. That's what my music is all about.

Steve started bringing folks over to my booth to meet me. One charming soul, 80 years young, was a woman who touched my heart with stories filled with the trials and triumphs of her life. Jesse Woods was full of flattery and compliments. Beating around the bush was simply not her style. She immediately insisted that we dance. This was in the midst of the noise and clutter of the workers arranging convention displays all around us. So, what was I to do? We danced. How she loved to dance. The setting didn't seem to faze her in the slightest. In fact, I don't even think she noticed.

Jesse spoke of her life as a child in Kansas and travels with her family. I vividly remember her eyes as she began to tell me her life's story. They were bright and glistened with moisture of tears in recalling old friends, hard times, joy and the young man who changed her life.

I could see the memories in her eyes
Of long ago, the man she loved, stories of her life
And as she spoke I watched her drift away
To the memories as warm as yesterday   ♫

After our dance, I sat with Jesse for more than two hours, enchanted by what she had to say and how she said it. I wrote as she retraced her life for me. Most of the time, she seemed far away as she spoke. My occasional question would redirect her focus to the present for only a moment. I was fascinated by her recollection of detail. Her stories were many, but they mostly revolved around one man, the stunt pilot who stole her heart at the tender age of 16.

Jesse told me of the night her father allowed and trusted her to attend the local dance, as long as she did not socialize with that "no-good daredevil," Jimmy Woods. She admitted openly to me that the previous year she became smitten with Jimmy when he had flown into town. Young Jimmy never left her mind that long year as she anticipated his return.

This cold night would be a turning point for Jesse. Her desire to see Jimmy again outweighed her father's orders to keep her distance. She was totally enamored of Jimmy. She wasn't about to let him leave again without her. Jesse left the dance alone. Saying good night to her parents, she went to her room and closed the door. She and Jimmy had a plan. In a heart-racing moment, Jesse rushed to pack only her nightgown, toothbrush and violin. In the dark of the night she slipped away, leaving the safety and comfort of her family. Their small Kansas farmhouse was soon miles behind her.

Jesse smiled and said that winter was cold
1928 in Kansas, where she met her beau
She broke her daddy's heart, never said goodbye
The night that she flew off with Jimmy into the sky

Interrupting her train of thought, I was compelled to ask, "Where did you go? How did you survive?" Jesse was only a young girl and Jimmy was a penniless daredevil pilot. They didn't have a dollar between them. Even after all these years, her infatuation with Jimmy remained undiminished. Jimmy was everything to her, and she'd follow him anywhere. And so she did. Jimmy was part of the Flying Aces Circus along with other barnstorming stunt pilots. Lord, she made me laugh and drew me into every tale.

Jesse relived in her eyes those hard times and confessed that she and Jimmy barely got by. Just about the time they'd scrape some money together, an airplane would need repairs. There was always one thing or another.

During their early years together, the Flying Aces would circle a town and perform aerobatics to draw attention and attract a gathering of locals to an area field. The pilots would offer rides for $1. The rides would hopefully earn them enough money for gas, oil, upkeep, and perhaps on a good day, some food. But money was scarce and the Aces needed some type of gimmick to create a sensation. The group was talking about how to increase the number of spectators and income. One member came up with an idea. He suggested they get someone to walk out on the wing and wave at the townsfolk. Jesse recounted to me that, in unison, all eyes slowly turned directly toward her. She said, "Oh, nooooo ya' don't!" But Jesse being the way she is, wound up being their first wing walker... Jesse On The Wing.

They flew across this country, not a nickel to their names
Above the town they'd form a crowd, for food and shelter from
*   the rain*
A dollar for a ride, to buy some gas then on their way
She winked at me and said those were the days
And the rushing wind would make the wires sing
There she goes, Jesse On The Wing

My songs come from the heart. Jesse and her stories touched me. This song that I wrote for her simply came to me in the days following our chance meeting. The sparkle in her smile and the light in her eye still grace a part of my being as a human and an aviator. These songs are for you. Enjoy!

Biography

KEN DRAVIS

Ken Dravis, "The Singing Pilot," has delighted audiences across the country in a variety of settings. His songs are original and his insight of aviation is unique. He has three aviation albums to his credit, *Songs of the Sky*, *Hooked on Flight*, and *Flying: Home to You*. Ken is the only professional entertainer/songwriter/corporate pilot in the world. Ken's love of aviation is obvious. As for his musical talents, he's a natural. He puts into words the incredible feeling that flight brings out in a pilot, with songs such as *Go Around, Take Me Away, Commuter Airline Blues, Don't Take Chances (With Your Life)*, and *Marry Me—Fly Free*. These are the songs you'll find yourself singing after hearing them. The kids like his singing too, especially *Air Show* and *(Daddy) Teach Me To Fly*. His latest album, *Rocky Mountain Memories, The John Denver Tribute*, is dedicated to his late close friend and cohort. They discovered that they shared a love of music and flying when Ken worked for John.

BETTY GEIGER-DARST

Betty Geiger-Darst, as Katharine Wright, presents a living biography. She provides her audiences with a rich historical cameo of Wilbur and Orville Wright's sister. Betty's interest in the Wright family was a natural extension of her exploration of the history of flight. Her research led to a relationship with the surviving Wright family and the unique opportunity to study Katharine, Orville and Wilbur through the generational tapestry of letters, diaries and family records. The depth of this research is immediately evident in Darst's portrayal when she greets her audience in a copy of a 1909 homecoming suit worn by Katharine as she greeted her brothers' return from Europe. Darst not only meets her audience in the persona of Katharine, she proceeds to share a remarkably personal account of the first family of aviation through a multimedia slide presentation and short vignettes based on Katharine's personal letters. Her insights of "Orv" and "Wil" are fascinating, inspiring and touching.

WRIGHT BROTHER QUOTES

This chapter represents only a few of the favorite quotes that symbolize the Wright story. Looking at what the Wrights and others had to say, one can quickly appreciate how truly gifted these two brothers were:

"It is not really necessary to look too far into the future; we see enough already to be certain it will be magnificent. Only let us hurry and open the roads." **Wilbur Wright in France 1908**

"I never knew a more simple, unaffected trio than Wilbur, Orville, and Katharine... Their heads were not in the least turned by the various attentions bestowed on them nor by the many great financial offers given to them to make demonstrations...." **Lord Northcliffe of England**

"When you have once made a friendship you can't unmake it. You take all the pleasure and privilege and responsibilities that go with it." **Katharine Wright**

"Regardless of any other recompense for our work, the fact that it has been the means of bringing us the friendship of several exceptionally congenial spirits was alone worth the effort." **Wilbur writing to friends in England 1911**

"In New York during the Curtiss suit, the judge asked Wil to explain how something worked. Wil went to a blackboard and drew a figure which anyone could understand. Afterward, the Curtiss lawyer said that if it hadn't been for Wil and his 'damned string and chalk' they would have won the case." **Katharine's letters**

"When Orv was in the air anyone could recognize who it was from the smoothness of his flying. And when he wished to test the control and stability of a plane, he would sometimes come down and make figure-eights at steep angles with the wing tip maybe not more than a few feet from the grass." **Katharine Wright**

WRIGHT BROTHER QUESTIONS AND ANSWERS

How did the Wright brothers become interested in flight?

Orville and Wilbur Wright grew up in a very supportive family. It was a family that believed if someone was interested in something, they should be encouraged. The Wright family philosophy provided the support needed to develop the special interests of these two inquisitive young men. These two brothers were always involved in projects that demonstrated their imagination and creativity. As a result, they developed many innovations in printing, created a calculating machine and even manufactured their own brand of bicycle. Fortunately for us, the 1890s was a time when the whole world was fascinated with the concept of flight. While ballooning was popular, it was an article on Otto Lilienthal and his gliders in the 1894 issue of McClure's magazine that captured Wil and Orv's attention. This challenged the brothers and inspired them to make the first heavier-than-air powered flight.

How did Wil and Orv solve the secret of flight when others failed?

They worked in tandem, finding strength in cooperation. Neither could have solved the problem alone. Although they always wore white shirts and ties when testing their flying machine, the brothers were very different. Wil would be covered with grease after a hard day's work in the bike shop. Orv, on the other hand, could work all day with nary a speck of dirt on his immaculate outfit. These two brothers present a case of contrasts while working in perfect harmony. And this was their special gift, which they used to their advantage. One would take the opposite side of an argument, saying "Tis so," while the other brother would say, "Tisn't either." They'd fuss long into the night until one had converted the other to his point of view.

According to their sister Katharine Wright, *"Oh, they have just had no end of fun learning to fly. To hear them argue around and knock the bottom out of each other's ideas, then at the end of three hours to find Orv where Wil started off, and Wil where Orv began, is just the killingest thing imaginable, and makes them both burst out laughing but it saved them no end of useless experiment...."*

Orville watching Wilbur at the controls with sister
Katharine as passenger. Pau, France 1909

Although they had their differences, the brothers trusted each
other implicitly. In fact, from the first time they entered business
together, they held a joint checking account and neither questioned the other on how the money was spent.

Why did the Wrights go to Kitty Hawk to conduct their experiments?

Three reasons: Wind, space and forgiving sand. Kitty Hawk
was selected after correspondence with the United States
Weather Service. It offered a reasonable number of windy, rain-
free days each fall. William Tate, Kitty Hawk's postmaster and
host to the arriving Wrights, described it as sandy land, free of
trees to break the wind current which often held to a steady 10 to
20 mph.

How old were Wilbur and Orville at the time of their first flight?

From Bishop Wright's diary, we find that Wilbur was 36 and Orville was 32.

How much did the first flying machine cost to develop?

On October 7, 1903, an airplane built by Samuel Langley fell into the Potomac river seconds after takeoff. The United States government spent $50,000 to have Samuel Langley build this aircraft. When Orv heard how much the government spent on Langley's expensive failure, he began figuring how much they had spent. The total came to less than $1,000, which included trips to Kitty Hawk. Some sources report this amount spent as $850. This came from the money they had saved from their bicycle business. When Bishop Wright sold a farm, he divided the money among his four sons. Wilbur and Orville had received a total of $3,000 from the farm sale but none of that was used in the development of the flying machine. Octave Chanute offered the brothers $10,000, which they refused.

Did Wil or Orv ever marry and did they have children?

Neither Wil nor Orv married. However, their two older brothers Reuchlin and Loren married and had children. They did a lot of babysitting for their nieces and nephews in the bicycle shop. At the age of 52, Wil and Orv's sister Katharine Wright married her math tutor from her Oberlin college days.

Why was Orville critical of Katharine's marriage at the age of 52?

Katharine provided an insight to this question in one of her letters. The Wright family was different from the typical family. For a long time Katharine was the only woman in the family and the other family members came to depend on her. She cared for Orv in the hospital at Fort Meyers, nursed Wil before his death from typhoid and cared for her aging father. She provided strong family support. She was also free from responsibility and had wonderful privileges as a sister of Wil and Orv.

Katharine once said that it was hard for her to leave Orv because of the on-going difficulties with the Curtiss lawsuit and the Smithsonian controversy. In one of her letters, dated January 13, 1926, she says:

"One of the things that makes it so hard for me to leave Orv, is the way that thing [Curtiss & Smithsonian problems] *has gone. Little brother has had so much trouble and he deserved just the opposite. For so many years I've tried to head off things that would worry him. I suppose sometimes I've kept to myself things that ought to have been told."*

Why was the United States so slow to recognize the achievements of the Wright brothers?

The U.S. government suffered from the embarrassment of Langley's unsuccessful flight attempts, having been heavily financed by tax dollars. It was hard to believe that two unknown people from Dayton, Ohio could possibly have mastered the secret of flight without any government assistance.

Where was the world's first flying school located?

In order to fulfill a contract with the French, the brothers had to train at least three pilots who would then train others in France. Wilbur had been flying at Le Mans, France, located just outside Paris. They needed milder weather to continue flying. Wilbur took the flying machine south to Pau which stands at the gateway to the Pyrenees Mountains. Pau became the home of the world's first flying school.

Who bought the world's first private airplane?

Charles S. Rolls of England's Rolls-Royce Automobiles was the first person in the world to purchase a private airplane. Rolls was a balloonist and an aviation enthusiast. He was one of the first to go to France to see Wilbur fly, recognizing that a miracle had just taken place. From that moment on, his ballooning was only for pleasure as he embraced mechanical flight. (In 1910 he was killed in an airplane crash in Bournemouth, England.)

Why were the Wright brothers successful when so many others had tried and failed?

The Wrights not only developed the world's first practical airplane, they also developed the science and technology to understand flight. For instance, they developed a wind tunnel in which miniature wings could be tested. They were the first to take useful measurements of the lift and drag and the travel of the center of pressure on curved surfaces. They were the first to compile tables that were helpful in designing airplanes. The accuracy of these measurements was instrumental in building the Kitty Hawk Flyer. In addition, they taught themselves and others how to pilot the craft. The Wright brothers opened the door for aviation as we know it today. Their tables and tests provided the resources that helped others to succeed.

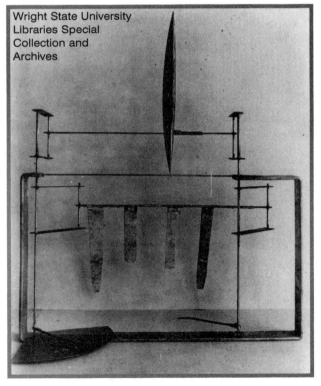

Wright State University Libraries Special Collection and Archives

The Wright Brother's early wind tunnel lift balance.
Circa 1901-02.

What did the Wright brothers think about women flying?

The Wright brothers were exposed to a technically capable woman early in their lives. Their mother was the engineer and mathematician of the family. She made things like sleds for the older boys. She taught Wil and Orv that it was a lot cheaper to make their mistakes on paper. Sister Katharine eventually became a supporting, non-technical and non-pilot partner to the brothers. At 18 years of age, Marjorie Stinson came to Dayton to learn to fly at the Wright School. Orville had someone call her parents to make sure they approved of such a young lady taking flying lessons. While waiting for the return phone call, Orville took Marjorie on a tour of the Wright factory.

How did Orville feel about the progress of the airplane in his lifetime?

Orv lived to see many advances in flight. He traveled in airplanes whose wingspans were greater than the length of the Kitty Hawk flight. Just 34 years after Kitty Hawk, the first jet engine was developed. After he stopped flying, Orv was often a commercial passenger. A number of pilots had their licenses autographed by Orville Wright. When airline pilots knew that Orville Wright was on board, he was frequently invited to the cockpit.

The last public photo taken with Orville was with around-the-world flyers Clifford Evans and George Truman in 1947. These two pilots stopped off to visit Orville in his home during the last leg of their world flight. He asked about their flight, they asked him about the early Wright brothers history.

How did the Wright brothers feel about their invention being used as a tool in warfare?

They never sought to exploit the emotion of patriotism or to suggest that national security required a multitude of martial wings. Wilbur died before the lethal capacity of the airplane was demonstrated.

Shortly after the outbreak of the First World War, the press noted that England was experimentally dropping oranges from an airplane to the deck of a seagoing vessel in an attempt to determine the feasibility of bombing ships. One of Orville's neighbors, who later became Dean of the School of Theology at Marion College, Indiana, took this news clipping over to Orville for his opinion.

Orville commented as follows: *"Up to the present time the wars of the world have been fought largely by the common people, while those who were responsible for declaring war remained at home. The airplane will change this. As a result of the use of the airplane, the palaces of kings and rulers will no longer be safe, but will be in danger of being blown up by bombshells dropped upon them from airplanes, I believe."* Orv concluded with, *"...the airplane will help to put an end to war, for when the men who make war find their own lives in danger, they will be less likely to decree war."* (From Kelly's Wright Brothers - page 290)

WRIGHT BROTHER'S INSIGHTS

How It Began

One of the most important letters ever received by the Smithsonian was written May 30, 1899 by Wilbur, who wrote, *"I believe that simple flight at least is possible to man and that the experiments and investigations of a large group of independent workers will result in the accumulation of information and knowledge and skill which will finally lead to accomplished flight.... I am about to begin a systematic study of the subject in preparation for practical work to which I expect to devote what time I can spare from my regular business. I wish to obtain such papers as the Smithsonian Institution has published on this subject, and if possible a list of other works in print in the English language. I am an enthusiast, but not a crank in the sense that I have some pet theories as to the proper construction of a flying machine. I wish to avail myself ...of what is already known and then if possible add my mite to help the future worker who will attain final success. I do not know the terms on which you send out your publications but if you will inform me of the cost I will remit the price."*

Richard Rathbun at the Smithsonian responded with information about booklets and referred the Wrights to Octave Chanute. (Octave Chanute was a civil engineer, aerial experimenter, and author of the book *Progress in Flying Machines* (1894). Chanute responded to the Wrights' inquiry. He followed their experiments closely and offered the services of his staff. The Wrights corresponded with Chanute until shortly before Chanute died in May 1910.

In Wilbur's letter to Octave Chanute on May 13, 1900, he writes, *"For some years I have been afflicted with the belief that flight is possible to man. My disease has increased in severity and I feel it will soon cost me an increased amount of money if not my life. I have been trying to arrange my affairs in such a way that I can devote my entire time for a few months to experiment in this field. It is possible to fly without motors, but not without knowledge and skill. This I conceive to be fortunate, for man, by reason of his greater intellect, can more reasonably hope to equal birds in knowledge, than to equal nature in the perfection of her machinery."*

A Promise by His Sons

Many lives had been lost in the experimenting. Wilbur and Orville had promised their father that they would not take any unnecessary chances. On July 26, 1901, Wilbur writes to his father, Bishop Wright, and says, *"We expect to be careful to avoid real risks. We do not think there is any real danger of serious injury in the experiments we make. We will not venture on thin ice until we are certain that it will much more than bear us."*

It Just Didn't Seem Possible

When I first began sharing the story of the Wrights, people often asked me what I thought of Bishop Wright's statement that man would not fly for a thousand years and that he did not believe that man should fly. The closest quote is credited to Wilbur. The brothers were returning home from disappointing tests at Kitty Hawk in 1901, and were feeling they had gone as far as they could go. He doubted if they would ever resume their experiments. Wilbur, in a state of melancholy, gave the quote that I find most believable. *"Man will not fly for one hundred years."* He felt that powered flight could not be achieved within his lifetime. At the patent hearings in 1912, Wilbur testified, *"When we left Kitty Hawk at the end of 1901, we doubted that we would ever resume our experiments.... At this time I made the prediction that men would sometime fly, but that it would not be within our lifetime..."*

Fortunately, according to Charlie Taylor, the man who built the engine for the world's first powered flight, *"They* [Orv and Wil] *were always thinking of the next thing to do,"* said Charlie. *"They didn't waste much time worrying about the past."*

Nevertheless, to provide a tonic for Wilbur's depressed spirits, Octave Chanute arranged for Wilbur to be invited to speak to the Western Society of Engineers in Chicago. Katharine is credited with nagging him into going. When she asked him whether his speech was to be witty or scientific, Wilbur replied that he *"thought it would be pathetic before he got through with it."*

Wilbur's speech gave to the world the information that experimenters needed in their journey towards powered flight. During the speech he shared what it was like to learn how to pilot the glider. Taking a piece of paper, he held it out at arm's length in full view of the audience, and then let it flutter to the ground. He explained, *"...it will not settle steadily down as a staid, sensible piece of paper ought to do, but it insists on contravening every recognized rule of decorum, turning over and darting hither and thither in the most erratic manner, much after the style of an untrained horse. Yet this is the style of steed that men must learn to manage before flying can become an everyday sport.... Now there are two ways of learning to ride a fractious horse: one is to get on him and learn by actual practice how each motion and trick may be best met; the other is to sit on a fence and watch the beast awhile, and then retire to the house and at leisure figure out the best way of overcoming his jumps and tricks. The latter system is the safest; but the former on the whole, turns out the larger proportion of good riders. It is very much the same in learning to ride a flying machine; if you are looking for perfect safety you will do well to sit on a fence and watch the birds; but if you really wish to learn you must mount a machine and become acquainted with its tricks by actual trial."*

In Bishop Wright's diary dated December 17, 1903, he writes, *"Wilbur is 36, Orville 32 and they are as inseparable as twins. For*

The first flight, December 17, 1903. Before the 120 foot, twelve-second flight, Orville positioned the camera, instructing Kitty Hawk resident, J.T. Daniels, when to activate the shutter. This was the world's first free, controlled and sustained flight in a heavier-than-air power-driven airplane.

several years they have read up on aeronautics as a physician would read his books, and they have studied, discussed, and experimented together. Natural workmen, they have invented, constructed, and operated their gliders, and finally their Wright Flyer, jointly, all at their own personal expense. About equal credit is due each."

According to Charmley, Wil is reported to have said just before his trial flight in 1903, *"Some day, somebody's going to make a plane with a motor powerful enough to raise it in still air, and then it'll make more than that speed—more than thirty miles an hour. Imagine it!"*

The French Go Crazy

In a letter from Wilbur to Orville dated August 25, 1908, Wilbur said, *"The excitement aroused by the short flights I have made is almost beyond comprehension. The French have simply become wild. Instead of doubting that we could do anything they are ready to believe that we can do everything.... People have flocked here from all over Europe, and as I wish to practice rather than give exhibitions it is a little embarrassing.... If the wind is more than five miles an hour I stay in.... Do not let yourself be forced into doing anything before you are ready."*

Wilbur's Most Remembered Speech

The speech people remember most often from Wilbur is not his earth-changing presentation at the Western Society of Engineers but the famous parrot speech. He was invited to receive an honor at a formal dinner of the Aero-Club of Sarthe, France on Sept. 24, 1908. He agreed to this, providing he would not have to make a speech to the group. The people in attendance, however, kept insisting that he speak. When he rose, he uttered his famous parrot speech. "I know of only one bird, the parrot, that talks, and it cannot fly very high or say very much." Immediately he sat down.

Wilbur Wright working the lathe at the
Wright Cycle Company, Dayton 1897.

Typhoid Takes Wilbur at Forty-Five

Bishop Wright's Diary, May 30, 1912 reads, *"This morning at 3:15, Wilbur passed away, age: 45 years, one month, 14 days...a short life, full of consequences. An unfailing intellect, imperturbable temper, great self-reliance and as great modesty, seeing the right clearly, pursuing it steadily, he lived and died."*

Flattery Seen a Mile Away

Regarding the fawning behavior shown to Wil and Orv, Katharine Wright said, *"...it is so easy to believe flatterers and they always surround anyone who is a little successful or prominent. It is so small-so childish; it shows such a lack of experience and observation and understanding of the great things in the world, to imagine oneself so wonderful and it shows that you don't know much about people if you believe all they say to your face. Orv is always warning me not to take too seriously the nice things people say to me about him for instance or anything else that is of great interest to me. My little Brother is not easily soft-soaped or deceived. Sometimes he makes mistakes but not often."* In September of 1925, while enroute to a meeting, Katharine remarked that she supposed the people who think the least of Orv will make the most fuss over him.

Orv is a Keeper

Orv never threw away anything. All of his personal checks were carefully packaged and tied with a light string and stored in the attic of Hawthorn Hill, the family mansion. They were packaged in order according to the year. Following Orv's death, the family disposed of unwanted possessions. The checks were in boxes that were sold. Susan Wright noted that the family later regretted that happening. These checks with Orville's signature were later sold in a frame mounting along with a photo of the first flight for a great amount of money. Some of the checks were written to help pay the way of deserving young people to college. Horace Wright, their nephew, was one of the recipients. He wanted to go to Massachusetts Agriculture College because of the excellent botany courses. Katharine said she would equal what

Horace saved by working. Orv, not to be outdone, said he would double what Horace saved. This is how Horace was able to afford a year of school in the east.

An Inventive Family

The Wrights were an inventive family. Mom Wright (the mathematician and engineer of the family) designed all her own clothes but first made a sketch of what she thought she wanted to make. She made all of Bishop Wright's clothes. She made a pattern, then tested the pattern on herself for size. She cautioned her children to try and make all of their mistakes on paper, as it would save them grief later.

Orville learned to make biscuits without use of milk. Father insisted that they were better than anyone else could make.

Wright State University Libraries
Special Collection and Archives

This photo, taken in Pau, France around 1909, shows Wilbur holding an anemometer, measuring the speed of the wind. Orville, to the left, is still using a cane because of injuries sustained in the 1908 Fort Meyers crash.

Another example of the inventive nature of Orville Wright is the balsa wood toy glider called the "Wright Flyer." Orville Wright also designed other toys, which were produced in brother Lorin's toy factory. Orv designed, among other specialized machines, a printing press that was used to put the advertiser's name on the wings of the Wright Flyer. Some of the family had to miss the dedication of the Kitty Hawk National Monument as they had to stay behind to fill a Quaker Oats' order for one million gliders to go into cereal boxes.

The Wright Inquisitiveness

Orv bought one of the first IBM electric typewriters. In his fascination with the typewriter, he tried to discover exactly how it worked and began to disassemble it. He toiled at it with screwdriver and pliers for three-quarters of an hour. He examined, explored, poked, and pushed with serious intensity. Finally, he had the floor covered with the parts of the machine and he didn't quite see how to put it together again.

His secretary, Mabel Beck, called for the IBM service man. *"He took one look at the parts,"* Orville's niece, Ivonette, recalled, *"and said, 'Look, I service these machines, but I don't assemble them'."* The service man gathered up the parts, sent them back to the factory and they sent him a new machine.

In their new home on Hawthorn Hill, Orv purchased a new gas stove ($35.00) for Carrie, the housekeeper. He asked her how the heat regulator worked and insisted on finding out for himself. Orv took apart the heat regulator and put it back together again. It never worked the same.

At another time Dayton Jewelers was unable to fix a complicated ship's clock which was a gift from his great friend, Griffith Brewer, a leader in British Aviation. Orville fixed it himself.

The Wright home on Hawthorn Hill had a central heating system. Orv rigged the wires and levers, which he understood but nobody else could. After his death the entire heating system had to be replaced. The house had a wonderful water system that Orv designed along with a central vacuum system that was quite unwieldy. It is still workable today.

Orv was always handy. There was a bathroom for each of the bedrooms and Orv always kept everything in working order. His own bathroom was quite large, done in white tile with built-in cabinets. He had installed a wooden rack from which he suspended bottles of shaving and hand lotion and mouthwash. The shaving lotion was a special concoction of his own made of bay rum and rose water with other ingredients. The huge shower was lined with pipes and fixtures which provided spray from many directions simultaneously. Orville designed the shower and it was built to his specifications with two shower curtains. One was an attractive turquoise blue, but behind it was a weather-beaten tarpaulin—part of the tarpaulin that had covered the original Kitty Hawk Flyer. His adjoining bedroom was quite small, in contrast to his magnificent bathroom.

Unfortunately, Orv never fully recovered from the Fort Meyers airplane crash. He continued to have difficulty getting up and down out of his chair. He didn't like to change records, so he began working on a phonograph record changer.

His niece Ivonette said, *"He'd pile up a lot of records and, consulting the chart with the names of the selections, he'd press a button to eject one and select another. I don't remember whether he*

Flying in Pau, France in 1909.

ever got it working right, but I do remember he came to our house and asked us if we had any old records. He was breaking so many he was running out of supplies." If one were to visit Orv's study today they would see a page turner mounted on the side of his chair with a book opened to the pages that he might have just been reading. His sciatica gave him difficulty. Turning the pages of a book would add strain.

In 1916 he vacationed in the area of Georgian Bay and saw Lambert Island, which became his summer home for more than 30 years. The cares of the world seemed to ease for him during the time he spent at the island. Blueberries thrived on the island. Orv especially liked blueberry pie.

He rigged up a railway to bring luggage and supplies from the dock, a water system, and his own type of security system which prevented break-ins when the Wrights weren't on the island. His boat also had many unique gadgets.

He fashioned a device to make toast over a kerosene stove by hinging two thin sheets of steel together. Then he clamped the bread between them and got toast free of kerosene fumes. Orv also had quite a sweet tooth. On Sunday afternoons he might like to make caramels on the excuse that the nieces and nephews wanted some. He was always concocting unique flavors of ice cream. One of his most unusual flavors was fig ice cream. Rigging the ice cream maker with a motor instead of turning the crank by hand saved them a lot of work. Unfortunately, Orv had not learned all of the tricks and the ice cream froze too fast.

Orville at the controls of the Baby Grand racing plane at Belmont Park, New York in 1910.

ADDITIONAL INFORMATION ABOUT THE WRIGHTS

* Had Orv not had the hobby of photography the world would have never seen the first flight photo (some folks think it to be more famous than the Mona Lisa).

* Orville and Wilbur's father kept a diary nearly every day of his adult life. The records were quite complete and provided valuable information during the patent hearings of 1912.

* Many people are unaware that the family had four brothers and one sister. Reuchlin was the oldest followed by Lorin. Wilbur was three-and-a-half years older than Orville. Katharine was the youngest, being exactly three years younger than Orv. There were also twins who died in infancy.

* Katharine was often described as vivacious and lively. She was the outgoing person in the family.

* None of the children in the family had middle names. The family had a nickname for Katharine, "Sterchens"—German for little sister.

* When Wil went to France, the public was hesitant to embrace him because he was so modest and unassuming. He wore the same type of overalls used by the workers in Leon Bollee's automobile factory where he had been given space. He set to work, keeping the same 10-hour day as the others and ate his lunch with them out of his own lunch pail when the noon whistle sounded. To the workmen, this casual behavior was extraordinary, so unlike the glamorized picture of Brazilian inventor-aeronaut Santos Dumont who did little work with his own hands and mixed only with his colleagues.

* On April 23, 1911, Wilbur visited the widow of Otto Lilienthal in Berlin to ascertain her financial situation and to view Lilienthal's old flying grounds. On December 2, 1911 the Wrights sent her a check for $1,000 as a token of their appreciation of Lilienthal's contribution to aeronautics.

Katharine speaking with an official. Orville and Wilbur Wright at right.

BETTY GEIGER-DARST

Betty is a student pilot and has flown a great deal of "copilot"
time with her husband in their airplane.

PETER V. AGUR JR.

DAD

My father, a naval aviator, was gone a lot, so my mother became a master at single-handedly parenting four small kids. One morning, when I was eight, during the chaos of getting two of us ready for school and feeding the other two, there was a knock on the front door. All activity stopped while my mother answered the door. It was a commander and a chaplain, with hats in hand. After a brief, hushed conversation at the door, the commander and chaplain adjourned to the living room to wait. My mother quickly finished getting the two of us out the door and on our way to school and then took the younger two kids to a neighbor so she could talk to her visitors in private.

They told her dad had ferried an aircraft to a naval air station in Japan and then boarded a Navy DC-7 for the long trip home. It was a two-stop trip, one at Midway Island and one in Hawaii. During the descent into Honolulu the plane struck a mountain. There were no survivors.

Word of a tragedy travels quickly in the naval wives' community. Mom later told me that by mid-morning the house was filled with friends and neighbors providing solace, helping with the babies, and bringing a feast of food. Shortly after the lunch dishes had been cleared, the front door opened and in walked my father.

During the refueling stop at Midway, he explained, he had gone into base operations and noticed another flight was two hours behind his. Since it was a nonstop flight he decided he could do some shopping and still be home at about the same time. He didn't know about the crash until he walked in the door. Happily enough, the Navy didn't have an accurate passenger manifest.

A FEW LESSONS IN LEADERSHIP
[Originally printed in *FAPA*, December 1992]

Vietnam's central highlands provided my first experience with "leadership" in the workplace. I was an Army aviator flying Hueys from one of the few airfields secured by South Vietnamese troops. Other more fortunate Army and Air Force airfields used the more effective U.S. ground forces to keep the bad guys on their side of the fence.

The Viet Cong knew our situation and took frequent advantage of it. We were the targets of light mortar harassment six to eight nights each month. Charlie would set up a mortar tube in the graveyard outside our perimeter and lob three or four shells into our compound to make sure we were all wide awake. Then he'd pack up and go home to bed while several hundred of us lost a couple of hours sleep guarding against a nonexistent ground assault.

Two or three times a year the Viet Cong spiced up their activities with a heavy pelting of mortars followed immediately by unwelcome visitors delivering satchel charges to our parked aircraft. These sapper attacks had a relatively low success ratio, but they were sure exciting!

Our platoon leader rotated home and was replaced by a new lieutenant. One of our guys thought it would be fun to brief him, over a few beers, on the camp's security situation. Since Army aviators have never been known to exaggerate, I must assume this new platoon leader had a vivid imagination because he slept in a bunker from that night on. During his second night in camp he experienced his first "three-shot-Charlie" event. The results were typical, plenty of noise and very little damage.

The next day our new lieutenant announced that enlisted flight crews (crew chiefs and door gunners), in addition to their flight schedules, would pull rotating duty as supplemental perimeter guards. Van, one of our most senior warrant officers, voiced strong concerns for the well-being of the crews. It was widely believed that a top notch crew chief and gunner were at least as valuable as "good luck" in making it through "365 days and a wakeup" to go home. Unfortunately, the lieutenant stood firm.

Van's reaction became legendary. What was expected of his crew was expected of him. He spent that night on the perimeter with his crew chief and gunner. As luck would have it, "three-shot-Charlie" delivered that night with the usual results.

The next morning, after only four hours rest, Van showed up at his helicopter for the day's mission. Doc, the company flight surgeon, wandered up to Van's ship, examined his eyes and grounded him for excess fatigue. Since we were short of pilots, an airworthy helicopter sat in its revetment that day. This did not look good on the company's operational readiness report, so some flight crew names disappeared from the guard duty roster later that day.

The moral to the story? The lieutenant may have been designated by the military system to a position of power, but Van proved to be the real leader. He kept the big picture in mind and knew success could be achieved by taking care of the basic needs of his people.

A LITTLE ENGLISH ON THE LANDING

I remember vividly my primary helicopter instructor, Rip Johnson, deftly demonstrating the techniques used in autorotation landings. He pre-briefed me, re-briefed me, and then described the decision cues as he demonstrated the first one. He was drop-jaw impressive. The next time around he asked me to lightly touch the controls as he did another one. Within a few laps of the field our shared efforts had shifted and I was doing most of the work.

Within a handful of tries I was consistently doing full touch-down autorotations without his assistance. Rip thought I was one of the sharpest students he had. What he didn't know was I have excellent peripheral vision and was watching his body language. At the bottom of the approach I could see his hand reach for the cyclic. This was the cue: time for me to flare. At the end of the flare, he'd reach for the collective. Time for me to cushion the touchdown. Since his timing was great, so was mine. He sent me on my first solo flight after about five hours total flight time. I'd never performed a truly unassisted autorotation. If the engine had quit during that flight I fully intended to make the landing as close to Rip as possible so I could see his helpful flinches.

Biography

PETER V. AGUR JR.

Pete Agur is a unique aviation business speaker. Audiences enjoy his informational and entertaining programs. His excellent academic credentials complement his extensive industry experience. He has worked with national service-based companies, Fortune 100 manufacturing companies, privately-held corporations, government organizations and public utilities on a broad spectrum of projects. These include, Strategic Planning and Implementation, Flight Department Start-up, Executive and Operational Personnel Selection, Organization and Teamwork Development, Operations Performance Measurement and Enhancement, Operations Consolidation, Flight Operations Cost-Benefit Analysis, Vendor and Equipment Selection and Acquisition and Disaster Response Preparedness. His work has been cited in *The Wall Street Journal, Aviation International News* and *Business and Commercial Aviation.* Pete is a contributor to *Business Aviation Management Journal, FORTUNE, Professional Pilot* and *Career Pilot* magazines. Pete's industry-leading work has been credited with making a significant positive impact for a number of companies on a variety of strategic and operational projects. Pete holds an MBA from Georgia State University, a B.S. (summa cum laude) in aeronautical sciences, an ATP certificate and multiple instructor ratings.

CATHERINE (CATHÉ) FISH

AIN'T NO ROOKIE

Being a female pilot does have its humorous side. On one of my charter flights, a passenger saw me in the pilot's seat and asked me if I really knew how to fly the thing.

Having heard this many times, I said with a straight face, "Well, you know, I'm not really sure." When we landed, he clapped and soon all the passengers were clapping with enthusiasm. I guess he was satisfied that I could really fly.

A female pilot friend of mine had a job flying aerial sightseeing tours in the African wilderness. One day a group of Japanese tourists arrived for the regular tour. They were puzzled when she met them at the plane and put their bags into the luggage compartment. In broken English, one asked her, "Where pilot?"

She thought she would have some fun. She looked around the tarmac and said, "I'm not really sure, but I'll look around." She gestured for them to get into the plane. Once they were seated and belted, she opened the cockpit door and with great exaggeration said, "Wow, here are the keys. And they left some instructions. Maybe I can fly the plane."

Slowly she read the checklist out loud, pondering each item, and eventually started the engine. She taxied down the dirt taxiway in an 'S' pattern, reinforcing the idea that she'd never taxied an airplane before. On takeoff, she continued the rookie persona, veering first towards one side of the runway, then the other, bouncing along on two, then one wheel before finally lifting off.

Once in the air, after a few steep turns, she gave the group an excellent tour. Then, with a smothered smile, she did a three-bounce landing.

Several weeks later, her boss called her in for a chat. He'd gotten a call from a Japanese tour coordinator wanting to schedule a tour. But they would only schedule if the company would let the lady baggage handler fly the plane again. The boss asked, "What's this about a lady baggage handler flying our planes?"

"Gulp."

CATCH 22

My dad is a retired captain of the Los Angeles fire department in California. On a visit with my parents, we were watching the 10 o'clock news. The newscaster informed us that a single engine airplane, identified as an Aero Commander, went down short of the Burbank airport. Both people on board survived.

The film footage showed the pilot, who was lucid, being cut out of the wreckage. On camera, the pilot said he ran out of fuel over Eagle Rock while trying to make the Burbank Airport.

The next camera shot was of the fire marshall in charge of the rescue. He looked into the camera and spoke with authority about the lack of fire saying, "They are just lucky there was no fuel on board."

Dad agreed. "You know how fuel feeds a fire. Remember when that plane hit the gas tanks at the Van Nuys Airport?"

"Oh, Daaaad," I said. "They wouldn't have crashed if they'd had fuel on board."

MULTI-ENGINE PILOT LADY

My husband and I have airplane-camped through much of the western United States and Mexico. We take the back seats out of our Cessna 172 in order to stow all our gear, including our bicycles with the handlebars turned sideways.

One spring, Doug and I got the itch for adventure. A three-week tour of mainland Mexico seemed the perfect cure. Most of the trip was wonderful and relaxing, sunny white sand beaches, turquoise water, great food, and lots of palm trees. Eating delicious lobster in Isla Mujeres stands out in my mind.

I quickly learned that talking to air traffic control in Mexico is quite different from in the states. When we flew into the airspace surrounding Acapulco, I called approach control and told them my position and intention to land. They handed me off to the tower, who told me "Cleared to land, lady." So I landed.

After I taxied off the active, I called ground control and asked for progressive instructions to the gas tanks. The same voice answered me: "Cleared to land, lady."

Thinking maybe that I should simplify my English, I said, "Where are the gas tanks?"

The reply was familiar. "Cleared to land, lady." I guess that was the only English he knew. My husband and I laughed uncontrollably as we taxied around the airport in search of the gas pumps. No one on frequency offered us further assistance.

On day eight, we landed in Palenque, seven miles from the famous Mayan ruins. Our intention was to pack our camping gear onto our bikes and ride to the campground near the ruins. No sooner had we landed, than a squad of very young Army soldiers armed with Belgian FN semi-automatic rifles surrounded us.

While the lieutenant went through all of our paperwork with a fine-toothed comb, the soldiers demanded to see every single piece of camp gear onboard. As each piece was taken out, such as our candle lantern or nested stainless steel cooking pots, each soldier had to "inspect" it. They were very polite about it, oohed and aahed and asked many questions. They were particularly impressed with our backpacking camp stove.

By the time they got to our soft-sided clothes bags, I was starting to get irritated. I reminded Doug of our carefully packed bribes of White Owl cigars. Doug ceremoniously presented one to each soldier, beginning with the lieutenant. Miraculously, just as Senterfitt's guidebook to Mexico indicated, as soon as the last soldier received his cigar, the search ended. The soldiers kindly offered to guard our airplane for us. They watched intently as we packed our bike panniers with our gear and rode off.

We continued to attract attention as we bicycled to town to find lunch. We stopped at a quaint restaurant in town and ordered the $3 fresh fish platters. We must have been riding the first mountain bicycles to be seen in this part of Mexico. Hundreds of villagers turned out to look at our bikes and touch

the tires. An hour later, we were still waiting for our fish platters. Turned out, it really was fresh—they sent someone out to catch the fish while we waited. The fish were huge, delicious and well worth the wait.

On day 15, in southern Mexico, we encountered unforecast marginal weather approaching our gas stop in Tuxla Gutiérrez. The field was below minimums and the whole area was socked in. There was not another airport with fuel for many miles. Approaching quarter tanks, we found the only airport that was above minimums was a nearby military field situated on higher ground. I didn't care to land there, but there was no alternative.

Taxiing in, we were surrounded by a horde of Mexican soldiers with semi-automatic rifles who directed us to park and shut down. A sergeant stomped out of a nearby building and headed straight for my husband who was sitting in the left seat. He pointed at Doug, who he assumed was the pilot, and told him to get out.

I suggested that Doug forget his fluent Spanish in this situation, so that we could feign ignorance. He got out and was immediately surrounded by armed soldiers. The sergeant insisted on speaking to the pilot in command. Doug was happy to point to me. The sergeant insisted on seeing his pilot license, which when finally produced, indicated *student pilot*. Then the sergeant demanded to know where Doug's instructor was while he was flying around Mexico. Again, Doug pointed at me.

After a lot more convincing on Doug's part in his pretend broken Spanish, reluctantly, the sergeant led me off to headquarters to face the commanding officer. I was scared. I tried to cajole the sergeant into letting Doug come with me. He said, emphatically, only the pilot in command. I had visions, due to the rumors I had heard, of being locked up for the rest of my life.

I can still see the look on the major's face when I entered the room. He started screaming at the sergeant, in Spanish, "I told you I wanted the pilot in command."

"But... she is the pilot in command, Major."

He didn't believe it, and in the next hour, he called in a handful of his staff members to ask them what to do with me. They were also incredulous.

Eventually they asked to see my pilot license. I brought all three out; commercial, flight instructor and ground instructor, and any other paperwork that looked impressive, including my last seven FAA medicals and my FCC radio operator permit. Each staff member had many comments as each studied every piece of my paperwork, turning them over and over and over.

Occasionally, they asked me questions. In broken Spanish I told them, "Mal tiempo, un poco gasolina." (Bad weather, little gas). They continued to argue about my disposition.

Finally, they agreed I had probably stolen the airplane, and they would arrest me if I didn't have the proper aircraft papers and visa. Fortunately, I was able to quickly produce all the proper paperwork.

The major seemed relieved. He actually smiled and slapped me on the back saying in English, "Multi-engine pilot lady, multi-engine pilot lady." He started calling in more staff members to meet the pilot lady. Two hours had now passed. They told me the weather had improved, and I could fly the seven or so miles to Tuxla Guiterrez to get gas.

Meanwhile, Doug's Spanish kept "improving" while everything we had onboard was slowly scrutinized. At the proper time, Doug pulled out White Owl cigars for each soldier. Once again, as soon as the last soldier received his cigar, the search ended. The soldiers spent the rest of the time asking Doug about our airplane engine and its performance.

When I was released from the building, I could hear Doug and the soldiers laughing. As I walked back to the plane, I could hear Doug asking the soldiers in Spanish, "When was the last time you shot a gringo?"

"Aye," one of the youngest soldiers confidently replied, puffing on his cigar, "the only gringos we shoot are drugistas."

What a relief, I thought.

LAST WORD

One of my flight students, now a Center controller, told me about a grouchy controller who must stay awake at night thinking up zingers to wing at pilots. One day grouchy was calling an aircraft on frequency, "USAir 123, Cleveland Center."

Pause

"USAir 123, Cleveland Center"

Pause

"USAir, you're just like my wife, you never listen."

"Cleveland Center, this is USAir 321. You might get her attention if you call her by her right name."

ONE OF A KIND

At the age of 79, my friend Pete Campbell died peacefully in his sleep, Christmas Eve 1999. While feeling very sad, one can't help smile in his memory as one recalls his antics. Pete was a pilot's pilot who always liked to have a good time. He loved to pull out his pilot's license and show his ratings. He was certified to fly in all aircraft. All. Period.

He was also a flight instructor's instructor. While working for the FAA, Pete pioneered the Flight Instructor Refresher Course. I had the privilege of working with him at the FIRCs. Pete bragged to me that he had, during his career, earned at least $150,000 teaching one particular unit on the magnetic compass. He could make that one hour so interesting, that the audience would be totally absorbed with his presentation.

One time in Nashville, Pete and I were standing outside the meeting room near the stage waiting for fellow instructor John Hammonds to finish his lecture.

Pete whispered to me, "Hey, you want to see me make John fall off the stage?"

"Sure," I said, "how are you going to do it?"

"Watch!" he said as he positioned himself so that John could see him, without the flight instructors in the meeting room being aware he was there. Pete pulled out his false teeth, and grinned a huge toothless grin at John.

John looked over at him and did a double take. John started laughing and he couldn't stop. Pete stood there flapping his naked gums at John with the most comical expression on his face.

The audience peered toward the door wondering what was so funny. Pete went straight-faced. I was doubled over with laughter watching John, who was still laughing hysterically, until he fell off the stage and had to call a classroom break. Pete quickly popped his teeth in and nonchalantly leaned up against the doorway as the puzzled instructors flowed out the doorway toward us.

Pete had his own style. He got away with saying things on stage that those of us younger than him could never have said. He was a Southern gentleman with a streak of naughty.

Once when he called me at home, the first thing he said was "You naked?" I would have never put up with that from anyone else, but coming from him, I laughed and laughed.

One Saturday afternoon at an Indianapolis FIRC, I was showing a video to the flight instructors on microburst. I walked outside the meeting room to call Pete on the house phone in the hallway to ask him about dinner plans. The first thing he said when he heard my voice was, "You naked?"

I replied, with mock indignation, "No, Pete, I am not naked. I am totally dressed." Immediately, an instructor rushed towards me out of the meeting room. "Catherine, did you know that your mic is still on?" Oops!

We sure miss you, Pete, and we'll always remember you. You kept us laughing!

Biography

CATHERINE (CATHÉ) FISH

Cathé Fish has taught motivating and entertaining aviation safety courses in all 50 states and Europe. She is a 17-year National Accident Prevention Counselor. Flying since 1973, she is a certified single-engine, multi-engine and instrument flight instructor. Her 6,000 hours of flight time include flying for a commuter airline, flying as a USDA contract pilot and teaching 300 students how to fly. Cathé was an instructor of aviation technology at Cochise College for five years. She has been one of the AOPA Air Safety Foundation's favorite lead instructors for 17 years, teaching 400 Flight Instructor Refresher Courses, 100 Pitch Hitter Seminars and many other safety programs. Cathé's *Flying Companion* and *Advanced Flying Companion* seminars repeatedly receive rave reviews. She challenges flight instructors in her *Become a 21st Century Flight Instructor* program. Expert in the latest GPS technology, pilots are eager to fully realize their investments with her *Practical Hands-On GPS Program*. This four-hour program brings welcome relief and confidence to pilots wanting to fill this void in their technical knowledge. Cathé amazes pilots at how quickly she makes time seem to fly by with her other fast-paced, lively programs, *Decision Making, Judgment Training, Risk Management* and *Human Factors*.

JAMES W. (PETE) CAMPBELL

ONE FLEW OVER THE HAYSTACK

Many people think the barnstorming days ended in the 1930's. This is far from the truth. Barnstorming was very active for about five years after World War II. Techniques had changed, but the spirit and the attitudes were the same.

In 1946, after flying 56 combat missions in a B-24 Liberator in the South Pacific, I became part owner of a flight school in Union City, Tennessee. To drum up business, nearly every weekend we would fly to some small town that didn't have an airport and haul passengers—barnstorm. This was different from the barnstorming days of the '20's and '30's when the barnstormers didn't have a home airport and went from town to town. We had just as much fun and probably as many wild experiences.

A fellow named Wayne, whose poor eyesight prevented him from passing his flight physical, loved airplanes and he loved to go flying. He was a bit older than the rest of us, in his mid 30s. Wayne used to hang around the flight school, so we took him flying with us on barnstorming weekends. Wayne would manage the ticket sales and then fly with us when we put on the little air show at the end of the day.

One barnstorming Sunday, I was flying passengers out of a hayfield near the small town of Clinton, Kentucky and Wayne was selling tickets. We had a very large crowd and business was really good. All afternoon I kept trying to think of something special to add to the air show at the end of the day.

The hayfield was about 2,500 feet long—plenty of space to put on the air show. The farmer had put the cut hay in one very big stack, 25 feet high, over on one side of the field. The wind was about 20 mph along the length of the field. I was flying a J-5 Cub Cruiser, which could take off and land at about 40 mph. With a headwind of 20 mph, my takeoff ground speed would be a very slow 20 mph. I got to thinking it would really be a good trick to fly over the haystack, very slow into the wind, and drop Wayne into the hay. His falling body would only be going 20 mph when it hit the hay. Wayne said sure, he would like to try it.

About sunset we quit hauling passengers, so I put Wayne in the back seat of the Cub and took the door off. We flew a couple of passes over the haystack, missing it by only a few feet. I was flying as slowly as I could without stalling. It looked as if it was going to be a cinch, so we decided Wayne would jump on the next pass.

Wayne said he could see the haystack okay, so when we got about 10 feet from the mound on the next pass he said he would jump. I came around into the wind and Wayne got out on the step with one foot. When I got close to the haystack, he jumped. I looked back and saw that Wayne had hit the haystack halfway up. I thought to myself, "That's the best trick I ever thought of. We'll get rich with this exciting stunt."

When I returned to the field and taxied up to the haystack, two men were holding Wayne up by each arm and walking him around. He looked dazed. "What's the matter?" I asked. "You hit right in the middle of the haystack."

We didn't know it, but the farmer had stacked the hay around a telephone pole to keep it from blowing away and the telephone pole was hidden from view by the hay. When Wayne landed in the haystack, his head had smacked right into the telephone pole, dazing him.

Wayne never did the trick again and nobody else ever tried. So went my chances for fame and fortune.

STUFFED CUB

The story you are about to hear happened a long time ago—in 1948. I hesitate to tell this tale, but today there are still several people alive who can confirm this event actually occurred. Folks, do not try this at home. I'd like to be able to say trained professionals accomplished this feat. But those people still alive would know the truth.

One morning a bunch of students and I were hangar flying and the question arose, how many people could fit in a J-3 Cub and still get airborne? Everyone has heard of packing kids into a phone booth. This is similar, except a phone booth doesn't have to get off the ground. Remember that the J-3 is a little two-seat tandem aircraft with a 65 horsepower engine and a design maximum takeoff weight of 1220 pounds. We decided to quit hangar flying and do some real flying to see for ourselves.

After quite a bit of configuring, calculating, and computing wing loading versus horsepower, we decided to try it with seven people. Here was the plan. We removed the stick from the rear cockpit and took off both doors. Chester would pilot the J-3 from the front seat with a small person on his shoulders. Billy, the heaviest, sat on the floor of the rear cockpit with his feet sticking out the open right door. I sat in the rear seat with my feet on Billy and another person on my shoulders. We packed the smallest person into the tiny baggage compartment behind the rear seat. The seventh person sat on the outside of the airplane, on the left lift strut where it joins the fuselage. He was to hold on to the windowsill of the open left window.

Six passengers and the pilot added up to 1025 pounds. Add the airplane, 750 pounds; two gallons of fuel, 12 pounds; and six quarts of oil, 11 pounds. This gave us a total gross weight of 1798 pounds; 578 pounds over the maximum approved gross weight, but still within the center of gravity range.

We had a lot of confidence in the J-3's structural integrity and figured the J-3 could carry the extra weight. (Don't think we were totally reckless. Airplanes flown overseas are flown over gross from all the extra fuel they have to carry to make it over the pond.) We'd find out soon enough if the 65 horsepower engine had enough thrust to get us off the ground.

Since the wind was about five mph out of the northwest, we decided to take off and fly straight to Uptown Airport five miles northwest. Chester would only have to fly one very shallow turn, which would prevent loss of vertical lift and decrease the possibility of stalling.

We arranged all seven people in and on the Cub, then Chester opened the throttle. After a very long ground run, we became airborne, but the Cub could not climb out of ground effect (10 feet). We had lots of runway left, so we landed straight ahead. When we stopped, Billy hollered, "I have had enough of this," and he crawled out from the bottom of the stack. Billy's leaving reduced our load by 195 pounds, so the remaining six bodies agreed to try again.

Chester shoved in the power and tried again. This time we broke out of ground effect, but still couldn't get over 200 feet of altitude. 200 feet was enough altitude, though, to make it to Uptown so we continued and landed without any further problems.

I never found out if this was a record or not. We were *very* reluctant to publicize the event. Even if the CAA (predecessor to the FAA) had heard that six adults had flown in a J-3 Cub, they wouldn't have believed it anyway.

TALES FROM A FLIGHT INSTRUCTOR - FOGGY

From 1951 to 1960 I worked as a flight instructor for California Eastern Airways. After being hired I started flight instructor training at a flight school in Columbus, Mississippi.

In addition to training instructors for commercial airlines, the school received many military contracts to train Air Force recruits to fly. All the employees of the flying school were civilians, including the staff meteorologist, a man we called "Foggy." Prior to each flight, Foggy would brief us on the weather. Foggy's weather briefings contained all the pertinent weather information we would need for flying and were usually pretty accurate.

In addition to being staff meteorologist, Foggy was my barracks chief in Columbus. He was a very sharp individual indeed, as I found out later.

After three weeks of refresher training at Columbus, I was sent to Craig Air Force Base in Selma, Alabama for six weeks of additional training. One day after leaving ground school class on my way to the mess hall for lunch, I ran into Foggy, the meteorologist from Columbus. I almost didn't recognize him. He was wearing the uniform of an Air Force first lieutenant, with Air Force wings on the left side of his coat and Navy wings on the right side. I said, "Hello!" and mentioned I didn't know he was a pilot. He replied, "Oh, yes. I'm over at Maxwell Field for a term of active duty. I'm in the reserves."

At the time I didn't give the chance meeting much thought. Later I found out Foggy was neither a pilot nor a reserve officer. In fact, he wasn't even a meteorologist. Foggy had written his own orders placing himself on active duty and making himself a pilot.

In the next month I learned Foggy had promoted himself to the rank of captain. When I returned to Columbus, I found out Foggy was in federal jail at Aberdeen, Mississippi. Foggy had, at another time, made himself a Navy officer and had been caught at that, too.

Foggy's enterprise didn't end there. After serving time for impersonating an officer at both Craig and Maxwell, he later made himself a colonel and enrolled in a jet pilot school in Texas. Foggy pulled this off for a while, but he was finally caught and put away again. It turns out he didn't do too badly as a pilot trainee in the jet school. Too bad someone didn't let Foggy keep his rank and put him in charge of something like security. Foggy's ambitious genius would have served a useful purpose.

Later, I heard a rumor Foggy had made himself a colonel again and was now a military attaché to a foreign country. Foggy's real name was Jack Brown, and the *Saturday Evening Post* (May 5, 1965) published a story of his life entitled *Fake Colonel: How He Fooled the Air Force.*

FEAR OF PSYCHOLOGY

Thanks to a nervous nut of a professor, psychology was one of the most interesting classes in flight instructor training. The professor's favorite subject was fear and flying. After one of his sessions on fear and flying, we were scared to go to the flight line and scared not to.

This professor didn't teach by boring lecture. He believed in teaching by demonstration. One Monday morning, after the kind of weekend when most of us were afraid we were actually going to live, the professor gave us one of his famous demonstrations.

Unbeknown to us, the professor had arranged to have one man dressed as a military prisoner and another dressed as an M.P. (military policeman) help with the demonstration. The classroom had an entrance at both the front and the rear. During the lecture, the front door banged open and the prisoner came running through pursued by the M.P. carrying a shotgun. When the prisoner was about halfway through the room, the M.P. shouted, "Halt!" three times. When the prisoner failed to stop, the M.P. shot him in the back.

We all thought it was real. A student sitting next to me jumped into my lap. Another student jumped out the nearest window. A third student crawled under the professor's table. While all of this was happening, the professor went around the room asking each trainee a simple question, such as, "What is your mother's name?" In response, he would receive such answers as, "Straight in the Back" and "Wah! Wah!" He asked me how old I was. I answered, "Three times!"

He proved his point. In times of extreme fear, one doesn't think too clearly.

GRADUATION

After completing flight instructor training, I returned to Columbus, Mississippi for my first teaching assignment. Each instructor was assigned four students. Six months later, my first students graduated. School tradition required that each graduation celebration include an awards dinner, an instructor-student dinner, a Friday stag night, and a Saturday night dance. Friday's stag night ended with the students attempting to outdrink the instructors. Since the students had to be in the barracks by midnight, the instructors won by default and decided to celebrate their victory at a local nightclub.

The bartender, an ex-con, was a little irritated when our large group of drinkers arrived so close to quitting time. He relented after we flashed our money and agreed to keep the bar open after midnight.

C. F. started having a little innocent fun by shaking a bottle of beer and squirting it on the bartender. The bartender didn't take to this too kindly, so he drew his pistol, and started over the counter after C. F. Most of the instructors noticed the commotion and instead of running for the nearest exit, ran for the bartender. Several instructors held his gun hand in the air, the gun pointing up at the ceiling, while the rest held his body.

Roy was sitting at a table with his back to the fight. About the time shots were fired, someone threw a broken glass that hit Roy in the neck. I heard him holler and went to see what was wrong. Roy said he thought he had been shot in the neck. I examined the wound. It was only a scratch, but I told Roy he had been shot and it looked bad. Then I said, "Look, Roy, if there is anything you think I should tell your folks, you should tell me now because it looks like you aren't going to be with us long." Roy turned as white as a sheet and fainted. He hasn't forgiven me since.

Meanwhile the bartender had dropped the pistol. An instructor held the bartender by his arms while C. F. was preparing to punch him in the mouth. C. F. drew back and swung at the bartender, but missed wide and hit J. L., who was standing nearby, in the temple. The blow knocked him out cold. Meanwhile, the bartender's wife had retrieved the pistol and was pointing it at the group of struggling flight instructors. Everyone held his breath until someone slipped up behind her and grabbed the gun.

Soon I was holding the bartender, and C. F. finally got to hit him in the mouth. J. L. came to, lowered his head and ran at the bartender, aiming to butt him the stomach. With his head down J. L. couldn't see where he was going. He missed the bartender and butted the oak bar. J. L. passed out cold again. Roy came to and was now crying with joy when he discovered he hadn't been shot.

The bartender began wandering around on the dance floor in a semiconscious condition with a broken nose until he finally fell into the jukebox. Someone had called the sheriff. By the time the sheriff arrived, the few instructors left were seated at a table having a sociable beer. The only person who looked drunk was the poor bartender sitting on the floor with his back against the jukebox. Someone had poured whiskey all over him and put the near empty bottle in his hand. The sheriff carried him away. We haven't seen the pistol-carrying ex-con bartender since.

RUNWAY DUTY

Paul, a buddy and fellow instructor, was an outstanding pilot and a great guy. Paul's only drawback was that he had worn false teeth since he was 21, but it never bothered him. One night Paul and I were assigned runway control duties. Runway control at the flight school meant sitting in the cab of a one-ton truck and giving instructions to approaching aircraft. If our communication equipment failed or the pilot didn't respond to our instructions, we were supposed to fire a flare gun in front of the approaching aircraft to signal a go around. We were equipped with two types of flare guns for the job: a handheld flare gun we fired out the cab window and a remote unit 300 feet down the runway, which was fired by electrical impulse from the cab. The flares were about the size of an eight-gauge shotgun shell. The handheld gun was a single shot. The remote was double barreled.

As controller in charge, I sent Paul to load the remote gun. As I watched him walk the 3,000 feet to the remote gun, I thought it would be funny to fire the gun immediately after he loaded it. As soon as I saw Paul close the barrels, indicating the gun was loaded, I fired both barrels. Whoopee! What a commotion that caused! Paul must have been within a foot of the gun when it went off, and of course it scared the devil out of him. When he jumped back from fright both denture plates fell out, too.

Paul wasn't hurt, but he was rather upset with me. When he got back to the control unit after washing and reinstalling his dentures, I knew he was really mad because he wouldn't talk to me at all.

Later that night an aircraft came in fixing to land wheels up. I hollered over the radio for the pilot to go around and shouted for Paul to fire the flare gun. Paul grabbed the hand flare gun and fired it at the aircraft. I couldn't tell if the aircraft went around or not. Paul forgot to open the cab window. The darn flare went around and around inside the control unit like the Fourth of July. I crawled under the console with Paul until the flare stopped its erratic flight. Now Paul was really mad at me. He said if I hadn't made him mad in the first place, he would have remembered to open the window before firing the flare.

BARREL OF DENTURES

Paul once had a French student who couldn't speak much English. Paul couldn't speak any French. When the student didn't respond, Paul would lose his temper and yell at him. One day Paul was teaching half rolls and reverses and the student wasn't catching on too quickly. So when they were upside down on a bad half roll, Paul lost his temper and started to holler at the student. When he opened his mouth, his teeth came out and fell on the canopy. Remember, they were upside down. Just as Paul reached for his teeth, the student rolled the aircraft back right side up.

Paul missed his teeth and they fell all the way to the bottom of the T-6. Now Paul was mush-mouthed and the student really could not understand a word he was saying. Paul took control and rolled the airplane back upside down. The teeth fell back to the canopy. But when Paul let go of the stick to reach for the teeth, the student took control and rolled the aircraft right side up. Paul missed his teeth again and watched them fall back to the belly of the aircraft.

By this time his teeth were covered with sludge from the belly of the aircraft, a few cigarette butts and some used chewing gum. Paul gave up trying to recover his teeth and they returned to the airport.

I was in the flight shack making out grade slips when I looked out the window and saw Paul, steaming, and the student, following meekly behind, returning from the T-6. Paul held something in his hand I didn't recognize. Man, was he flapping his gums when he came in to wash his teeth and reinstall his choppers in his face.

BOOTS ARE MADE FOR WALKING

In 1953, we used PA-11's (Piper Cubs) to supplement the T-6 training. A student started out in the Cub. If he did okay after 10 hours in the Cub, we moved him up to the T-6. If he washed out, it was cheaper on the student's pocketbook and the T-6's.

The Cub is a very small tandem seat trainer. The instructor sits in the rear, the student sits in the front. The rear seat rudder pedals are located on each side of the front seat. So when both instructor and student are seated, the instructor's feet rub against each cheek of the student's rear end.

Paul always wore half boots when he flew. One day, his student got sick in the Cub. When the student leaned over to throw up, he missed the door and filled Paul's half boot full. Paul landed immediately and pulled off his boot. I watched him coming toward the flight shack with the boot in his hand. He looked upset and went straight to the toilet. I didn't know what was wrong and followed. I walked in on Paul with his foot in the commode, flushing it. I thought he had lost his mind until he told me what happened. We had lots of fun with Paul. He is one of the finest pilots I have ever flown with.

THE WALKING PILOT

The only time I made the newspapers in Columbus was not from my flying escapades, but from my bet on the 1952 presidential election. I was Chairman of the Craig Air Force Base (CAFB) Democratic Committee and Hugh McCloud was Chairman of the

CAFB Republican Committee. So naturally, in 1952, I bet on Stevenson and McCloud bet on Eisenhower. The loser agreed to walk the nine miles from CAFB to the town of Columbus—barefoot.

As any student of history knows, I lost. I started the walk at the base guard gate. I was easy to spot. I was wearing a sign on the front and back of me stating "I BET ON STEVENSON" and I was leading a line of cars extending a half-mile behind me. The folks in the cars offered me encouragement, food, and drink, mostly drink.

By the time we reached Columbus, my feet were bleeding, but I was so juiced, I didn't noticed. My wife, Linda, met me at the Columbus city limit. When she saw the shape of my feet, she almost had a seizure. She wanted me to ride the rest of the way, but I informed her I would rather walk on bloody nubs than renege to a Republican. Linda went home and prepared a tub of salt water to bathe my feet. Over 100 people, including newspaper and radio reporters, greeted me when I arrived home. The event, including pictures, made the United Press (U.P.) hookup. Folks sent me dozens of letters, a $50 Stetson hat and 20 pairs of shoes.

My feet were so sore I could not wear shoes for a week and had to fly in my socks. One day, when flying the T-6, my right foot slipped off the brake and caught in the rudder pedal. I almost wet myself before I got it loose. My right foot stayed sore for an additional week.

It took me 20 years to wear out all those pairs of shoes, but I won't ever forget that bet.

UPGRADING

In 1951 the Air Force delegated primary flight training to civilian contractors. Between 1951 and 1960, nine contract schools conducted this training and California Eastern Airways was one of them. Because we had overtrained, the Air Force had more pilots than cockpits and needed to place some of the overflow in the cockpits of the primary trainers. So the Air Force took back all primary flight training in December of 1960.

The practice of upgrading to new aircraft, and staying proficient in all aircraft was an ongoing job, and had to be performed in our off duty times. Even though we were assigned to our students only five hours per day, the rest of the day was usually taken up with upgrading or proficiency flying.

One event that was very humorous happened when we were upgrading from the T-28 to the T-37. The upgrading to the T-37 was performed in the following manner. Five of the California Eastern instructors went to the Cessna factory in Wichita, Kansas where the T-37s, the little twin engine trainers, were built. First the factory pilots checked out the five instructors in the T-37. Then these instructors brought the new T-37s to our base at Mission, Texas. Each of these instructors then checked out four other instructors; they in turn checked out four other instructors, until all instructors were checked out. Then 16 instructors went to Wichita, Kansas and picked up 16 more T-37s.

This starts a class, and then the process is repeated until all the classes are phased into the new aircraft. Four classes required approximately 100 T-37s. Remember, there must be enough aircraft for dual and solo to operate at the same time. Only half of the students are on the flight line at one time. The other half are in ground school. At noon they switch.

Back to the humorous event! One day instructor Deb Vallee was checking out another instructor, Jim Brown. They went to practice phase-four spins, about the hairiest maneuver anyone can think of. The T-37 failed to recover from a spin and Deb and Jim had to eject. Remember, the T-37 is a two-place, side-by-side aircraft and each pilot has a separate ejection seat.

When Deb Vallee, the instructor pilot in command, shouted, "Eject!" they both fired their ejection seats at the same time. This resulted in their automatic parachutes opening at the same time. This caused them to float toward the ground within a few hundred feet of each other.

While floating toward the cactus-covered Texas desert, Deb shouted to Jim, "You ain't the best trainee I ever checked out."

Jim shouted back to Deb, "That ain't all. You ain't the best check pilot I ever had either."

When they landed, Deb was not injured at all, but Jim hurt his knee a little, and he got some cactus pricks. Of course, the aircraft splattered when it hit the ground.

Deb Vallee had been wearing slip-on oxford shoes that day. He should have been wearing lace-up shoes or boots. The T-37 does not have ejection stirrups for your feet, so Deb was fired right out of his slip-on oxfords. They were found at the crash site, undamaged.

This was Jim Brown's first flight in the T-37. Therefore, he had one takeoff and no landings.

Pete Campbell holds a model of the B-24, the plane he flew during WW II. His wife, Linda, holds the plague signifying the renaming of the Everett-Stewart Airport terminal in Tennessee in Pete's honor.

In Memory of

PETE CAMPBELL

Pete Campbell passed away in his sleep on Christmas Eve in 1999 at the age of 79. Aviation lost an icon. With his wild aviation stories and bold sense of humor, Pete was a character and pilots just loved him. He had such a joy for life. If Pete was in the room, there would be laughter. He logged 22,000 hours flying airplanes (piston and jet), gliders, rotorcraft, balloons and ultra lights. He flew 56 South Pacific combat missions in a B-24 and was still flying acrobatic shows in his Cessna 150 in his seventies.

As an FAA employee, Pete was the major instigator of the Flight Instructor Revalidation Clinics and the FAA Accident Prevention Programs. Pete would say, "You can't prove that penalizing a pilot improves safety, but I can prove that education does!" And he did. The numbers proved him right. One cannot fathom how many pilots he has touched with his safety messages as each instructor has passed these lessons on to their students, and their students to the next generation. He taught hundreds of aviation safety seminars and gave 2,800 lectures to 28,000 CFIs across the country. The Everett-Stewart Airport Terminal in Tennessee was named the Pete Campbell Terminal, honoring his tremendous contributions to aviation. Pete taught us well. He made us laugh like no other could. His incredible contribution to aviation safety is mind-boggling. We will miss you Pete.

Production Crew

Getting the stories on paper was the challenge. It took seven years of coaxing, note taking, audiotaping, transcribing and rewriting. Some speakers are prolific writers. For some this will be their first book.

Jeannette and Diane

Diane Titterington had the vision for *Speaking of Flying*. She is the designer, compiler, managing editor and producer. This is her third book project. Flying since 1973, she is a commercial/instrument pilot and was a radar air traffic controller at Houston Center for five years. Diane is now President of The Aviation Speakers Bureau.

Jeannette Walder, assistant editor, also wrote four stories for a contributor after listening to his storytelling. She is an instrument pilot whose travels include flying in the Caribbean. Diane and Jeannette have flown air races together including the Palms to Pines Air Race (photo). Jeannette has a master's degree in engineering and is a patent attorney for a prestigious law firm in Chicago.

Brian

Brian Weiss, senior editor, has written for and edited magazines, books and periodicals in a career spanning 25 years. He is an instrument pilot who previously served as associate editor of *Psychology Today*, medical/science editor for *Aviation Safety Magazine*, editor of *Baja Explorer*, and author of the nationally syndicated newspaper column and magazine *FREEBIES*. He founded the marketing, consulting and communications firm WORD'SWORTH in 1977.

The Aviation Speaker's Bureau

Since 1986, The Aviation Speakers Bureau has been assisting clients in selecting speakers to add excitement and substance to their events.

We provide high quality and distinguished educators, entertainers and experts in the aviation industry.

The best part? Our services are free to you! We match the best possible speaker to meet your needs and budget.

This book showcases a number of our speakers. Visit our web site to meet more of our speakers and to preview audio and video clips. If you have another topic or speaker in mind, please ask.

Our professionals shine and
make you look good every time!

www.aviationspeakers.com

FOR SPEAKER AVAILABILITY & BOOKING INFORMATION CALL:

949-498-2498

P.O. Box 6030

San Clemente, California

92674-6030

TOPICS

ACES
ACCIDENT REVIEW
AEROBATICS
AGRICULTURAL SPRAYING
AIRCRAFT DESIGN
RESEARCH & DEVELOPMENT
AIRCRAFT RESTORATION
AIRLINE CAPTAIN
AIRSHOW PERFORMER
AIRSPACE
BUSINESS
MANAGEMENT
CAREERS IN AVIATION
CHARACTER PORTRAYAL
COLUMNIST
COMMUNICATION
CREW RESOURCE MGMT
CUSTOMER SERVICE
DECISION MAKING
DISASTER PLANNING
EMERGENCY LANDINGS
FARS
EMERGENCY MANEUVER TRNG.
FIGHTER PILOTS
FIRSTS
FLYING COMPANION PROGRAM
FUTURIST
GOAL SETTING
HISTORICAL
HOLDING PATTERNS
HUMAN FACTORS
HUMOR
IN-FLIGHT EMERGENCIES
INSPIRATIONAL
INSTRUMENT FLYING
LAW
LEADERSHIP
MOVIES & TELEVISION
MULTI ENGINE
MUSIC—AVIATION
NEWS/REPORTING
OVERCOMING OBSTACLES
PERSONAL DEVELOPMENT
PSYCHOLOGY
SAFETY
SALES
SPACE PROGRAM
STALL/SPIN AWARENESS
STRESS
STUNT (PRECISION) FLYING
SUPERSONIC
TEAM BUILDING/TEAMWORK
TEST PILOTS
WAR
WEATHER
WEATHER RADAR
WOMEN IN AVIATION
WRIGHT BROTHERS
YOUTH PROGRAMS

Index

I

J

K

L

M